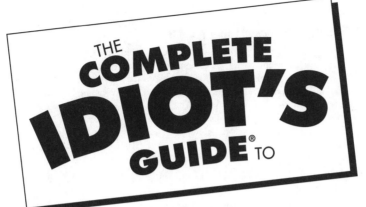

THE
**COMPLETE
IDIOT'S
GUIDE®** TO

JavaServer Pages™

by Robert Brunner

ALPHA

A Pearson Education Company

International Standard Book Number: 0-02-864320-8
Library of Congress Catalog Card Number: 2002103791

04   03   02   8   7   6   5   4   3   2   1

Interpretation of the printing code: The rightmost number of the first series of numbers is the year of the book's printing; the rightmost number of the second series of numbers is the number of the book's printing. For example, a printing code of 02-1 shows that the first printing occurred in 2002.

Printed in the United States of America

Note: This publication contains the opinions and ideas of its author. It is intended to provide helpful and informative material on the subject matter covered. It is sold with the understanding that the author and publisher are not engaged in rendering professional services in the book. If the reader requires personal assistance or advice, a competent professional should be consulted.

The author and publisher specifically disclaim any responsibility for any liability, loss, or risk, personal or otherwise, which is incurred as a consequence, directly or indirectly, of the use and application of any of the contents of this book.

For marketing and publicity, please call: 317-581-3722

The publisher offers discounts on this book when ordered in quantity for bulk purchases and special sales.

For sales within the United States, please contact: Corporate and Government Sales, 1-800-382-3419 or corpsales@pearsontechgroup.com

Outside the United States, please contact: International Sales, 317-581-3793 or international@pearsontechgroup.com

Publisher: *Marie Butler-Knight*
Product Manager: *Phil Kitchel*
Managing Editor: *Jennifer Chisholm*
Acquisitions Editor: *Eric Heagy*
Development Editor: *Michael Koch*
Senior Production Editor: *Christy Wagner*
Copy Editor: *Cari Luna*
Illustrator: *Chris Eliopoulos*
Cover/Book Designer: *Trina Wurst*
Indexer: *Tonya Heard*
Layout/Proofreading: *Angela Calvert, Svetlana Dominguez, Stacey Richwine-DeRome*

Contents at a Glance

Contents

Introduction

If you're like a lot of people, when you log on to a fancy website, you're probably curious about what makes all that cool stuff work. You might think that the answer to that mystery is a well-guarded secret that only a special few are privy to. But the fact is that powerful website creation techniques are available to just about anyone. The only difference between you and the people who designed that impressive website is that the latter folks have spent many years perfecting their craft.

One of the technologies that makes such websites possible is JavaServer Pages (JSPs), the technology you learn about in this book. The truth is that JSP pages are just plain text documents that can contain something called template data, as well as server-side scripts, that enable the generation of dynamic content for your website. But from this simplicity comes a whole world of web programming that will forever change the way you design web content.

In this book, you start by seeing why you need to learn about JSP pages. By looking back on the evolution of web-based technologies, you'll be able to see how JSP pages fit into the big picture and why they make sense to use. But JSP doesn't work alone. In fact, there are lots of technologies that fall under the term *web*. Here, you'll explore several, including JavaBeans, tags, and objects. By the end of the book, you'll be able to combine all these technologies to produce dynamic web content.

Whom This Book Is For

There was a time when *The Complete Idiot's Guide* series was aimed only at complete novices, who had no experience whatever with the technology discussed in the book. However, this particular *Idiot's Guide* fits into a different category. Specifically, this book is for people who are new to JSP, but who have some experience with other related web technologies, especially HTML. That is, if you're a complete novice with all web technologies, you should skip this book for now and instead start with a book such as *The Complete Idiot's Guide to Creating a Web Page*.

How This Book Is Organized

This book is divided into five parts.

Part 1, "Getting Started with JSP," reviews the basics on which JSP pages are built. This includes TCP/IP, the web, and the HTTP communication process. This part also covers the installation of the Tomcat server, and show you how to build, deploy, and test your first JSP page. The part concludes with a quick tour of the different JSP technologies.

Part 2, "Getting Into JSP," is designed to show you how to build JSP pages by directly adding Java code to your web pages. In this part I describe the fundamentals of using Java variables and methods, as well as Java classes. I'll also show you how to use some of the built-in capabilities of JSP containers to work with multiple JSP pages. I conclude by showing you how to package all the files necessary for your web application together, which enables you to easily distribute your web application to other people and servers.

Part 3, "Working on the Client," takes a break from JSP technology, and focuses on improving the presentation of your data on the client. This includes a discussion of using XHTML and the sort of documents that you can create with it, as well as a discussion of cascading style sheets. When you need to perform processing on the client, such as validating form data or directing the server to perform specific tasks, you can use JavaScript. Finally, this part concludes with a discussion of working with Java on the client, as I demonstrate how JSP pages and Applets can work together.

Part 4, "Working on the Server," looks at advanced JSP concepts that enable you to remove Java code from the JSP page. This enables you to simplify the development and maintenance of the JSP pages in your application, while also promoting code reuse. This is accomplished by using JavaBeans to encapsulate data and Servlets to control the processing of the JavaBeans. I'll also introduce and develop custom actions, which enable you to replace large chunks of Java code in your JSP page by a simple tag.

Part 5, "Entering the Real World," uses the concepts and techniques from the earlier parts to tackle real-world problems, including security, globalization, sending mail, and generating XML. After reading these chapters, you'll have a better understanding of what it takes to build an online business.

At the end of the book you'll also find a troubleshooting appendix that provides potential solutions to the inevitable problems that can arise when you are trying to work with Internet technologies, as well as a glossary that helps you talk the JSP and Internet talk.

All the examples in this book were tested using the open source Jakarta Tomcat JSP/Servlet container. The first reason for selecting this server is that it is free. The second, and most important reason, however, is that this server is the reference implementation for the official JSP and Servlet specifications. Thus, if it works on Tomcat, it has to work on any other compliant JSP server.

In order to make things easier for you to get started, you can either follow along with the book trying new things out as you go along, or else you can grab a complete working archive of the server that has all the JSP, HTML, XML, CSS, and JavaScript files. Unlike other books, I won't tell you to only use one approach. I believe that you should understand all the different possibilities, their advantages and disadvantages, and then select whatever works best for you. All the code is available for free online. Also, although the examples in this book were developed under Windows 2000, the information presented is valid with any operating system that supports the technologies covered in this book.

Extras

This book also features extra tidbits called sidebars. These asides are designed to supply you with extra information, tips, and cautions. Here's what you'll find …

Coffee Break

This is where you'll read about interesting topics related to the discussion at hand.

Tagged

This is where you'll find definitions of the technical words you need to know as a programmer.

Fresh Brew

This is where you'll read about tricks and tips that can make programming more fun and convenient.

> **Hot Java** _____
>
> This is where you'll find important information about problems you may run into as you write your programs.

Acknowledgments

Until you have done it, you never appreciate just how hard it is to write a book. As hard as it has been for me, it was undoubtedly harder for my wife, who had to take care of our three kids, while also cooking our fourth. For a while it was questionable who would finish first—our new baby or this book. Hey Cookie, thanks for holding in there.

I also must thank the rest of my children: Anastasia, Aleyna, and Jarrett, for not getting too angry that Daddy had locked himself in the office, yet again.

Great thanks are due to my agents, Neil and Vicki from StudioB, for not only finding me this challenge, but also helping me to manage it. I also am grateful to my research collaborators at Caltech, Microsoft Research, and John Hopkins, for not noticing that I was only putting in 40-hour weeks.

While my name may be on the cover, a great deal of work was done by a lot of other people, including Eric Heagy, who demonstrated amazing restraint, despite the constant delays; Michael Koch, who appreciated the ever-changing contents; and the rest of the crew at Alpha Books—keep pushing out oranges, because who wants a lemon.

Special Thanks to the Technical Reviewers

The Complete Idiot's Guide to JavaServer Pages was reviewed by two experts who double-checked the accuracy of what you'll learn here, to help us ensure that this book gives you everything you need to know about JavaServer Pages technology. Special thanks are extended to Sue Spielman and Christopher McGee.

Trademarks

All terms mentioned in this book that are known to be or are suspected of being trademarks or service marks have been appropriately capitalized. Alpha Books and Pearson Education, Inc., cannot attest to the accuracy of this information. Use of a term in this book should not be regarded as affecting the validity of any trademark or service mark.

Part 1

Getting Started with JSP

Ready to get started? Great! This part will get you started developing JavaServer Pages applications. In the next four chapters, you'll learn first about the foundations for JSP technology and what makes web applications work. Next, you'll get to install the Tomcat server so you can build your own JSP pages. Finally, I'll show you how simple or complex your JSP pages can be. So get set, now go!

The Backgrounder

In This Chapter

- A brief history of the web
- How Internet communication works
- How the web works
- Generating dynamic content
- The Java Servlet life cycle
- JSP technology and the web

If you are anything like me, after buying this book (you did buy it, right?) you are probably quite eager to jump in and start writing your own JavaServer Pages (JSP) documents. Maybe you want to build an e-commerce site, amaze your friends, or impress your boss. Right now, however, I am going to ask you to temper your enthusiasm for a little while, as you absorb some necessary background material first. After all, JSP technology didn't grow on trees, and it wasn't invented overnight. It builds on existing technology and community needs. Understanding the grand picture will make a lot of what comes later make more sense.

A Brief History of the Web

It's hard to imagine that the web is just over a decade old. It was in 1991 that Tim Berners-Lee released the HTML and HTTP specifications to members of the High Energy Physics community via the very first web server.

Three short years later, the explosive growth of the web led Tim to found the World Wide Web Consortium (W3C). The W3C is an open consortium where parties who are interested in the future of the web can come together to define new protocols that will lead to the continued growth and evolution of the web.

In order to get new users for the web, HTML clients needed to be made available for a diverse range of users in different operating systems. There also needed to be web servers that could be used to deliver hypertext content running on a wide range of different hardware systems.

Out of the National Center for Supercomputing Applications (NCSA) in Urbana-Champagne, Illinois, came the Mosaic browser and the NCSA HTTP Server. These tools gained widespread use and eventually drove the creation of two revolutionary tools, the Netscape web browser and the Apache web server.

Eventually the popularity of the Netscape web browser and the clamor for more online content drew the attention of Microsoft, an early critic of the web. To its credit, Microsoft quickly changed directions, developed the Internet Explorer (IE), and the browser wars ensued. Competition between Netscape and IE became intense, but eventually Microsoft prevailed, in part because they made IE available for free, claiming it was part of the operating system. Of course, this resulted in legal entanglements that are still being decided.

How the Web Works, or the HTTP Model

JSP is a web-based technology, so you need to understand the World Wide Web and its underpinnings to have a solid understanding of JSP technology.

The web is built on Internet communications, which is predominantly done via TCP/IP, HTTP, and HTML. In the following subsection, I go over each of these protocols in a bit more detail.

TCP/IP

TCP/IP stands for Transmission Control Protocol over Internet Protocol, which is just fancy terminology for describing a syntax that computers can use to communicate with each other over a network. During the days of early networking, different computers communicated using different languages, sort of how we humans talk to each other around the globe.

The basic premise of TCP/IP is that messages between computers are broken into short pieces called packets. Before sending a packet, a computer creates a special packet header, which, in part, indicates the destination address. TCP uses IP to form addresses, which are enumerated by a series of octet, or one-byte, numbers, in what is known as "dotted decimal notation." For example, in IPv4, which is currently the most commonly used version of IP, a network address is encoded in four bytes such as 18.7.14.127. The Internet Assigned Numbers Authority (IANA) formally assigns these numbers, so don't think you can just grab any old number you like.

Fresh Brew

If you want to know more about how IP addresses are assigned, take a look at the IANA website at www.iana.org. For more information on the next version of the Internet Protocol, look at the IPv6 website at www.ipv6.org. If you really find this stuff fascinating—and who doesn't—stroll over to the Internet Corporation for Assigned Names and Numbers, or ICANN, at www.icann.org. ICANN is the new controlling body for IP addressing, naming, and port assignments.

Some of the numbers used to represent IP addresses have special meanings, such as a Loopback adaptor, or private networks (which you might have if you have a personal firewall device on your PC). With the explosive growth of the Internet, the pool of available numbers is rapidly diminishing, leading to the creation of IPv6, which uses 6 bytes to form the network address.

Coffee Break

The Internet, which uses TCP/IP as its communication protocol, is like a spiderweb. At home, your personal computer connects to the Internet via a service provider that forms one node on the network. Each node is connected to many other nodes, which is formally described as a graph. This means that two nodes on the network can communicate with each other via many different paths through the network, providing a very flexible and robust connection mechanism. In reality, there is a hierarchy of nodes, classified in terms of different tiers; the spiderweb analogy is still very relevant.

This flexible nature of the TCP/IP standard was an inherent design choice to allow the network to survive limited attacks. Since the network itself determines the exact route network packets take, failure (for whatever reason) of any given node would not prevent communication across the network. For example, if all network nodes in one city were turned off (you can almost hear the contractor utter, "Oops!") traffic would be re-routed via other network nodes.

Since the pool of IP addresses is limited, especially until the support for IPv6 becomes more widespread, many computers are connected to the Internet via dynamic IP addressing. This connection scheme allows Internet Service Providers to reuse a pool of addresses across a group of users. This mechanism, however, does not work too well if you want to run a server, such as a web server, since your computer receives a new IP address every time it connects to the Internet. In this case, you would want a static IP address, where your machine always uses the same IP address whenever it connects to the Internet.

Numbers are all fine and good for computers, but humans tend to stop remembering number sequences once they get larger than seven digits (which is, incidentally, why your phone number has seven digits). To make things easier for humans, an address-naming scheme, called Domain Name Service (DNS) was developed to allow people to indicate destination IP addresses by name only.

As with numerical IP addresses, domain names can't be picked at random; and, because they can be a valuable commodity, they aren't free. To buy them, you need to go to a registered domain registrar, who assigns you the domain name. Once you know the name a server uses (for example, like www.w3c.org), you can now communicate that information to someone else. However, since computers only deal with numbers, a domain name still has to be mapped to the correct numerical IP address for network communications to work properly. This name-number translation is performed by a name server, which your Internet Service Provider may have told you about.

Hot Java

Note that not all Domain Registrars are created equal. On the one end are the industry giants like Network Solutions, Inc., which is significantly more expensive than its competitors, and on the other end you have fly-by-night organizations that take your money and run. If you take your time and do your homework, you can find good deals with reputable firms. A worldwide list of official name registrars is available from the Internet Corporation for Assigned Names and Numbers at www.icann.org/registrars/accredited-list.html.

At this point, you understand all about IP addresses and domain names, which allows network communication to travel between computers. However, many computers perform multiple roles, including web servers, FTP servers, database servers, packet routing, name servers, mail servers, news servers, and so on.

You may be wondering how a computer knows what network packet goes to which server application. The last piece to the puzzle is a port number. Just as the IP address tells the network to which computer a packet should be sent, the port number tells the receiving computer which running application should receive the packet. To illustrate, think of an IP address as your street address while a port number is the mailbox on your house. You need to have both the IP and the port to deliver a packet the same way that you need a street address and a mailbox to receive your postal delivery.

Coffee Break

When is a server not a server? When it's a server. The term *server* is somewhat overused in techno babble, and it can get confusing. A server can be the hardware machine itself, or it can be software that runs on the machine. It's common to refer to software programs that perform specific tasks as servers. A web server deals specifically with web-related things, usually HTTP. An FTP server is used for transferring files between two physical machines. If software is being referred to as a server, it is usually preceded by a noun, as in database server, name server, mail server, and so on.

While all port numbers aren't as tightly controlled as IP addresses and domain names, some are, and there are standard port numbers for specific services. For example, web servers, which utilize the HTTP protocol, listen by default to port 80. Port numbers below 1024 are termed "Well-Known" ports and generally require root (or Administrator) privilege to invoke the corresponding service. While you can run other applications on nonstandard ports, doing so can result in bizarre consequences.

If you would like to see a more detailed listing of port numbers, try the IANA website at www.iana.org/assignments/port-numbers.

Clients and Servers

All this talk about computers communicating over a network might inspire you to wonder why computers need to talk to each other at all. If you have used computers for a while you might even recall a time when your computer did everything by itself. In this model of operation, your computer contains all software it needs to operate, and you exchange data with others by physically transporting it on floppies, tapes, CD-ROMs, or similar media.

This model is not very efficient; especially for IT departments, which need to install the same software on all computer systems, including every patch or software upgrade. With the now ubiquitous networks, software and data can be stored and deployed from a central location. When a computer (or its user) needs data or software, it can be obtained directly from a single repository. This model is called a *client-server* architecture, because one server can provide resources for multiple clients.

Coffee Break

The very first network was called "sneaker net." A floppy disk was put in a drive on one machine, filled with data and then removed by an engineer who ran it over to the next machine. While this wasn't very productive in terms of network response time, it did keep the engineers in good shape.

A third model is starting to develop, which is called a *peer-to-peer* architecture. In this situation, nothing is centralized, as data and software can be located on multiple different computers. When you need something, you look up the closest location that has what you need and you request it.

HTTP

Okay, so now that you understand about network packets, you might be asking yourself what is inside those packets. With the explosive growth of the World Wide Web, chances are pretty good that any random packet you inspect is related to the web, which employs a client-server architecture. To communicate, web clients and servers communicate with each other using a very simple, easy-to-implement protocol with only a handful of commands that are communicated in plain text—HyperText Transfer Protocol (HTTP). HTTP is a pure request/response protocol. For each and every request made to the web server, there is a corresponding response sent back to the client. This is important—as you'll see when we start diving into JSP technology—because the requests and responses are packaged up for you in the JSP world.

Fresh Brew

The list of HTTP commands include HEAD, GET, PUT, POST, DELETE, TRACE, OPTIONS, and CONNECT. For more information, the official resource is the HTTP/1 Request for Comments (RFC), which is available at ftp://ftp.isi.edu/in-notes/rfc2616. txt. RFC dates back to the days when the Internet was starting out. The people working on it were highly distributed and worked in a very loose federation. When someone wanted to publish and receive feedback on a new method or technique for performing some functionality, they sent it out to the members of the Internet community and re-quested comments. The action stuck as the name for these eventual standards. The list of request for comments is available online at www.rfc-editor.org.

A more subtle aspect of HTTP is that it only supports stateless transactions. In this model, a client makes a request to a web server for a specific resource, which can be a web page, an MPEG video, or an MP3 audio file. The server processes the request and returns a response, which can either include the requested resource or an error condition. Once the server sends its response to the client, it moves on to the next request, retaining no "memory" of previous transactions. This means that web developers need to implement their own state-persisting mechanisms, which is the reason for web cookies.

If you want to see how easy it is to communicate with a web server, open up a shell window (or command prompt on a Windows operating system). Since HTTP uses plain text, you can use the telnet program to establish a TCP/IP connection to a web server, and just enter your particular HTTP request. Since HTTP is stateless, the server will process your request and close the connection, so be ready to either capture the output in a file or be sure to leave the telnet window open so you can read the response. As a starter, if you want to talk to a web server at www.persistentjava.com, you would enter the following to establish the connection:

```
telnet www.persistentjava.com 80
```

which tells telnet to connect to the machine with www.persistentjava.com as its domain address on port 80. Once the connection is established, you can type a legal HTTP request to the server to get a response. For example, the following request is to retrieve the web server's root document:

```
GET /
```

Coffee Break

In many systems, data and resources are shared among different users. It's necessary to maintain and pass this information between users. When a piece of information is maintained, it is referred to as statefull. If the information is only valid for the short period that it is being used in that instance, then it is referred to as stateless. This will become more important as you dive into JSP and how information is passed between pages.

HTML

HTTP is only half the story, however, for the explosive growth of the Internet. The other half is due to the simple format used in the web model to write a document in a platform- and language-independent manner. This format is known as HyperText Markup Language (HTML). Originally, HTML utilized a small number of markup commands to indicate how a document should be displayed: things like a title, the body, or a link to another document. Of course the subsequent "Browser Wars" increased the size and complexity of the HTML vocabulary, but a small number of markup commands still provide most of the functionality of HTML.

HTML markup tags are special instructions that indicate how things should appear when a document is rendered, or presented, to the client. In HTML, a markup tag is specified by surrounding the command with a less-than sign (<) and a greater-than sign (>). A markup command can have optional attributes, which are included inside the less-than and greater-than signs with the name of the command, and it can have associated data, which is enclosed between a start and end tag. Thus, to write the HTML markup that specifies that something should be written in boldface, you would write `<b>here is` important text</b>. Since a picture is worth a thousand words, take a look at Listing 1.1, which shows very simple HTML document, and try to guess what the markup is intended to accomplish.

> **Fresh Brew** _____
>
> If you remember from a few pages back, an international body, known as ICANN, strictly controls the physical mechanisms that run the Internet. The web, on the other hand, is not controlled in this manner. Instead, there is an international organization, known as the World Wide Web Consortium (W3C) that publishes recommendations detailing specific technologies. The W3C has no power to enforce these recommendations, something that was made painfully clear during the struggle between Netscape and Microsoft for control of the web browser market. The W3C relies on the power of peer pressure to enforce all implementers of web technology to faithfully adopt its recommendations. For more information on the W3C, go to www.w3c.org.

Listing 1.1   A Simple HTML Document

```html
<html>
<head>
<title>A Simple HTML Document </title>
</head>
<body>
<h1>Hello World</h1>
<hr>
This is a <i>simple</i> example that is designed to
demonstrate how <b>simple</b> it is to write HTML documents.
</body>
</html>
```

Give up? Figure 1.1 shows how the Microsoft Internet Explorer web browser renders this HTML document. Don't worry; since this book is not designed to teach you HTML, I am not going to spend any more time on it. If you want to know more, take a look *The Complete Idiot's Guide to Creating a Web Page*, by Paul McFedries. All you need to know at this point is HTML is the means by which information is transported across the Internet.

> **Coffee Break** _____
>
> If you already have a firm grasp of web application, you may wonder why I haven't mentioned any other web acronyms. Good question, but everything in its own time. Later in this book, I will discuss how cascading style sheets (CSS) and JavaScript can be used to improve the look and functionality of a JSP web application. We also, among many other cool things, will generate XML documents using JSP.

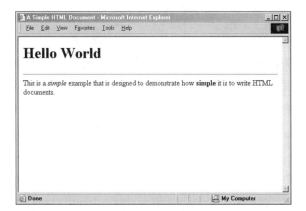

Figure 1.1

This is a simple HTML document as rendered by Internet Explorer.

What About Dynamic Content?

If you were paying attention during the last section, you saw a simple little HTML document. This simplicity allows anyone to create their own web pages, which can include images, audio, movies, or who knows what. By and large, however, these web pages are almost all static in nature. This is not a good model; after all, who wants to reread the same newspaper everyday?

In the static world, to change a web page—or in more formal terms the HTTP response to a specific HTTP request—someone needs to rewrite the web page. Fortunately, better (and cheaper) solutions were invented. Some of the more popular include Common Gateway Interface (CGI), Microsoft's Active Server Pages (ASP) technology, and the open source server scripting language PHP. Many of the websites you visit everyday, such as www.google.com or www.amazon.com, utilize technologies like these that generate dynamic content. Often the response these sites generate is based on input that you provide, perhaps through an HTML form as demonstrated in Listing 1.2 and shown in Figure 1.2. (Whenever you see a place to enter data in a web browser, you are viewing an HTML form. A form contains HTML elements that specify what type of input it will receive. When you enter a username and password to gain access to a website, you are typing information into an HTML form. This information is sent to the web server as part of the request from the browser.)

Listing 1.2   A Fictitious HTML Form Document

```
<html>
<head>
<title>A Simple HTML Document </title>
</head>
<body>
<h1>Hello World</h1>
```

continues

Listing 1.2 A Fictitious HTML Form Document (continued)

```
<hr>
<form method="POST" action="http://www.myserver.com/Hello">
<p> Enter your name:
<input type="text" name="username" size="20"/>
<input type="submit" value="Submit" name="B1"/>
</p>
</form>
</body>
</html>
```

Figure 1.2

Our simple HTML form document as rendered by Internet Explorer.

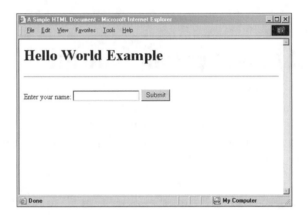

Let's take a closer look at the form document. The <HTML> tag tells the browser that this is an HTML document. The <HEAD> tag specifies any prolog information for this file. Items such as the title are contained within the closing </HEAD>. Everything else in the HTML document is contained within the <BODY> tag. You have a "Hello World" text that will be displayed, followed by a horizontal line rule <HR>.

The form tag has a number of attributes associated with it. In this example, you are telling the form to execute the HTTP POST request and send all of the information to the location www.myserver.com/Hello. The information in a form is only sent to the server when the Submit button is pressed. More on this shortly.

On this form, users are asked to enter their name. This is followed by an input field that allows text to be entered. When the information is sent to the server, you will be able to access what the user entered by looking at the "username" attribute specified as the name. In this sample, I've limited the text a user can enter to 20 characters.

Last but not least, there is the Submit button. Here's where the action takes place. When the user presses the button that is displayed, all of the information in this form will be sent to the server. Through this type of mechanism you are able to gather input from a user and pass it along to the web server. Forms play an important role in JSP technology because they are the mechanism for getting input from the user to the server.

Hot Java _____

While it is possible to have multiple forms on a given HTML page, you can't have nested forms. If you take Listing 1.2 and add a nested form, the code would look like this:

```
<form method="POST" action="http://www.myserver.com/Hello">
<p> Enter your name:
<input type="text" name="username" size="20"/>
<form method="POST" action="http://www.myserver.com/Hello">
<input type = "submit" value="Submit" name="B2"/>
</form>
<input type="submit" value="Submit" name="B1"/>
</form>
```

This is not valid HTML. It's necessary to plan how your data input works to avoid this situation.

Many of the most popular websites are almost completely dynamic in nature. This does not mean that they do not contain any static content; instead, they present the static content in different formats or in different combinations.

For example, one of the most popular web search engines is Google (www.google.com), shown in Figure 1.3, which generates a list of web pages that is bound to satisfy any given query. Another example would be an e-commerce website such as the Barnes and Noble website, shown in Figure 1.4, where you search the store for items that interest you. One last example are websites that search e-commerce sites for best deals, such as the BestBookBuys site for the book industry or the Qixo site for the airlines industry, shown in Figure 1.5.

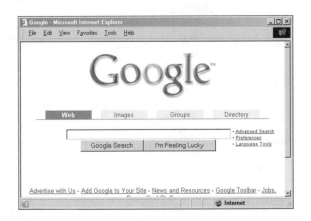

Figure 1.3

The Google web search engine website, where a simple query can find you whatever you want on the Internet.

Figure 1.4

An example of an e-commerce site: the Barnes and Noble online bookstore, where dynamic content is a necessity in order to effectively serve the customer.

Figure 1.5

The BestBookBuys website, where you can price-shop multiple online bookstores to find who has the best prices on any book.

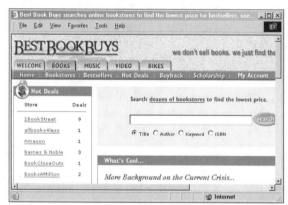

Figure 1.6

The Qixo website, where you can price-compare multiple airlines for a given travel itinerary.

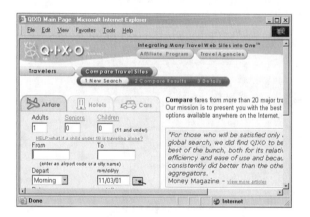

All of these, and other, less popular alternatives that I didn't list, allow a web developer to generate a new response for each client request, depending on a wide range of different factors. None of these solutions, however, are Java-based, and thus I can't talk about them since this is a Java-based book. Seriously though, these other solutions don't enjoy the many benefits of Java, including platform and vendor probability, scalability, efficiency, security, and the access to many built-in enterprise technologies like database access. Fortunately, a Java solution was also developed.

Primordial Java

The Java solution came into being as part of the evolution of web technology. Initially, all web-based processing was done on the client. The client means just in the browser. This is when technologies like JavaScript and Visual Basic (VB) script came into play.

Coffee Break

Java and JavaScript have nothing in common other than they both use the word Java. They are completely different beasts. It has been confusing to many people to have two different technologies named so similarly. Java is a programming language. JavaScript is a scripting language. The way you use them is completely different, so don't be fooled into thinking you know one because you might know the other.

As dynamic content became more popular, the client wasn't very exciting anymore. Things moved to the server-side. It was here that a number of new technologies began to arise. It is also here that it became possible to get true dynamic content by using databases.

First in the server-side game was CGI (Common Gateway Interface); that provided a clumsy and slow way to get to dynamic data. Because CGI had such poor performance, something called FastCGI (how original) became popular.

The next step was to improve on FastCGI and somehow get the web request processing right inside the web server. That's when Server Side Includes (SSI) was born. Many web server providers jumped on the bandwagon, but the problem was that each provider had their own set of rules for how SSIs worked. This posed problems for developers and along came the mighty engine of Microsoft to tame the beast.

Microsoft introduced Active Server Pages (ASP). The real benefit of using ASP was that as a developer, you could now specify your own custom way of doing things instead of being told what to do by a provider of SSI. Some might consider this a "two steps forward, one step back" proposition, because by using ASP you're still tied to the Microsoft environment.

So next came Java Servlets, a generic server extension. But Servlets can be cumbersome to work with and you need to be a programmer fairly well versed in Java to write servlets.

That's where JavaServer Pages technology comes into the picture. JSPs are an extension of Java Servlets. You get almost the same benefits using JSP, but you don't need to be a true Java programmer to use it. In fact, most JSP programmers are web content providers. They are interested in getting the pages to look and layout nicely, but also want to get the added features of dynamic content.

The Life and Times of a Servlet

This Java solution is Servlets. Originally introduced in 1997, Java Servlets have since grown to provide a robust Java-based mechanism for generating dynamic content. Servlets are not the easiest technology to use for generating dynamic HTML.

Coffee Break

In case your Java is a little rusty, let me refresh your memory. Java applications are portable because they are not tied to a particular machine or operating system. This is different than most software, which is designed to run on a specific type of hardware. Instead, Java applications run inside a Java Virtual Machine (JVM). A virtual machine is a program that runs like non-Java programs and provides a special environment for Java programs to execute. It looks like a real machine to Java applications, but is really a virtual machine since the actual machine does not exist.

Normally, when an application is compiled, it can only be installed and executed on a single type of computer, like an Intel-based personal computer running Microsoft Windows. Since Java applications are compiled to run inside a JVM, they can be installed on any computer that has a JVM, which nowadays is almost any computer in the world. This makes Java programs very portable.

Historically, this meant that Java programs ran slower than similar programs that were designed to work directly with particular hardware. With significant improvements in Java compilers and JVMs, this is no longer as big of a concern as it used to be. Even more interesting, some hardware vendors are actually looking to create a hardware implementation of a JVM, which would run Java applications even faster, as it wouldn't be very virtual!

Servlets are Java programs must run inside a Java Virtual Machine (JVM). Because most web servers are not written in Java, you need a program that implements the Servlet specification. This program is called a Servlet container—when an application runs that uses Servlet technology, the Servlet itself is actually running inside the Servlet container.

Servlets have a well-defined life cycle, which is managed by the Servlet container. First, the Servlet class must be loaded into a JVM and instantiated. After this, the Servlet is initialized, during which time it can obtain current runtime parameters or establish database connections. Once a Servlet is properly initialized, it is ready to handle requests. Finally, when a Servlet container determines that a Servlet is no longer needed, say your toddler pushed the shutdown button on your server, the Servlet is destroyed, and all acquired resources are released.

 Hot Java

The application that provides support for a Servlet (or JSP) document is a Servlet (or JSP) container. You may also see this called a Servlet engine, which is the old name. Don't show your age—call them containers.

Why JavaServer Pages?

At this point, you may be wondering when, if ever, I am going to get around to talking about JSP—"Robert, this is a book on JavaServer Pages, right?" Never fear, because in a roundabout way, I already have. JSP technology is translated into Java Servlets before they are executed inside a Servlet container. For more details see Chapter 3, "Building Your First JSP."

 Fresh Brew

Unless you want to embarrass yourself at the office holiday party, never refer to JSP as Java Server Pages. The official name is JavaServer Pages. Of course you are always safe with JSP.

JSP pages are just plain text documents that can contain regular text, known as template data, and server-side scripts to indicate how dynamic content should be generated. There is syntax defined in the JSP specification that allows for all sorts of neat things to be done. You will be learning about those features later on in the book but for now, take a look at your first JSP, shown in Listing 1.3. This JSP page creates a web page that dynamically generates a response that looks identical to the web page in Listing 1.1. Compare this to Listing 1.2 and you should see one reason why JSP is much better. (Hint: Which is easier to read?)

Listing 1.3   A Dynamic JSP Page

```
<html>
<head>
<title>
Hello World Example
</title>
</head>
<body>
<h1>
<% out.println("Hello World"); %>
</h1>
</body>
</html>
</html>
```

The JSP looks very similar to the HTML page we walked through earlier, with one exception: the new addition of the line `<% out.println("Hello World"); %>`. What makes this line important is that you are now getting data on the fly and adding into the final HTML document that will be displayed to the user. You will see shortly that this is one of the key features of JSP.

Perhaps the best reason, however, to use JSP is that it is a specification. In Chapter 2, "Playing with Pets," I show you how to install everything you need to learn how to write and execute JSP pages. Primarily, this will involve the Jakarta Tomcat Servlet container, which provides the official JSP and Servlet reference implementation, and most importantly is free. But Tomcat isn't the only game in town, just the cheapest. You are free to select a JSP container from any vendor, and as long as it is standard compliant, everything you learn about JSP in this book will work.

The Least You Need to Know

♦ Internet communication primarily relies on TCP/IP, domain names, and port numbers.

♦ HyperText Transfer Protocol (HTTP) is the language web applications use to communicate.

♦ HyperText Markup Language (HTML) is used to encode documents for use on the web.

♦ JSP pages are turned into Servlets.

♦ JSP technology provides a cool way to generate dynamic content.

Playing with Pets

In This Chapter

- ◆ Installing Java
- ◆ Acquiring and installing Tomcat
- ◆ Defining and looking at IDEs
- ◆ Finding JSP web hosting sites

Chapter 1, "The Backgrounder," presents the foundation on which JavaServer Pages (JSP) technology is built. Before you can start whipping up JSP documents, however, you need to make sure you have everything installed to actually produce them. Having your own computer, preferably with an Internet connection, to develop and test your JSP builds is an obvious requirement; I won't walk you through that step. However, I will walk you through the rest of the process, which includes acquiring and installing a Java Virtual Machine (JVM), a Servlet container, and (optionally) a Java Integrated Development Environment (IDE). One other thing I discuss in this chapter is finding a web-hosting site for your newly created JSP files.

Installing Java

With the perplexing zoo of acronyms that the Java language has become, installing the right software has become a little more difficult. Perhaps you're anxious about knowing you have installed the right software. To make sure this doesn't happen to you, I will guide you through the Java maze. At the end, you will have installed the Java 2 platform, and, hopefully, will have a better understanding of what all this Java nonsense means—just think how you will amaze all of your colleagues at the next company picnic—and not just because you can scoff down 10 hot dogs in less than five minutes!

Tagged

In case you're wondering what the difference is between a **Java software development kit** (JDK or **Java SDK**) and a **Java runtime environment** (JRE): The JDK provides you with all the tools you need to build and run Java applications; the JRE only enables you to run Java applications. Because you want to develop and not just run JSPs, you will want to download the Java 2 SDK as detailed later in this chapter.

The Java 2 Platform

Back in the beginning, you could identify the original Java version by the version number of the corresponding Java development kit (JDK) you were using. This started with version 1.0.2 in the first widespread release of the Java language, and eventually went through several JDK 1.1.x versions. In one of the greatest marketing ploys of all time—at least in their own minds—the Javasoft marketing team decided to change the name of the Java language version to Java 2 following the release of the JDK version 1.2.

Not since the introduction of new Coke has a marketing ploy been met with such amusement. With the release of the next version of the JDK, however, things became a little less humorous. Suddenly, the name became "version 1.3 of the JDK for the Java 2 platform," which is more than just a mouthful. But, to get back to the topic at hand, the current version, and what I will be using throughout this book, is version 1.4. The official Javasoft website for the Java 2 platform is www.javasoft.com/java2. You can reach the main Javasoft website at www.javasoft.com or java.sun.com

By the way, if you're confused about why I continually reference Javasoft and not Sun Microsystems when I discuss Java, don't be. Javasoft is just an operating group within Sun that is responsible for the development and promotion of Java.

Unfortunately, the situation recently became even more complicated (as you will discover if you look at the Java 2 website), although this time the reason is more understandable. Due to the growth in the size and complexity of the JDK, the Javasoft engineers decided to release the kit in three different flavors, which were each targeted toward different market segments. The three flavors are the Java 2 Platform, Standard Edition (J2SE); Java 2 Platform, Enterprise Edition (J2EE); and Java 2 Platform, Micro Edition (J2ME). (There's also a cherry flavor, but I won't mention it again, because it leaves all Java developers with sticky fingers and gooey, red rings around their mouths.)

You can safely ignore J2ME for this book, as it is aimed at developers who are building applications for the mobile devices market, including cell phones. J2SE is for the majority of Java developers, and includes the bulk of the original Java development kits such as the graphical interface classes, the System classes, and the input and output classes. (If you don't know anything about Java classes, wipe that puzzled look off your face. You'll find out about them soon enough!) At the other end of the spectrum is J2EE, which is aimed at developers building large applications that need to provide business services to a large number of users. One example of this type of application would be banking services, such as ATM transactions, or online banking capabilities. (Note to self: Use J2EE to write software that will automatically add $10,000 to my account on a daily basis. Whoops! Did I say that out loud?)

The Java 2 Platform, Standard Edition

Officially, both Servlets and JSP are part of the enterprise edition, and you would, therefore, need to download the J2EE in order to use all that JSP cool stuff. For various reasons you don't need to know, however, you can stick with the J2SE product. The J2SE website (www.javasoft.com/j2se/) contains a link to the download sites for the JDK software for the Solaris operating system, the Windows operating system, and the Linux operating system.

If you are using one of these operating systems, you are all set; just follow the links to download version 1.4 of the Java 2 software development kit (SDK). Once you have downloaded the appropriate SDK, installation is straightforward—just follow the included directions. For example, the Windows installation process will do everything for you, all you need to do is tell it where to install the files.

For those that need a little extra hand-holding, here's a step-by-step guide that I like to call *The Complete Idiot's Guide to Installing the Java SDK on Windows*. Note that, because websites are in a continual state of flux, I can't guarantee that the web pages referenced in the following instructions will still exist when you read this. You might have to start at the main URL of java.sun.com/ and adapt the following process as necessary.

1. Load up your web browser and go to this URL: java.sun.com/j2se/. The Java 2 Platform Standard Edition web page appears.
2. Under the Current Releases head, click the "Java 2 SDK, Standard Edition, v 1.4 Beta 3 (SDK)" link. The "Java 2 SDK, Standard Edition, v 1.4.0 Beta 3 (J2SETM)" web page appears.
3. Click the "Download Windows" link. The "Download Java 2 SDK, Standard Edition, v1.4.0 Beta 3 for Windows 95/98/ME/2000/NT 4.0 (Intel Platform)" section of the web page appears.
4. Click the Continue button right under the heading. The "Terms and conditions of the license & export for Java(TM) 2 SDK, Standard Edition, Beta 3 1.4.0" web page appears.

5. Read the agreement (yeah, right), and then at the bottom of the page, click the Accept button. The "Download Java(TM) 2 SDK, Standard Edition, Beta 3 1.4.0" web page appears.

6. Click one of the download buttons. Windows asks whether you want to Open or Save the file.

7. Choose Save, and download the file to your Desktop. Because the file is 35MB, unless you have high-speed Internet access, you might as well go paint a house or something until the download completes.

8. When the download completes, double-click the resultant file. The Java installer starts. Follow the onscreen instructions to complete the process. That wasn't so hard, was it?

> **Fresh Brew** _____
>
> Throughout this book, I will primarily demonstrate how to do things on a Windows platform, in my case that is Windows 2000 Server. Since JSP technology is almost exclusively platform independent, this should present few problems if you are working on a different platform. In the small number of situations where confusion might arise, such as directory structures, I will include a discussion in the text, or utilize a sidebar, like this one, to indicate what you should see or do on a UNIX or Linux platform.

If you are using a different operating system, all is not lost, as various vendors have developed either JDKs or JVMs for a wide range of operating systems. Javasoft maintains a list of Java platforms for some of the more obscure or less popular operating systems at www.javasoft.com/cgi-bin/java-ports.cgi. As you can see in Figure 2.1, almost any computer you want to use is supported by the Java 2 platform. Other JVMs exist for both the Windows and Linux platforms, so you have a lot of options if you don't want to achieve higher performance or are looking for a better licensing arrangement.

Figure 2.1

This website lists ports of the Java 2 platform available to other operating systems.

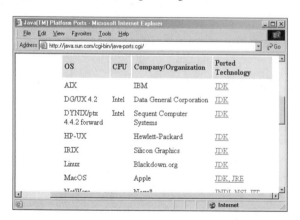

Introducing Apache, Jakarta, and Tomcat

Once you have installed the appropriate JDK (which is the same thing as the Java SDK), the next step is to acquire a curious thing called, by people in the know, a Servlet container. This thingy will serve your JSP documents as a web application. Even if you already have access to a commercial JSP and Servlet container via your employer, I strongly encourage you to follow along with the directions in this section to download and install the Tomcat Servlet container, because Tomcat provides a completely functioning Servlet and JSP container. Tomcat comes in several different versions (for details see the following section). In this book, I use Tomcat version 4, which, of course, means that you should, too.

Coffee Break

You may have heard about Apache—it is the world's most popular web server. In fact, more web sites use the Apache web server, or its derivatives, than all other web servers combined. The Apache web server is an open source software project (which means anyone can get the source code and modify it), and relies on developers around the globe for continued maintenance and development.

The Apache project has grown beyond its roots, however. Nowadays, software projects covering Java, XML, and PHP fall under the Apache umbrella. To simplify the legal aspects and rights of the Apache project, the Apache Software Foundation (ASF) was started.

One of the big benefits of creating the ASF was that corporations could support the work of the Apache projects. This has allowed Sun to provide and support the development of Java projects, including the JSP reference implementation. If you are interested, you can join the ASF, and contribute to the world of quality, free software.

The Jakarta project (jakarta.apache.org) manages all of the Java-specific projects "owned" by the Apache Software Foundation. This includes the Tomcat Servlet container, as well as other popular Java projects like the Ant build tool, the log4j logging tool, and the Struts library.

Getting Your Own Tomcat

Okay, so now you are convinced that Tomcat is the greatest thing since sliced bread—if not, reread the last section! Now it is time to actually get your own Tomcat, which is amazingly simple. Just go to the Jakarta project website at jakarta.apache.org, shown in Figure 2.2.

Figure 2.2

The Jakarta project manages the Java-specific projects for the Apache Software foundation, including the Tomcat Servlet container.

On the left side of this web page, you will see a bunch of links under the "SubProjects" heading. If you follow the Tomcat link, you will travel to the Tomcat website, which is shown in Figure 2.3. Be sure to keep your head about you, despite all of the different possibilities on this web page. You want to download a binary version of Tomcat, which is one of the options on the left side of the Tomcat website, under the "Download" heading. Just click the Binaries link to get there.

Figure 2.3

The Tomcat website is the home of the Tomcat Servlet container. Tomcat is the official reference implementation for Servlet and JSP technology.

At this point, you will see the Jakarta project web page that lists all available downloads. You probably have noticed that there are three different versions of software available:

♦ **Release Builds** are production-quality versions that are stable and have been thoroughly tested.

♦ **Milestone Builds** are basically Beta products that provide new functionality, but have not been thoroughly tested.

♦ **Nightly Builds** are the current state of the development effort, and are only for experts who are contributing to the development of a particular project.

You will want to download the latest release build for Tomcat, which, at the time of this writing, is version 4.0.1. When you select this link, you go to the Tomcat download site, where you can obtain either binary or source versions. Click the Bin folder near the top of the page, and then click on the jakarta-tomcat-4.0.1.zip file (or whatever the latest version is). Download this file to your Desktop. Because the file is a relatively slim-and-trim 5MB, you won't have time to paint a house, but you might get a living room done! (By the way, information on downloading versions of Tomcat for other operating systems is available in the README file that is displayed along with the Tomcat download web page.)

Installing Your Tomcat

After you have downloaded version 4 or later of Tomcat, you can now proceed to the installation phase. You can either attempt to figure it all out for yourself (good luck!), or you can use the following *Complete Idiot's Guide to Installing Tomcat on Windows:*

1. Make sure that you have installed the Java SDK.

2. Open your Start menu, and select Run. The Run dialog box appears.

3. In the Open box, type sysedit, and then click OK. The Sysedit application appears.

4. Select the AUTOEXEC.BAT window, and add the following line to the end of the file: **SET JAVA_HOME=*X*:\j2sdk1.4.0-beta3**, where *X* is the drive on which you installed the Java SDK.

5. Reboot your computer so that the new environment variable becomes active.

6. Double-click the file you downloaded, and unzip its contents to your hard disk. (If, for some insane reason, you don't have the software you need to unzip files, point your web browser to www.winzip.com.)

Note: If you are using a different operating system, like Linux, you can download the appropriate zip or tar.gz file and follow the online directions for installing and running Tomcat. These instructions are located at the URL jakarta.apache.org/tomcat/tomcat-4.0-doc/RUNNING.txt. Essentially, all you need to do is unpack the downloaded file into the appropriate installation directory. After all is said and done, you should have a directory structure similar to the one shown in Figure 2.4.

Figure 2.4

After installing Tomcat, you should take a look at the installed directory structure, as we will be working in various directories throughout the book.

Now What?

The last step in the process is to start up the Tomcat server. Several scripts in the jakarta-tomcat-4.0.1\bin subdirectory control the operation of the Tomcat server. On Windows platforms, you will use the startup and shutdown batch files (startup.bat and shutdown.bat), while on the UNIX platforms, you will use the startup and shutdown shell scripts (startup.sh and shutdown.sh). In order to properly set up and reclaim server resources, you should always use these scripts to start (using the startup script) and stop (using the shutdown script).

At this point, assuming you already didn't jump the gun, go ahead and start your Tomcat server. To test your installation, you can open a web browser and enter the following URL in your web browser: localhost:8080/. If your browser looks like the one in Figure 2.5, you have done everything successfully. If not, be sure to read the Release notes that came with your copy of the Tomcat server.

Figure 2.5

Once Tomcat has been installed, start it up. If you browse to localhost:8080/ and see this web page, you know your installation worked.

You should also check that you have properly installed your version of the Java software development kit. Go to your Start menu, and look under Accessories for Command Prompt. Click this selection to open a shell window (a command prompt), and type the following (exact details will depend on your operating system and command shell):

```
echo %JAVA_HOME%
```

Or ...

```
echo $JAVA_HOME
```

If you don't get the directory where you installed your Java SDK, you will need to set the JAVA_HOME environment variable properly before starting Tomcat. For more information, refer to the Tomcat installation directions earlier in this chapter.

Once Tomcat is running properly, you should pat yourself on the back for a job well done. Heck, go get a hot fudge sundae! Now the fun begins. By following the links on the Tomcat welcome page, you can take a look at some JSP example pages that are included with the Tomcat server. From the Tomcat JSP example page, shown in Figure 2.6, you can try out the examples, look at the JSP source code, or both.

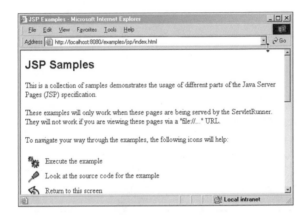

Figure 2.6

The Tomcat Servlet container comes with several JSP samples. You can either see the source code for the JSP document, see the JSP document in action, or both.

Using an Integrated Development Environment

At this point, you have everything you need to build and test JSP pages. However, the development of any Java application, including JSP- and Servlet-based web applications, can be greatly simplified by using a Java Integrated Development Environment (IDE). An integrated development environment pulls together all the tools you need—editor, compiler, debugger, and so on—into one cohesive software package. Some specific benefits of an IDE include the following:

- Syntax highlighting or coloring
- One-click compilation and execution
- Integrated debugging
- Code completion and templates
- Complete project management

Specific IDEs that have explicit support for JSP development include the following:

- Forte for Java, which is available from Sun
- VisualAge for Java, which is available from IBM
- JDeveloper, which is available from Oracle
- JBuilder, which is available from Borland

If you are going to be developing a large JSP web application, I strongly suggest that you take a look at these products. On the down side, these products often are rather expensive, sometimes do not automatically support the latest version of the JSP specifications, and generally have a steep learning curve to become fully functioning within the environment.

Coffee Break

If you are on a tight budget or are just playing with JSPs, you may not feel like laying down the necessary cash to purchase a Java IDE. In this case, you have two primary options. First, you do not need an IDE to develop Java applications, including JSP. You can always use the JDK you downloaded earlier and a simple text editor like Notepad or Emacs to develop your applications.

However, if you really enjoy the integrated environment, all is not lost. Many popular IDEs include a free version—such as the Forte for Java, Community Edition—that can be used for many projects. Another option is to use an open source and completely free IDE, such as NetBeans, which is available at www.netbeans.org.

Thinking About JSP Web Hosting

At this point, the last thing you are probably thinking about is where you are going to set up your new JSP web application. (You're probably still thinking about that hot fudge sundae!) However, we might as well talk about it now. Many ISP and web hosting services do not (yet) provide support for JSP web applications. Before you have built your attention-grabbing, world-domination JSP website, be sure to select a web service provider that will enable the public to view your masterpiece as you intended. Two prominent JSP providers are hostjsp.com and ejip.com. You can find a listing of some of the JSP providers online at www.jspinsider.com/services/hosting.view.

However, to be perfectly clear, in order to learn about JSP technology or to just follow along with the examples in this book, you do not need a JSP-capable web hosting service. You only need a web hosting service if you want to provide access to a JSP-enabled website, which you want someone else to manage for you.

If you have a permanent Internet connection, such as DSL or a cable modem, you can always run your own site, subject to the terms of your ISP agreement, of course. If you have a static IP address, this is rather easy, just buy the domain name you want, and register it to point to your static IP address.

If you have a dynamic IP address, things are more difficult, but still possible. First, you can upgrade your ISP connection to a static IP address, which is generally called a business package. Second, you can follow the directions for the static IP case and as long as you never disable your Internet connection you should be okay. If you do lose your Internet connection and are assigned a new dynamic IP address, you will need to reregister your site with your DNS registrar. This process will generally take a few days to become effective, which may be rather bad for business. Finally, you can look for a DNS forwarding service, where you can have traffic forwarded from your domain, which is managed for a small fee, to your personal website, which you maintain.

The Least You Need to Know

- The official Javasoft website for the Java 2 platform is www.javasoft.com/java2. You can download the Java SDK from this website.

- To get your own copy of Tomcat, go to the Jakarta project website at jakarta. apache.org.

- Before running Tomcat, you must have the Java SDK installed properly on your computer.

- To start and stop the Tomcat software, you should use the script files located in the jakarta-tomcat-4.0.1\bin subdirectory.

- To test your Tomcat installation, open a web browser to the URL localhost:8080/. If your browser displays the Tomcat introduction page, you're in business.

Building Your First JSP

In This Chapter

◆ Saying hello JSP style

◆ Deploying your JSP

◆ Looking at the gory details of a JSP

◆ Seeing the results

I can already hear the grumbling—"Two chapters and we still haven't written a JSP"—so I won't hold you back anymore. In this chapter, you get your chance to shine. Building on a simple JSP example, you will learn how to write and deploy a JSP document, what happens to the JSP, and how to view the results. This simple example you build is the classic "Hello World" example, which made its first appearance in the classic programming book, *The C Programming Language*, by Brian W. Kernighan and Dennis M. Ritchie. I picked this example because it's easy and demonstrates the basics of JSP. In truth, we will actually build several different sample JSPs, so this chapter could be called your first, second, third, and maybe more JSP.

Saying Hello

In order to show you how to write, deploy, and view a JSP-generated page in action, without getting bogged down in complex JSP constructs, I am going to start with the aforementioned "Hello World" demonstration and follow all the steps from writing the page to seeing it viewed in a browser window. The directions in this chapter are for the Tomcat version 4.0 web server. If you are using a different Servlet container, you may see something different or require slightly different instructions.

Looking at the JSP Itself

First, you need to create your first JSP document, which is shown in Listing 3.1. As you can see, this JSP doesn't do a whole lot, just prints out "Hello World!" In fact, if you are very observant, you may have noticed that this example is actually an HTML file. Don't worry; this is intentional, and perfectly legal. By starting with this example, you will have a good baseline that helps you see what changes when you start adding JSP elements into this simple example.

Listing 3.1   A Simple JSP

```
<html>
    <head>
        <title> Hello World Example </title>
    </head>
    <body>
        <h1> Hello World! </h1>
    </body>
</html>
```

Here's how to get this example typed and saved to your hard disk:

1. Start Notepad (or some other text editor).

2. Enter Listing 3.1 into the new document.

3. Save this file, under the name hello.jsp, to the webapps\examples\jsp subdirectory of your Tomcat installation, as shown in Figure 3.1. (If you went with the installation defaults, the full path is *X*:\jakarta-tomcat-4.0.1\webapps\examples\jsp\hello.jsp, where *X* is the hard drive to which you installed Tomcat.)

Important note: If you use Notepad to create and save your file, be aware that Notepad likes to tack the extension .txt onto every file name. This means that your JSP file may end up with the name hello.jsp.txt. If this happens, you'll need to manually change the name back to hello.jsp. If Tomcat can't find your file, check that the file name is correct. To stop Notepad from adding the .txt file-name extension, change the file type in the Save As dialog box from "Text Documents (*.txt)" to "All Files."

Another important note: If you're using a text editor other than Notepad, be absolutely sure that you save the file as plain text! Tomcat can't understand things like Word .doc files. Tomcat can't understand David Lynch films, either, but who can?

Congrats on creating your first JSP file! Of course, creating the file is just the start. The next step is to have Tomcat turn this JSP into one of those Servlet thingies we talked about earlier.

Figure 3.1

This figure shows the directory structure of the Tomcat installation, focusing on the directories where you will be deploying your JSP documents.

Seeing Is Believing

Before you can use your JSP page, it must be translated into a type of file that Java can understand. This type of file is called a compiled Java class file. The translation process is known as the *translation phase* (Oooh! We're really sounding geeky now!) and consists of two steps:

1. The JSP file is converted into a Servlet.

2. The Servlet is compiled into the JSP implementation class, which is the form that Java can run. (In more geek terms, you would say that "The servlet can be run inside the *JVM*, or *Java Virtual Machine*.")

The translation phase automatically occurs the first time a browser loads the JSP page. This translation process can take a few moments or more, depending on the size of the JSP file. In these cases, one cool thing the pros do is precompile their JSP pages in order to minimize any delays when a browser loads the pages.

In order to tell a Servlet container to generate the corresponding Servlet for a JSP page, all you need to do is request the JSP page from your web browser. Here's how to do this with your hello.jsp file:

1. Start Tomcat using the startup script. (If you forgot how to do this, refer back to Chapter 2, "Playing with Pets.")

Tagged

Java applications run inside a **JVM**. (A gold star to every reader who remembers that JVM means **Java Virtual Machine**.) To do so, they are first compiled into a Java class file. This class file is what the JVM loads and runs.

2. Start your web browser.

3. Direct your browser to localhost:8080/examples/jsp/hello.jsp. (To do this, type the URL `localhost:8080/examples/jsp/hello.jsp` into your browser's address box and press Enter.)

After a brief pause (translation phase, remember?), you should see the resulting web page in your browser, as shown in Figure 3.2. Not only was your JSP page translated into a Java class file, but it also was turned into the HTML file you're now admiring in your browser. How cool is that? The processing phase is the second step performed by the Servlet container. As long as the original JSP file remains unchanged, the translation step (the first step) is not repeated. This means that the next time you want to display your hello.jsp page, it'll pop up almost immediately.

Figure 3.2

This figure shows the end result of the JSP translation and processing phases.

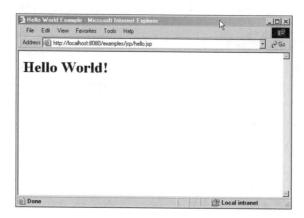

The Generated Servlet

While it produces the HTML file for your web browser, the Tomcat server also generates a Servlet, which Tomcat saves in a temporary work directory. You can view this Servlet by opening the hello$jsp.java file, located in the jakarta-tomcat-4.0.1\work\localhost\examples\jsp directory as show in Figure 3.3.

Figure 3.3

The Tomcat Servlet container stores generated Servlets under the work subdirectory of the Tomcat installation.

When you look at the hello$jsp.java Servlet, keep in mind that your Servlet may look slightly different. This can be due to several reasons:

♦ You have a different version of the Tomcat server.

♦ You created a slightly different version of the hello.jsp file.

♦ You have different Servlet containers.

With that warning, let's jump into action and stroll through the hello$jsp.java Servlet, shown in Listing 3.2.

Listing 3.2   The Generated Servlet for Our Simple JSP

```java
package org.apache.jsp;

import javax.servlet.*;
import javax.servlet.http.*;
import javax.servlet.jsp.*;
import org.apache.jasper.runtime.*;


public class hello$jsp extends HttpJspBase {


    static {
    }
    public hello$jsp( ) {
    }

    private static boolean _jspx_inited = false;

    public final void _jspx_init() throws
org.apache.jasper.runtime.JspException {
    }

    public void _jspService(HttpServletRequest request, HttpServletResponse
response)
        throws java.io.IOException, ServletException {

        JspFactory _jspxFactory = null;
        PageContext pageContext = null;
        HttpSession session = null;
        ServletContext application = null;
        ServletConfig config = null;
        JspWriter out = null;
        Object page = this;
```

continues

Listing 3.2 The Generated Servlet for Our Simple JSP (continued)

```java
String   _value = null;
try {

    if (_jspx_inited == false) {
        synchronized (this) {
            if (_jspx_inited == false) {
                _jspx_init();
                _jspx_inited = true;
            }
        }
    }
    _jspxFactory = JspFactory.getDefaultFactory();
    response.setContentType("text/html;charset=ISO-8859-1");
    pageContext = _jspxFactory.getPageContext(this, request, response,
            "", true, 8192, true);

    application = pageContext.getServletContext();
    config = pageContext.getServletConfig();
    session = pageContext.getSession();
    out = pageContext.getOut();

    // HTML // begin [file="/jsp/hello.jsp";from=(0,0);to=(7,7)]
        out.write("<html>\r\n    <head>\r\n
        <title> Hello World Example </title>\r\n
        </head>\r\n    <body>\r\n
        <h1> Hello World! </h1>\r\n
        </body>\r\n</html>");

    // end

} catch (Throwable t) {
    if (out != null && out.getBufferSize() != 0)
        out.clearBuffer();
    if (pageContext != null) pageContext.handlePageException(t);
} finally {
    if (_jspxFactory != null)
_jspxFactory.releasePageContext(pageContext);
    }
  }
}
```

Wow! I don't know about you, but that sure is a lot of Java for such a simple example. In fact, the single Java statement in boldface is where the specific HTML is generated. The rest of this class provides the necessary framework for what you will learn in the rest of this book. Don't worry if this seems overwhelming or you don't get something, you still have the rest of the book to go through the details.

You also may have noticed that a few methods in the Servlet—such as the `jspx_init()` method—have no source code inside them. Since your JSP is so simple, being only HTML, these methods have nothing to do, thus they are empty.

See that list of `import` statements near the top of the listing? You know, the lines that look like this:

```
import javax.servlet.*;
import javax.servlet.http.*;
import javax.servlet.jsp.*;
import org.apache.jasper.runtime.*;
```

These statements ensure that the Servlet has access to the parts of the Java API the Servlet requires. The next interesting thing to notice is that the Servlet extends the `HttpJspBase` class, which is the base class for Servlets generated from JSP pages.

That last sentence was a bit of a mouthful, eh? If you're confused, here's the code line in question:

```
public class hello$jsp extends HttpJspBase {
```

Looking at this line you can see that the name of your class is `hello$jsp`. After the name, you see the words `extends HttpJspBase`. All this means is that your `hello$jsp` class adds stuff to the already existing HttpJspBase class. Get it?

In Chapter 1, "The Backgrounder," I briefly talked about the Servlet life cycle. This life cycle has nothing to do with being born, paying taxes, and then dying. Rather, it has to do with the order in which the Servlet does what it needs to do. This stuff happens in this Servlet's `jspx_init()` method for the initializing stage (when the Servlet first starts up) and the `jspService()` method for the service stage (the stage that does what the Servlet is programmed to do). Because this JSP page does nothing complicated, you don't need a destroy method, which is kind of the opposite of the `jspx_init()` method.

Fresh Brew

Web browsers have evolved into powerful applications that can display or manipulate data in a bewildering array of formats. Because of this, a browser must be told what type of data it is being sent. Formally, this is done with something called MIME types (see Chapter 19, "You've Got Mail," for more information). In JSP and Servlets, you tell the browser what's coming by setting the content type of the HTTP response. Several examples of Content types include text/html, text/plain, and text/xml. If this all sounds to you like Greek spoken backward, just know that I will discuss different content types later in this book.

If you are focusing on the jspService() method, you should notice the call to the setContentType() method, which looks like this:

```
response.setContentType("text/html;charset=ISO-8859-1");
```

This method specifies the type of content you want to send to the browser. In this case, it is just plain old HTML.

After this method call, the Servlet sends the HTML in the original JSP page directly to the browser. Notice how this HTML text isn't changed at all; it is just written as a Java String object, like this:

```
// HTML // begin [file="/jsp/hello.jsp";from=(0,0);to=(7,7)]
    out.write("<html>\r\n      <head>\r\n
<title> Hello World Example </title>\r\n
</head>\r\n      <body>\r\n
<h1> Hello World! </h1>\r\n      </body>\r\n</html>");

// end
```

This is an example of what is known as *template text* in a JSP page. Template text is always left exactly as is. You probably also noticed the two control characters \r\n, which are the carriage return and linefeed characters used on Windows platforms to indicate a new line. If you are using a UNIX platform, you would only see a single line feed character, that is \n, because these operating systems encode new lines differently.

Finally, notice the error-handling code near the end of the jspService() method. That stuff looks like this:

```
    } catch (Throwable t) {
        if (out != null && out.getBufferSize() != 0)
            out.clearBuffer();
        if (pageContext != null) pageContext.handlePageException(t);
    } finally {
        if (_jspxFactory != null)
_jspxFactory.releasePageContext(pageContext);
    }
```

Since I did not indicate any special error-handling capabilities in this JSP page, the Servlet is set up to handle any possible problem (known in geek-speak as an *exception condition*). In general, you will want better error handling—unless, that is, you don't mind losing customers! In Chapter 6, "Getting a Free Lunch," you learn to properly handle error conditions in a JSP application. Unfortunately, that chapter really has nothing to do with food, so if you're hungry, get a snack now.

Where There's a Will, There's a Way

Since you might feel a little cheated from the last example—after all, it didn't really contain any JSP elements—let's take a look at a few more examples. Both of these two examples produce the same result in your web browser, but they do the deed in different ways.

CAUTION

Hot Java

If your JSP examples don't work, first be sure that your Tomcat server is running. To check this, open a browser and go to the URL localhost:8080/. If you see the Tomcat welcome message, your Tomcat server is running. If you see the "Sexy Ladies in Leather" page, you're probably doing something wrong.

Another problem could be that you placed your JSP page in the wrong place or that you are using the wrong URL. To simplify matters, I suggest that you always place your JSP file in the jakarta-tomcat-4.0.1\webapps\examples\jsp subdirectory that the Tomcat server placed on your hard drive.

Another Greeting

The next example is a minor variation on the first. As you can see in Listing 3.3, rather than just enter the HTML text directly, in this example, I use a JSP expression to print out my greeting. The code indicates the JSP expression with the <%= tag. (Again, don't worry about the exact JSP details, as we will cover these thoroughly in this book.) To get this example ready to go, perform the following, now familiar, steps:

1. Start your text editor.
2. Enter Listing 3.3 into the new document.
3. Save this file, under the name hello2.jsp, to the jakarta-tomcat-4.0.1\webapps\ examples\jsp\hello.jsp subdirectory of your Tomcat installation.

Listing 3.3   A Second Greeting

```
<html>
    <head>
        <title> Hello World Example </title>
    </head>
    <body>
        <h1> <%="Hello World!"%> </h1>
    </body>
</html>
```

Now, open a browser window and go to localhost:8080/examples/jsp/hello2.jsp. After a brief pause, while Tomcat both translates and processes the JSP page, your browser displays the same web page you saw with the first example. If you take a look at the generated Servlet, which is called hello2$jsp.java and is located in the same directory as the first generated Servlet, you will notice a few changes. In Listing 3.4, I show the relevant part of the Servlet where the HTML output is produced (notice the boldface statements). As before, the HTML, which is just Template text, is not processed, but sent directly to the browser. The JSP expression, however, has been turned into a separate call to the print() method.

Listing 3.4   A Portion of the Generated Servlet

```
// HTML // begin [file="/jsp/hello2.jsp";from=(0,0);to=(5,13)]
    out.write("<html>\r\n      <head>\r\n
    <title> Hello World Example </title>\r\n
    </head>\r\n      <body>\r\n          <h1> ");

// end
// begin [file="/jsp/hello2.jsp";from=(5,16);to=(5,30)]
    out.print("Hello World!");
// end
// HTML // begin [file="/jsp/hello2.jsp";from=(5,32);to=(7,7)]
    out.write(" </h1>\r\n      </body>\r\n</html>");

// end
```

Yet Another Greeting

Before you finish this chapter and get back to the Sexy Ladies in Leather website, take a look at one more example program. Again, this program is a minor variation on the greeting theme. As shown in Listing 3.5, this time, however, I am using a JSP scriptlet—which is enclosed in the <% and %> tags—to print out the line "Hello World!" As before, you should create and save this file (this time as hello3.jsp) in the webapps\examples\jsp subdirectory of your Tomcat installation.

Listing 3.5   A Final Greeting

```
<html>
    <head>
        <title> Hello World Example </title>
    </head>
    <body>
        <h1> <% out.println("Hello World!") ;%> </h1>
    </body>
</html>
```

If you point your browser to localhost:8080/examples/jsp/hello3.jsp, you will see your old friend "Hello, World!" yet again. But this time, there is one small change, which is only visible if you look carefully. First, look at the generated Servlet in the hello3$jsp.java file. You should notice that the HTML output (which is indicated in boldface in Listing 3.6) is passed unprocessed, but the scriptlet is actually placed directly within the Servlet.

Listing 3.6   The Generated Servlet

```
// HTML // begin [file="/jsp/hello3.jsp";from=(0,0);to=(5,13)]
    out.write("<html>\r\n        <head>\r\n
    <title> Hello World Example </title>\r\n
    </head>\r\n      <body>\r\n           <h1> ");

// end
// begin [file="/jsp/hello3.jsp";from=(5,15);to=(5,45)]
    out.println("Hello World!") ;
// end
// HTML // begin [file="/jsp/hello3.jsp";from=(5,47);to=(7,7)]
    out.write(" </h1>\r\n      </body>\r\n</html>");

// end
```

Notice that the Servlet now calls the `println()` method, not the `print()` method, when printing the greeting. The difference is that there is now an extra new line in our generated HTML file, as you can see if you view the HTML source for hello3.jsp, which is shown in Listing 3.7.

Listing 3.7   The Generated HTML

```
<html>
    <head>
        <title> Hello World Example </title>
    </head>
    <body>
        <h1> Hello World!
 </h1>
    </body>
</html>
```

While seemingly minor, this example demonstrates an important point. Small changes can have subtle effects, which might only be noticeable as bugs or inconsistent behavior.

The Least You Need to Know

- ◆ JSP files are just simple text files.
- ◆ The first step in processing a JSP page is the translation phase. During this stage, the JSP page is translated into a Servlet and the Servlet is compiled into a Java class file or a JSP page implementation class.
- ◆ The second step in processing a JSP page is the processing stage, where the client request is received and invoking the JSP page implementation class generates the server response.
- ◆ There is always more than one way to do something in JSP, including saying "Hello!"

A Quick Tour of JSP

In This Chapter

♦ Understanding JSP web application design

♦ Using JavaBeans, tags, and JSP

♦ Introducing implicit objects

♦ Taking stock of JSP elements

Now that you have gotten your feet wet with a few JSP files, it's time to take a look at the big picture. In this chapter, I introduce the main JSP concepts and constructs that I cover in more depth later in the book. First, however, let's talk about JSP application design. Be forewarned, this chapter contains some scary-looking stuff. Just keep in mind that all of this stuff gets explained in detail in later chapters.

Understanding JSP Application Design

All of the JSP examples I present in Chapter 3, "Building Your First JSP," were quite simple, because they were intended to demonstrate a single point. These examples followed a simple design philosophy popularly called *page-centric design*. In this scenario, you focus on writing JSP pages that accomplish a simple task; and, if necessary, you combine several simple JSP pages together to perform more difficult tasks.

In the real world, however, life isn't so simple. Just try to eat a plate of spaghetti without getting sauce on your shirt, and you'll see what I mean. As far as JSP goes, though, this complex world forces you to tackle such complex issues as the following:

◆ **Authentication.** Making sure of a person's identity

◆ **Personalization.** Presenting information that's been personalized to the user

◆ **Localization.** Presenting information in a way that's appropriate to a particular culture or area of the world

◆ **Persistence.** Storing information for later retrieval

Sure, these are way-cool sounding tech words that will impress your friends. Unfortunately, these and other complex issues can make developing JSP applications ... shall we say ... difficult. To overcome these challenges, some folks came up with a different design strategy. This design strategy is named FCBTPB, which stands for Forget Computers Because They're a Pain in the Butt. Okay, I'm lying. The name of the design strategy is actually called the Model-View-Control, or MVC for short. You will frequently see the MVC design strategy referred to as Model 2 in a lot of technical specs. You'll learn more about the Model 2 design strategy in a few minutes and see why it plays such an important role in JSP design.

The Page-Centric Design Model

Although often downplayed in many JSP books, page-centric design can be very useful for something called *prototyping*, which is a fancy word for quickly putting together a model of how something is going to work. One of the primary benefits of the page-centric development process is that debugging (figuring out why something isn't working) is considerably easier, because all of the programming stuff is in one place. Another advantage is that page-centric design makes the initial design process easier. This is because a single page (or more likely, several pages working in concert) provides the whole package.

On the other hand, the page-centric model has several disadvantages. First, talking about this stuff in mixed company is a sure way to never get another date. But more to the point, a page-centric approach tends to mix web development with programming, making it much harder to effectively work on your JSP application. That is, it's much more difficult to combine web-page design with the programming that makes everything work than it is to keep the design separate from the programming. Second, the page-centric approach makes it harder to use your JSP application in other areas of the world or to approach new problems.

The Model 2 Design Paradigm

The alternative to page-centric design is the Model 2 strategy, which essentially uses the very hairy sounding Model-View-Controller (MVC) approach to JSP application development. (Say that three times fast!) To put it more simply (you're welcome), with MVC you're not allowed to put much, if any, programming code into a JSP page. Instead, a JSP page is only responsible for the *view*, which is how information is presented to the user. A Servlet, or possibly a tag library, which you'll learn about later, performs the actual heavy lifting (come on, put some muscle into it!). This Servlet is called the *Controller*. It determines how and when things happen based on some information from the user. Sort of like the Godfather. Finally, interaction with the actual data is controlled by a JavaBean, and is known as the *model*. The model is where all information internal to an application is stored and manipulated. This is commonly referred to as "Business Logic." The model maintains the business logic of an application. JavaBeans are one mechanism in Java that are used to code your business logic. You'll find out more about JavaBeans later in this chapter, but, just for clarity, know that they have nothing to do with that brown stuff you drink in order to wake up in the morning.

The MVC strategy enables you to develop complex applications that are considerably easier to maintain and extend than the applications you get using page-centric models. In other words, if you follow the rules of the MVC design strategy, you'll find that working on your JSP pages is easier. More importantly, once you get to be a JSP pro, you'll find that you have a lot fewer headaches maintaining your JSP applications if you follow the MVC strategy correctly. This is due to the fact that data and how that data is manipulated and viewed are divided into separate processes. The only main disadvantage of this approach is that debugging and prototyping can be tougher due to the complexity of even simple applications. I discuss MVC development in more detail in Chapter 15, "Introducing Servlets."

Fresh Brew

The MVC programming paradigm has been around for a long time. Originally the paradigm, along with many other innovative concepts, was developed at Xerox. In the MVC model, the Model handles the data and all interactions with the data, the View presents the data to the user, and the Controller holds all the programming that performs the application logic.

Implicit Objects

The JSP container provides information to a JSP page through special Java objects known as *implicit objects*. These objects are declared as variables within each JSP page and are provided to you courtesy of the Java language. You don't have to do anything special to have these objects created, it's all done for you by the magic of the JSP container. You are free to use these implicit objects anywhere within a JSP. If you look at Listing 4.1, which is an abbreviation of Listing 3.2 in Chapter 3, you can actually see how the generated Servlet declares these so-called implicit objects, even for our simple JSP example. All of the code listed here is provided for you, free of charge. I'm listing it here just so you can see how they are created under the covers when the Servlet code is generated. Remember … all JSPs actually get compiled into Servlet code.

Listing 4.1   Implicit Objects Declared in the jspService() Method

```
    public void _jspService(HttpServletRequest request, HttpServletResponse
response)
        throws java.io.IOException, ServletException {

        JspFactory _jspxFactory = null;
        PageContext pageContext = null;
        HttpSession session = null;
        ServletContext application = null;
        ServletConfig config = null;
        JspWriter out = null;
```

In this code snippet, you can see what objects are implicitly available at the start of a JSP page. Inside the parentheses of the jspService() method call, you can see both request and response objects, appropriately named request and response. See 'em? In addition, the first few lines of the method declare a group of variables, including a pageContext object, a session object, an application object, and an out object. These variables are the implicit objects provided by the JSP container to the JSP page. I discuss implicit objects in more detail in Chapter 7, "Talking to the Container."

JavaBeans

A JavaBean, or Bean for short, is just a special kind of Java class. You can think of a Bean as a kind of mini-program that provides a specific service. For Beans to work, you must program them using special programming techniques. Originally, JavaBeans were developed to simplify the development of graphical interfaces, but they are extremely useful when building web applications, because you can use them to encapsulate the data that gets processed with a JSP page. What's that fancy word "encapsulate"? I have no idea! I just thought it sounded cool. Actually, encapsulate means to hide data inside an object such as a class.

Examples of data that you might encapsulate with a JavaBean in a JSP application are people, bank accounts, stock information, products, or shopping carts. (Of course, by "shopping carts," I mean online shopping information, not those metal things that leave dents in your car.) The data elements stored in a JavaBean are referred to as *attributes*, and a JavaBean provides access to these attributes via *setter* and *getter methods*. For example, if an attribute is called `age`, access to this attribute must be provided by a `setAge` method and a `getAge` method. This naming scheme is one of the rules of Bean programming. Setter and getter methods are also known as Mutator and Accessor methods, respectively. Many times the terms are used interchangeably in fancy documentation, so if you see methods referred to by either name you'll know what they're talking about. I discuss JavaBeans in more detail in Chapter 11, "Using Cascading Style Sheets."

Fresh Brew

Scope refers to the area within a JSP web application where a Java object is considered valid and is available to other objects. In JSP, there are four different scopes defined in a hierarchy: page, request, session, and application. You can explicitly set the scope attribute for any JavaBeans you use within a JSP application.

Page scope, which is the default, implies that an object is valid (or can be used) only within a given JSP page. Request scope implies that an object is valid only during the processing of a single request. Session scope implies an object is available through-out a single client-server session, such as an e-commerce transaction. Finally, an application scope means that an object is valid throughout an entire JSP web application and is shared among all users of the application.

JSP Tag Libraries

One of the more recent additions to the JSP specification is the Tag Library facility. A Tag Library provides a powerful method for creating name labels for all programmers working on a project. No, wait! Actually, a Tag Library provides a powerful method for encapsulating application logic behind simple tags that appear to the JSP developer as new JSP tags. What is really cool about tags is that they hide much of the coding complexity for JSP developers. Usually a Java expert will write the Java code for specific tags. The tags are then made available to JSP developers in a much simpler fashion and require no knowledge of how to actually write Java code. Yet, you can still get to use the functionality that was written in Java. Tags and Tag Libraries are portable across JSP applications, and essentially provide a new syntax that can feel more natural to JSP developers. Tags and Tag Libraries are discussed in more detail in Chapters 12, "Controlling the Client," and 13, "Using Forms and Applets," respectively.

Taking Stock of JSP Elements

JSP is actually nothing more than HTML pages with some added goodies. The goodies are called JSP elements and are defined with a special syntax that the JSP compiler understands. The JSP elements are what make a JSP. Otherwise it would be just another HTML page. JSP elements come in three types: directive, action, and scripting elements. Elements are constructs within the JSP page that are recognized by the Servlet container. Anything that is not an element is known as template text. In the current JSP specification, all JSP elements can be created using an XML notation, although scripting elements are generally still indicated using the original JSP notation. I discuss JSP elements in more detail in Chapter 5, "Exploring Scripting Elements."

JSP Directives

Directives provide a mechanism for a JSP page to communicate directly with the JSP container, and they do not produce any output on the current request output stream, generally refereed to as out. Remember the implicit objects I mentioned earlier? "Out" is one of those objects that we get for free. The JSP syntax for encapsulating a JSP Directive is to use the <%@ start tag and the %> end tag. The three JSP directives are …

◆ page, which is used to define page-dependent properties and communicate them to the JSP container.

◆ taglib, which declares to the JSP container that the current JSP page uses a JSP tag library.

◆ include, which is used to substitute text and/or JSP code during the JSP translation stage.

Hot Java _____

If you have experience with Java applications, you are probably aware of the ease by which you can write multithreaded, or concurrent, Java applications. Since a web server, and thus a Servlet container, must serve multiple, concurrent users, they are generally multithreaded to improve performance. As a result, different threads can call your JSP page concurrently.

In order to prevent contention issues, or data inconsistencies, you need to declare the threading model your JSP page uses and develop your application accordingly. You can indicate whether your JSP page is thread-safe by setting the isThreadSafe attribute on the **page** directive. If you set it to true, you will need to properly synchronize all shared data access.

JSP Actions

While directive elements provided information to the JSP page during the translation stage or when it's being compiled, action elements provide information to the JSP page during the processing stage, or during runtime; runtime is when the user is actually on the page viewing it in the browser. Action elements follow the XML notation, and utilize the jsp XML namespace. Standard action elements are defined in the JSP specification, and include the following:

- `<jsp:useBean>`
- `<jsp:setProperty>`
- `<jsp:getProperty>`
- `<jsp:include>`
- `<jsp:forward>`
- `<jsp:param>`
- `<jsp:plugin>`

As the names suggest, these actions either relate to the use of JavaBeans in a JSP page, or are used to include content, forward a request to another page, provide information to another JSP page, or to include the specific HTML that is required to indicate a web browser needs to use the Java 2 plugin.

In addition to the standard actions, there are also custom actions, which are used to interact with a tag library. JSP actions are discussed in more detail in Chapters 8, 11, and 12.

JSP Scripting Elements

The last type of JSP element is the scripting element, which connects the other JSP elements and the Template text together. Scripting elements provide a mechanism to add Java code to your JSP page; and, beyond the prototyping stage of your application development, they should be used cautiously. The reason that they should be used cautiously goes back to the MVC model I mentioned earlier. If you use scripts in your JSP, you are basically coding Java into your page. This violates the MVC model because if you have code in your JSP you are more than likely doing something that should be in the Model portion of your application. Remember, JSPs are considered "Views." Not to mention the fact that having Java code in your JSPs make them messy and difficult to read through. Scripting elements are generally indicated using the original JSP syntax; however, the current JSP specification provides an alternative XML syntax that is designed to be used by authoring tools or other automatic generations mechanisms. Currently all scripting elements must be in Java, per the JSP specification, although this restriction may be relaxed in the future.

Scripting elements come in three different categories:

♦ **Declarations,** which are used to declare constructs, either data or methods, that can be used anywhere within a JSP application. Since declarations create constructs that have application, or global, scope, they are generally not recommended.

♦ **Expressions,** which provide a mechanism for embedding a Java expression within a JSP page, that is evaluated and the result is converted to a Java String object.

♦ **Scriptlets,** which are used to embed Java code fragments directly in the JSP page. The scriptlets are processed during the request processing stage.

Scripting can be used in special situations and has its purpose. Sometimes it's just the lazy way out. But when something is easy, it tends to cause problems later. If you are coding Java into your JSPs, take a step back and consider carefully if you really want to be doing so. Usually the answer is no.

The Least You Need to Know

♦ JSP forces you to tackle such complex issues as authentication, personalization, localization, and persistence.

♦ Page-centric design can be useful for prototyping, which means quickly putting together a model of how something is going to work.

♦ On the downside, the page-centric approach tends to mix web development with programming, making it much harder to effectively work on your JSP application.

♦ The alternative to page-centric design is the Model 2 strategy, with which you're not allowed to put much, if any, programming code into a JSP page.

♦ Implicit objects are declared as variables within each JSP page and are provided to you by the Java language.

♦ A JavaBean is just a special kind of Java class that provides a specific service. For Beans to work, you must program them using special programming techniques.

♦ JSP is actually nothing more than HTML pages with JSP scripting elements, which come in three types: declarations, expressions, and scriptlets.

Part 2

Getting Into JSP

In this part you'll learn more about the basics of building a JSP-backed web-site. First, you'll learn how to add Java code to web pages. Next you'll see how to process requests, make responses, and interact with the web server. Finally, you learn how to make multiple JSP pages work together, and then wrap everything up into an actual web application.

Exploring Scripting Elements

In This Chapter

- ◆ Declarations
- ◆ Expressions
- ◆ Scriptlets
- ◆ Comments
- ◆ Quoting

Most of the other books and articles that talk about JSP technology downplay or ignore using Java directly in a JSP page. This is because, in large projects, developers with different expertise and backgrounds are given responsibility for specific parts of a web application. For example, web designers control page layout, database developers control how an application interacts with the corporate data store, and Java developers make the entire thing work. (You also have to consider the "gopher" who keeps everyone stocked with potato chips, gummy bears, and diet soda, but that's not something we'll go into here.)

In order to simplify website development and maintenance, this multideveloper approach requires that a developer never place Java programming code in a JSP page. The page should contain only HTML (or XHTML or XML), JavaBeans, and JSP tag libraries. The reason is simple: A web designer does not know Java and will therefore not know how to use it. Hiding all of the programming details inside JavaBeans and/or JSP tag libraries allows web developers (or more likely their tools) to use only the syntax with which they're familiar when designing a web page.

On the other hand, I don't like being told to do things in a certain way, and I doubt you do, either. As a result, I have taken an alternative approach in this book; I show you all of the possibilities, present their advantages and disadvantages, and let you decide how you want to proceed. In any event, the best course of action in any JSP project is often to first do all of your programming directly in the JSP page, and once everything works, move the programming into JavaBeans, Servlets, or a tag library.

All right, enough of the highbrow stuff. Even I'm getting a headache. It's now time to get down and dirty. In this chapter, I am going to cover the basics of writing JSP pages, including declarations, expressions, scriptlets, comments, and quoting rules—more cool terms to add to your growing techie vocabulary. So start your editor, fire up your Tomcat, and let's get busy.

I Declare!

You use a JSP declaration to declare variables or methods for use within a JSP page. The declaration must be a legal statement for the scripting language used in the JSP page. (Right now, Java is the only language you can use; more on this in Chapter 6, "Getting a Free Lunch.") Declarations produce no output; they just give to the page information about the data and methods you're going to use.

You can write declarations in two ways: JSP syntax or XML syntax. For example, to declare an integer variable named `index` and initialize it to have the value of 10, the JSP syntax would be …

```
<%! int index = 10 ; %>
```

While the XML syntax would be …

```
<jsp:declaration>
int index = 10 ;
</jsp:declaration>
```

One important point to notice is that a semicolon (;) terminates these declarations. The semicolon is necessary, because the declarations must be complete legal statements.

Global or Local?

The most important point to remember when using declarations is that any variable or method declared inside a declaration has *global scope* within the JSP page. A variable or method with global scope can be accessed anywhere within the page. In general, global scope is a bad thing. To see why, take a look at Figure 5.1, which contains a global and local variable.

Listing 5.1 shows the JSP page that produces the web page seen in Figure 5.1. Don't worry about the local variable declaration or the variable accessing; I will cover those later in this chapter.

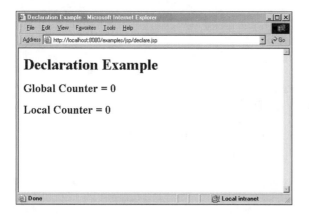

Figure 5.1

This is a simple JSP declaration, showing a global and local variable on the first request.

Listing 5.1   declare.jsp

```
<%! int global = 0 ; %>
<html>
    <head>
        <title> Declaration Example </title>
    </head>
    <body>
        <h1> Declaration Example </h1>
        <h2>
        <% int local = 0 ; %>
        Global Counter = <%=(global++) %>
        <p/>
        Local Counter = <%=(local++) %>
        </h2>
    </body>
</html>
```

To show the difference between the global and local variables, take a look at Listing 5.2, which is the Java file that contains the generated Servlet for the JSP page in Listing 5.1. If you place declare.jsp in the webapps\examples\jsp subdirectory of your Tomcat installation, you can run this example for yourself. The URL for the JSP page in this example is localhost:8080/examples/jsp/declare.jsp. If you have followed along, you can take a look at the generated Servlet by opening the declare$jsp.java file for yourself, which is in the work\localhost\examples\jsp subdirectory of your Tomcat installation.

Listing 5.2 declare$jsp.java

```java
package org.apache.jsp;

import javax.servlet.*;
import javax.servlet.http.*;
import javax.servlet.jsp.*;
import org.apache.jasper.runtime.*;


 public class declare$jsp extends HttpJspBase {

    // begin [file="/jsp/declare.jsp";from=(0,3);to=(0,21)]
        int global = 0 ;
    // end

    static {
    }
    public declare$jsp( ) {
    }

    private static boolean _jspx_inited = false;

    public final void _jspx_init() throws
org.apache.jasper.runtime.JspException {
    }

    public void _jspService(HttpServletRequest request, HttpServletResponse
response)
        throws java.io.IOException, ServletException {

        JspFactory _jspxFactory = null;
        PageContext pageContext = null;
        HttpSession session = null;
        ServletContext application = null;
        ServletConfig config = null;
        JspWriter out = null;
        Object page = this;
        String  _value = null;
        try {

            if (_jspx_inited == false) {
                synchronized (this) {
                    if (_jspx_inited == false) {
                        _jspx_init();
                        _jspx_inited = true;
                    }
```

```
            }
        }
        _jspxFactory = JspFactory.getDefaultFactory();
        response.setContentType("text/html;charset=ISO-8859-1");
        pageContext = _jspxFactory.getPageContext(this, request, response,
                    "", true, 8192, true);

        application = pageContext.getServletContext();
        config = pageContext.getServletConfig();
        session = pageContext.getSession();
        out = pageContext.getOut();

        // HTML // begin [file="/jsp/declare.jsp";from=(0,23);to=(8,8)]
            out.write("\r\n<html>\r\n      <head>\r\n
            <title> Declaration Example </title>\r\n
            </head>\r\n      <body>\r\n
            <h1> Declaration Example </h1>\r\n
            <h2>\r\n              ");

        // end
        // begin [file="/jsp/declare.jsp";from=(8,10);to=(8,27)]
            int local = 0 ;
        // end
        // HTML // begin [file="/jsp/declare.jsp";from=(8,29);to=(9,25)]
            out.write("\r\n          Global Counter = ");

        // end
        // begin [file="/jsp/declare.jsp";from=(9,28);to=(9,39)]
            out.print((global++) );
        // end
        // HTML // begin [file="/jsp/declare.jsp";from=(9,41);to=(11,24)]
            out.write("\r\n          <p/>\r\n          Local Counter = ");

        // end
        // begin [file="/jsp/declare.jsp";from=(11,27);to=(11,37)]
            out.print((local++) );
        // end
        // HTML // begin [file="/jsp/declare.jsp";from=(11,39);to=(14,7)]
            out.write("\r\n          </h2>\r\n      </body>\r\n</html>");

        // end

    } catch (Throwable t) {
        if (out != null && out.getBufferSize() != 0)
            out.clearBuffer();
        if (pageContext != null) pageContext.handlePageException(t);
    } finally {
```

continues

Listing 5.2 declare$jsp.java (continued)

```
            if (_jspxFactory != null)
_jspxFactory.releasePageContext(pageContext);
        }
    }
}
```

Don't worry about the length of this code listing for now; the relevant sections are in boldface. As you can clearly see, especially if you remember the examples from Chapter 3, "Building Your First JSP," the declaration of the global variable is way off by itself. In fact, global is declared with class scope, which means that every single instance of the declare$jsp class will share one copy of the global variable. Any changes by one declare$jsp object will be seen by all of the other copies.

If you reload the JSP page in Listing 5.1, you see how the global variable is increased every time, while the local variable never changes. For example, if you reload declare.jsp 10 times, you see the web page shown in Figure 5.2.

Figure 5.2

This figure shows the same simple JSP declaration as in Figure 5.1 after 10 requests. Notice how the global variable has been updated every time a new request is handled, while the local variable is reinitialized with every new request.

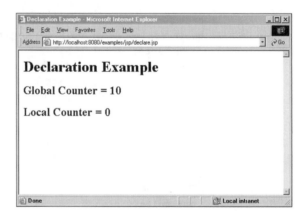

Global variables are almost always a bad idea, because they can cause drastic side effects. This is especially true in multiuser or multithreaded environments (that is, concurrent environments, where many things are happening all at once). You may think that a hit counter (a variable that counts the number of times the page has loaded) might be an acceptable use for a global variable; however, even in this instance it is a bad idea. Different processes in a multithreaded web server could interfere with each other and produce inconsistent results. Now you know why declaration elements are not recommended.

Methods or Madness?

Declaration elements can be useful, though, especially during the prototyping phase. You can use them to declare methods that you want to use in the rest of your JSP page. For example, say you need a method to return the sine of an angle that is entered in degrees.

Because the `sin()` method requires that the given angle be in radians, you need to convert between degrees and radians, as shown in Listing 5.3. (And you thought you'd never have a use for all that high-school math.) In this listing, I've declared a new method named `sind()` that itself calls `sin()` with the converted argument.

Listing 5.3   sin.jsp

```
<%!
  private static double sind(double angle) {
    return(java.lang.Math.sin(angle * (java.lang.Math.PI/180.0))) ;
  }
%>
```

Listing 5.4 shows the relevant part of the generated Servlet, which now contains a new method.

Listing 5.4   sin$jsp.java

```
public class sin$jsp extends HttpJspBase {
    // begin [file="/jsp/sin.jsp";from=(1,3);to=(5,0)]

        private static double sind(double angle) {
            return(java.lang.Math.sin(angle * (java.lang.Math.PI/180.0))) ;
        }
    // end
```

Notice how the method was copied directly as written in Listing 5.3 into the Servlet.

If you remember from Chapter 1, "The Backgrounder," as part of its life cycle, a Servlet has an init phase, a service phase, and a destroy phase. The JSP container automatically generates the service phase when the JSP page is first requested. The `init` and `destroy` methods, however, are not, and they can be explicitly defined if necessary by placing the method inside a declaration element. One example of why you might want to do this would be to record processing information in a special log file, which is demonstrated in Listing 5.5.

Listing 5.5   demolog.jsp

```
<%!
  java.io.File fh ;

  public void jspInit() {
    fh = new java.io.File("tmp.log") ;
  }
```

continues

Listing 5.5   demolog.jsp   (continued)

```
    public void jspDestroy() {
      fh.delete() ;
    }
%>
```

Just an Expression

You have already seen several different examples of JSP expression elements; for example, I displayed the value of the global and local variables using expression elements. In general, JSP expressions are Java expressions, not statements, that are evaluated every time the JSP page is requested. The JSP expression is converted to a string, which is written to the response output stream.

Expressions can be written in JSP syntax ...

```
<%= global++ %>
```

... or in XML syntax:

```
<jsp:expression> global++ </jsp:expression>
```

For a simple example of using an expression, Listing 5.6 uses an expression to generate the current time and data.

Listing 5.6   date.jsp

```
<html>
    <head>
        <title> Expression Example</title>
    </head>
    <body>
        <h1>
            Currently, at the server it is <br/>
            <%= new java.util.Date() %> <br/>
            and all is well!
        </h1>
    </body>
</html>
```

When your browser requests this JSP page, the system provides the current time and date and returns it as part of the HTML response to the client, as shown in Figure 5.3. You may wonder how this works; the trick is that every Java class has a toString() method, which generates a string representation of a given object. When a String object is needed, such as in the body of a JSP expression element, the toString() method is implicitly called. Since the date object is created inside an expression element, each time you request this JSP page, you will get a different response.

Figure 5.3

The current date and time on the JSP server displayed to the client. Each time this JSP page is requested, the current time and date are returned.

Scriplets

JSP scripting elements enable you to place multiple lines of Java in your JSP page. This can be very useful; for example, you can easily use loops or conditional statements to change the appearance of a JSP page. To demonstrate, the JSP page in Listing 5.7 creates a multiplication table, which is shown in Figure 5.4.

Listing 5.7   multiply.jsp

```html
<html>
    <head>
        <title> Scriptlets Example</title>
    </head>
    <body>
        <h2> A Multiplication Table </h2>
        <hr>
        <h2>
        <table border="2">
            <tr>
                <th> </th>
            <% for(int i = 1 ; i < 10 ; i++) {%>
                <th> <%= i %> </th>
            <% } %>
            </tr>
            <% for(int i = 1 ; i < 10 ; i++) { %>
                <tr>
                <td> <b> <%= i %> </b></td>
                <% for(int j = 1 ; j < 10 ; j++) { %>
```

continues

Listing 5.7   multiply.jsp   (continued)

```
            <td> <%= (i * j) %> </td>
        <% } %>
        </tr>
    <% } %>
        </table>
        </h2>
    </body>
</html>
```

Notice how easy it is to generate a large HTML output, in this case an HTML table, by mixing scriptlets, expressions, and HTML elements.

Figure 5.4

This is the multiplication table generated from our JSP page.

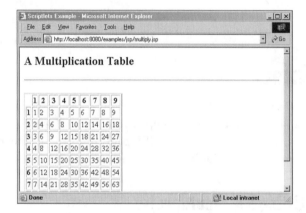

Of course, abusing (read: overusing) scriptlets can be very dangerous, as you can quickly end up with a large mess of spaghetti code. For small projects, or just to prototype a new feature, scriptlets are great—just be careful!

Any Comments?

One important technique for making your JSP page more readable is to comment everything appropriately. While this is generally true for any application, it is especially true for JSP pages, which undergo considerable transformation, from JSP to Servlet to HTML (or XML). To handle all three stages, there are three different types of comments that you can use in a JSP page:

- ◆ Hidden comments
- ◆ Scripting comments
- ◆ Output comments

Hidden Comments

Hidden comments are actual JSP comments and use the JSP syntax:

```
<%-- Hidden Comment Goes Here! --%>
```

They are called hidden since the JSP container removes them when generating the Servlet, thereby hiding them from the client who requested the JSP page. They are useful when commenting JSP elements. Listing 5.8 demonstrates a simple hidden comment.

Listing 5.8   hcomment.jsp

```
<html>
    <head>
        <title> Hidden Comment Example</title>
    </head>
    <body>
        <h2> Can you see the hidden comment?</h2>
        <hr>
        <h2>
            <%-- Print out the numbers from 1 to 10. --%>
            <% for(int i = 1 ; i < 10 ; i++) {
                out.println(i) ;
              } %>
        </h2>
    </body>
</html>
```

Scripting Comments

Scripting comments are used to comment the Java code you are using in a JSP page, and use one of the following different Java comment syntaxes. For inline comments (comments on the same line as an expression) use ...

```
int i = 0 ; // i is the indexing variable
```

For block comments (comment on their own lines) use ...

```
/* The following code computes the area of an arbitrary shape */
```

For a JavaDoc comment use ...

```
//* The user can choose one of the following options
<ul>
    <li> continue </li>
    <li> exit </li>
```

```
</ul>
 after entering the name of the file
*/
```

Scripting comments are carried through to the generated Servlet, and can be quite useful when prototyping JSP applications.

Output Comments

Output comments are perhaps the most interesting, as they are considered template data by the JSP container and passed through to the client. Output comments follow the HTML comment syntax ...

```
<!-- HTML Comment goes here ->
```

... and can contain embedded expressions, which means you can have dynamic comments (comments that change) in your JSP page. Since many advanced HTML elements are embedded inside HTML comments, this can be a powerful technique, as shown in Listing 5.9.

Listing 5.9   ocomment.jsp

```
<html>
    <head>
        <title> Output Comment Example</title>
    </head>
    <body>
        <h2> Look at the HTML source to see the output comment?</h2>
        <hr>
        <h2>
            <!-- File was generated at <%= new java.util.Date()  %> -->
            Hello World!
        </h2>
    </body>
</html>
```

If you look at the generated HTML source, you will see the HTML comment ...

```
<!-- File was generated at Wed Oct 31 12:00:39 PST 2001 -->
```

... Embedded inside the HTML file (okay, your comment will have a different time and date!)

Can I Quote You?

If you are familiar at all with HTML or XML, you know about character entities. If not, don't worry, they are easy to understand. Basically, because markup languages treat certain characters as special—the characters used to signal markup commands—if you want to use these characters in your HTML or XML file, you need to quote them. For example, these five characters are special in markup languages, and must be quoted properly, in order to be displayed: less than, greater than, ampersand, single quote, and double quote. In JSP, the same condition holds true, and you must quote special characters as demonstrated in Table 5.1.

Table 5.1   JSP Quoting Rules

Context	Character	Quote
Template Date	<%	<%
Template Date	%>	%>
Script	<%	<\%
Script	%>	%\>
Element	'	\'
Element	?	\?
Element	\	\\
Element	<%	<\%
Element	%>	%\>

Now that you know something about using scripts in JSP pages, it's time to move even further forward. In the next chapter, you get into all sorts of cool stuff like request objects, response objects, and HTTP sessions.

The Least You Need to Know

♦ The most important thing to understand is when and where it is acceptable to use JSP scripting elements.

♦ You use a JSP declaration to declare variables or methods for use within a JSP page.

♦ Any variable or method declared inside a declaration has global scope within the JSP page.

♦ JSP expressions are Java expressions, not statements, that are evaluated every time the JSP page is requested.

◆ JSP scripting elements enable you to place multiple lines of Java in your JSP page.

◆ One important technique for making your JSP page more readable is to comment everything appropriately.

◆ There are three different types of comments that you can use in a JSP page: hidden comments, scripting comments, and output comments.

Chapter 6

Getting a Free Lunch

In This Chapter

- ◆ Understanding web application scoping rules
- ◆ Using the request object
- ◆ Using the response object
- ◆ Working with HTTP sessions
- ◆ The rest of the implicit objects

In the previous chapter, I showed you how to work with JSP declarations, expressions, and scriptlets. In this chapter, I take advantage of free objects that the JSP container provides, which encapsulate specific concepts related to web applications. I already talked about these objects briefly in Chapter 4, "A Quick Tour of JSP." They are formally called *implicit objects* and they provide access to the JSP's runtime environment. One very important point about implicit objects is that they can be used only in scriptlets and expressions and not in declarations or template text. To understand why, in this chapter, I also briefly review what happens to a JSP page when it is requested by a client.

Tagged

They are called **implicit objects** because they are created for you by the JSP (or Servlet) container. Thus, they are implicitly available and do not need to be explicitly created (using the **new** operator) before you can use them. For example, with an explicit object, you need to create it before using it.

```
myObject explicit = new MyObject() ;
explicit.someMethod() ;
```

With an implicit object, you don't need to create it, that's already done; you just start using it.

```
implicit.someMethod() ;
```

Reviewing Client Requests

To refresh your memory, JSP pages are first translated into Servlets and then compiled by the JSP container. For simple JSP pages, the translation process basically places all of the JSP scriptlets and expressions inside a special _jspService() method. Remember when you looked at this method back in Chapter 3, "Building Your First JSP"? If not, take a moment to review that chapter. Got it? The arguments to this method are two implicit objects that represent the HTTP request and response, as shown in the following code snippet:

```
    public void _jspService(HttpServletRequest request, HttpServletResponse
response)
```

Depending on the contents of your JSP page, other implicit objects are also available in the _jspService() method, although they are explicitly created at the beginning of the _jspService() method, as shown in the following code snippet:

```
        PageContext pageContext = null;
        HttpSession session = null;
        ServletContext application = null;
        ServletConfig config = null;
        JspWriter out = null;
```

As you can see, the implicit objects are only valid inside the _jspService() method, which is where scriptlets and expressions are placed. Before jumping into a lengthy discussion of these different implicit objects, however, you need to understand the overall architecture of a web application, especially how it affects the scope, or visibility, of implicit objects.

Scoping It Out

When you are building your website using JSP technology, you will work with Java objects, intentionally or not (remember, this chapter is about implicit objects that are created for you automatically). Any object in a JSP or Servlet has an area within the web application in which it is visible to other objects, expressions, or scriptlets. This visibility concept is formally known as *scope*.

For your web applications, there are four different levels of scope:

- ◆ Page
- ◆ Request
- ◆ Session
- ◆ Application

These different levels build hierarchically upon each other, like Russian dolls. Understanding the scope rules become more important as the complexity of our web applications increases.

Page Scope

The first level is page scope, which is restricted to a single JSP page. Any object that is created with page scope is only accessible within the page where it is created. Once the HTTP response has been sent to the requesting client or the original HTTP request has been forwarded to another web component, all references to objects with page scope are released and the objects become candidates for garbage collection. (Garbage collection is when the system destroys unused objects, thus removing them from memory. This is much like how you take your kitchen garbage out to the curb for collection, except with computer garbage collection, you don't get that awful odor—at least, not usually.) This means that any processing or results that were calculated by a specific JSP page are lost and must be recomputed with every new request.

So far, I have only shown you how to work with single-page web applications, and, as a result, everything you have done has used page scope. This will soon change, because you will begin to work with multiple JSP web applications. In order to provide access to objects with page scope, the implicit `pageContext` object maintains references to all objects with page scope. You saw the `pageContext` object being initialized in the `_jspService()` method, like this:

```
PageContext pageContext = null;
```

Request Scope

The next level in the scope hierarchy is request scope, which refers to all processing needed to satisfy a single HTTP request. (An example of an HTTP request is when your browser displays web content.) As I already mentioned, your previous JSP examples have used one JSP page per HTTP request. More complex examples, which demonstrate "real-world" applications, often have multiple JSP pages, and possibly JavaBeans, Servlets, and JSP tag libraries working together to satisfy a single request.

For example, if a website requires you to log in, you might interact with multiple JSP pages. Or you might have to search a product catalog at an e-commerce site. Your request will probably be processed by a controlling Servlet, the data will be stored in multiple JavaBeans, and a JSP page will present the results to the client (usually a web browser). Objects with request scope are valid until the request has been completed. This means that objects with request scope, which are stored in the request object, can be shared among multiple JSP pages.

Session Scope

If you think about this e-commerce example a little bit more, you realize that you often will have multiple related requests. For example, when you buy products online at a web store, you often browse the catalog, which is one HTTP request, and when you find something you like, you add it to your shopping cart, which is another HTTP request. If you have a lot of items to buy, you may repeat this process, until eventually your shopping cart is full, which requires many more HTTP requests.

Obviously, all of these requests are related, and the website developer needs to share information, such as the contents of the shopping cart, between the different requests. In order to do this, you can make use of an HTTP session, which allows different requests to share information. You can associate objects with a HTTP session, which allows objects to have session scope. Objects with session scope are valid throughout the duration of a session. Sessions can be terminated by a direct request, such as when a user purchases the items in a shopping cart, or indirectly, after a specific amount of time has expired without any activity, such as when someone leaves a shopping cart inactive for a day or two. You saw the `session` object being initialized in the `_jspService()` method, like this:

```
HttpSession session = null;
```

Application Scope

Our fictitious little e-commerce example has worked quite nicely as a scope demonstrator. So far, the web store works great, as a client can browse and shop at her leisure; but it only works for a single user! If you want your web store to be profitable, you need to serve many, simultaneous (or concurrent) clients. Sometimes, different sessions need to share data, or objects. For example, you would want different sessions to share inventory information, so that you can tell clients whether the product they want is in stock or not.

In order to share information between sessions, you can use the application object, which provides a higher level of application scope and enables different sessions to share information. If, for some reason, a specific JSP page (or pages) does not participate in an HTTP session, it can still utilize application scope to share information between HTTP requests. You saw the application object being initialized in the _jspService() method, like this:

```
ServletContext application = null;
```

Coffee Break

At this point, you may be wondering if there is anything more encompassing than application scope. After all, some web stores basically encapsulate different applications, or product categories, in different applications. For example, a web store might sell toys, books, electronics, and host an auction site.

While this is true, there is no higher level of scope than application scope. If these different "stores" need to share information, either they work together as a single application, or they need to implement an additional mechanism, such as using a database. Otherwise, the stores act as independent entities.

Seeing the Request

As I mentioned while discussing request-level scope, the request implicit object holds all information about a specific HTTP request. This information includes request parameters that are generated as part of an HTTP GET or POST operation; attributes, which can be set by the JSP container or by a JSP or Servlet before forwarding the request; and HTTP headers.

Coffee Break

I have been making exclusive mention of HTTP as the protocol used in a JSP application. While certainly the most dominant protocol, other protocols are also allowed under the JSP specification, although not everything, such as sessions, transfers cleanly to other protocols. Since HTTP is the dominant protocol, I will focus solely on HTTP in order to keep the discussion concise.

Request Parameters

Anytime you fill out a form at a website and click Submit, your browser transfers the information to the server as HTTP parameters. The two mechanisms for sending this information are the HTTP GET and the HTTP PUT operations. The GET method appends the data to the URL, which you may have seen before. The PUT method, on the other hand, encodes the data in the HTTP message body.

This process is demonstrated in Listing 6.1, which is a JSP page that displays all parameters passed to it, via either GET or PUT. If you call this JSP page with the following parameters, you will get the web page shown in Figure 6.1.

```
http://localhost:8080/examples/jsp/paramcheck.jsp?query=hello&query=goodbye&password=sun
```

Take special notice of the way I've tacked the parameters onto the paramcheck.jsp request. In previous examples, to display a JSP page, you simply provided a URL that included the path to the page. For this example, such a URL looks like this:

```
http://localhost:8080/examples/jsp/paramcheck.jsp
```

Adding the following to the URL adds the parameters to the page request:

```
?query=hello&query=goodbye&password=sun
```

I use request parameters frequently throughout this book, because they are the primary means for an HTTP client to communicate with a server. For example, they can be used to log in to a website, select products from a catalog, or enter a query string.

Listing 6.1 paramcheck.jsp

```jsp
<%@
  page
  import="java.util.*"
%>

<html>
<head><title>Display Parameters JSP Page</title></head>
<body>

<h1> Parameter Names and Values </h1>
<hr/>
<%
  String name ;
  String[] values ;
  for (Enumeration names = request.getParameterNames();
       names.hasMoreElements();)
  {
    name = (String)names.nextElement() ;
    values = request.getParameterValues(name);
```

```
   %>
   <p/>
   <font size="4"><%= name %></font>
   <ul>
   <%  for(int j = 0 ; j < values.length ; j++)
       { %>
          <li> <%= values[j] %> </li>
          <%
       } %>
   </ul>
   <%
 } %>
</body>
</html>
```

The first thing you probably notice about this JSP page is the use of the page directive, which looks like this:

```
<%@
  page
  import="java.util.*"
%>
```

Right now, just ignore this directive; we will cover it in Chapter 7, "Talking to the Container."

After the page directive are several HTML elements that compromise the bulk of the static HTML content:

```
<html>
<head><title>Display Parameters JSP Page</title></head>
<body>

<h1> Parameter Names and Values </h1>
<hr/>
```

A JSP scriplet follows the HTML stuff. This script extracts the names of all request parameters from the HTTP response object. Notice how you can just use the request operator; you don't have to create it yourself—that's why it's called an implicit object.

Okay, you ready for some techno babble? Try this: In order to display the names, the JSP scriptlet iterates over the parameter-name enumeration and displays the names it finds there. Yow! "Enumeration" is just a fancy name for a collection of objects. In this case, the enumeration is a collection of names named, appropriately enough, names. The scriptlet gets this enumeration by calling, in the for loop, the request object's getParameterNames() method:

```
Enumeration names = request.getParameterNames()
```

That brings us to the word "iterate," which simply means to start at the beginning of a collection and look through it one step at a time. In this case, the for loop continues as long as the call to the names object's hasMoreElements() method returns true:

```
names.hasMoreElements()
```

For each step in the iteration, the scriptlet gets the next name in the enumeration and gets the value (or values) associated with the parameter name, storing it in the values array:

```
name = (String)names.nextElement() ;
values = request.getParameterValues(name);
```

When displaying parameter names, the JSP page increases the font size, so that the names stand out:

```
<font size="4"><%= name %></font>
```

Since parameters can have multiple values associated with a single parameter name, the page needs to loop over (iterate over) all possible parameter values, which it does in the second for loop:

```
<%  for(int j = 0 ; j < values.length ; j++)
    { %>
      <li> <%= values[j] %> </li>
      <%
    } %>
```

Figure 6.1

This figure shows the JSP Parameter check page displaying the result of the specified URL request.

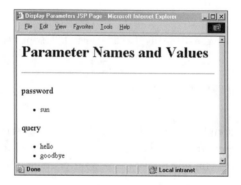

Attributes

I said previously that the request object stores those objects that have request scope. This is accomplished by request attributes. The ServletRequest class has setAttribute() and getAttribute() methods, which allow you to associate any Java object to a name, so that the object can be shared between different JSP pages that are participating in handling a particular request.

The following two JSP pages demonstrate this feature. Listing 6.2 shows a JSP page that extracts as strings all attributes that are available to it and generates a web page that displays the result. Unlike request parameters, only one value can be associated with a given name, thus you do not need to loop over all possible values. Instead, you can just print out the name and value for each attribute.

Listing 6.2   AttributeCheck.jsp

```
<%@
  page
  import="java.util.*"
%>

<html>
<head><title>Attribute Parameters JSP Page</title></head>
<body>

<h1> Attribute Names and Values </h1>
<hr/>
<%
  String name ;
  String value ;

  for(  Enumeration names = request.getAttributeNames();
        names.hasMoreElements() ;) {
    name = (String)names.nextElement() ;
    value = (String)request.getAttribute(name) ;
%>
<p/>
<font size="4"><%= name %></font>: <%= value %>
<% } %>
</body>
</html>
```

In order to demonstrate the use of request attributes, you need to first set them and then call the attribute-listing JSP page. In Listing 6.3, you have a JSP page that first sets several attributes, including using the same name for two different objects (in this case the objects are just Java String objects) to demonstrate that only the most recent binding is retained. At the end of this JSP page, we have a forwarding directive, which will be discussed in more detail in Chapter 8, "Mixing and Matching JSP Pages."

Listing 6.3 CallAttributeCheck.jsp

```
<%
request.setAttribute("query", "hello") ;
request.setAttribute("query", "goodbye") ;

request.setAttribute("database", "jdbc") ;
request.setAttribute("user", "java") ;
request.setAttribute("password", "sun") ;
%>
<jsp:forward page="AttributeCheck.jsp"/>
```

Confused about how to work this example? Here are the details:

1. Run your copy of Tomcat.

2. Type Listing 6.2, and save it to your jakarta-tomcat-4.0.1\webapps\examples\jsp directory under the name AttributeCheck.jsp.

3. Type Listing 6.3, and then save it to the same directory under the name CallAttributeCheck.jsp.

4. Start your web browser and give it the URL localhost:8080/examples/jsp/ CallAttributeCheck.jsp.

After calling CallAttributeCheck.jsp, you get the web page shown in Figure 6.2. This shows how the first object that was associated with the attribute named "query" is not stored. Using attributes is a powerful technique for sharing information, like login data, between different JSP pages.

Figure 6.2

This figure shows the JSP Attribute check page displaying the result of the objects passing between JSP pages.

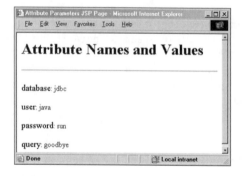

Headers

Part of the HTTP specification includes a discussion of HTTP headers, which are predefined names that can have one or more associated values. These headers are used to communicate specific information concerning the abilities of the client (for example, a web browser) or the format or encoding of data being sent. There are two categories of HTTP headers associated with an HTTP request:

- General headers—includes Cache-Control, Connection, Date, Pragma, Trailer, Transfer-Encoding, Upgrade, Via, and Warning.
- Request headers—includes Accept, Accept-Charset, Accept-Encoding, Accept-Language, Authorization, Expect, From, Host, If-Match, If-Modified-Since, If-None-Match, If-Range, If-Unmodified-Since, Max-Forwards, Proxy-Authorization, Range, Referer, TE, and User-Agent.

As you can probably guess from these lists, these headers dictate everything from the types of character encodings to the types of languages a client understands and accepts. Enough of the pesky details; it's about time for another example.

In Listing 6.4, all request headers are extracted for the issuing request object. In this JSP, only a single value is extracted for each header, using the getHeader() method of the request object; while in general, some headers can have multiple values. A demonstration of this JSP page in action is shown in Figure 6.3.

Fresh Brew

The full HTTP version 1.1 specification is available online at ftp://ftp.isi.edu/in-notes/rfc2616.txt. It includes lengthy discussion on each of these headers as well as a wealth of information on HTTP in general.

Listing 6.4   HeaderCheck.jsp

```
<%@
  page
  import="java.util.*"
%>

<html>
<head><title>Headers JSP Page</title></head>
<body>

<h1> Header Names and Values </h1>
<hr/>
<%
  String[] names = {"Accept",
                    "Accept-Charset",
                    "Accept-Encoding",
                    "Accept-Language",
                    "Authorization",
                    "Expect",
                    "From",
                    "Host",
```

continues

Listing 6.4   HeaderCheck.jsp   (continued)

```
                    "If-Match",
                    "If-Modified-Since",
                    "If-None-Match",
                    "If-Range",
                    "If-Unmodified-Since",
                    "Max-Forwards",
                    "Proxy-Authorization",
                    "Range",
                    "Referer",
                    "TE",
                    "User-Agent"} ;
%>
<p/>
<%  for(int i = 0 ; i < names.length ; i++) { %>
<font size="4"><%= names[i] %></font>: <%= request.getHeader(names[i])  %>
<p/>
<%  } %>
</body>
</html>
```

Figure 6.3

This figure shows the JSP Header check page displaying the values of some of the available HTTP request headers.

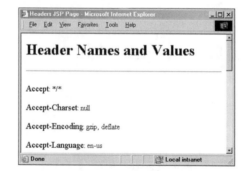

Making a Response

Now that you have seen the request object, take a look at its opposite, the response object. The response object is used to control the server's response to the client. If you recall from the generated Servlets you have seen, all of the template text in a JSP page is added to the response by being explicitly printed to the out object, which is another one of those implicit object thingies you learned about. For example, here's how a JSP page from Chapter 3 prints HTTP to the out object:

```
out.write("<html>\r\n    <head>\r\n        <title> Hello World Example
</title>\r\n    </head>\r\n    <body>\r\n        <h1> Hello World! </h1>\r\n
</body>\r\n</html>");
```

The response object provides a great deal of control over the communication between the client and the server. Part of the response is a status code, part of it is a series of headers (just like with the request object), and the bulk of it is the template text and dynamic content that is produced by your JSP page.

Another use of the response object is to set the content type of the response. Basically, this is just the MIME type of the response, which is used to indicate whether plain text, HTML, images, movies, audio files, or whatever is being returned to the client, along with the character set of the response, which is also known as the locale. For example, to indicate that the response is HTML and you want to use the default locale, you would do something like this:

```
response.setContentType("text/html") ;
```

In order for things to work properly, you need to set the content type and the locale before any of the response gets written. This means that you need to specify the content type before using any template text. Fortunately all of this is easier than it sounds, as you will see in Chapter 7.

Status Codes

If you do a lot of web surfing, you will undoubtedly run across a web page that has either moved, is no longer available, or requires some authorization that you didn't provide. Inevitably, your browser displays an error page that might have specified a number, like 307 or 401. The rest of the page might have been specific information detailing what happened, like the web page has moved and you will be redirected in five seconds.

These error codes and corresponding messages are called HTTP status codes and are controlled by the response object. There are five categories of status codes, which are distinguished by the first number of the three-digit code:

- Codes that begin with a one (1XX) are informational
- Codes that begin with a two (2XX) indicate success
- Codes that begin with a three (3XX) indicate a redirection (being referred to another web address) is necessary
- Codes that begin with a four (4XX) indicate a client error
- Codes that begin with a five (5XX) indicate a server error

You can set a response status code during the processing of a client's request by calling either the setStatus() or the setError() methods of the response object, depending on whether you need to indicate an error condition or not. For example, to indicate that a given resource could not be found, you would use the following statement.

```
response.setError(SC_NOT_FOUND) ;
```

On the other hand, to indicate that a request was successful, you use this statement:

```
resonse.setStatus(SC_OK) ;
```

Coffee Break

If you are curious, the following list shows all of the defined HTTP 1.1 status codes along with their meaning. If you surf the web a lot, several of these, such as 401 or 404 are probably familiar to you. The javadoc listing of the HttpServletResponse class lists the available status codes.

Code	Meaning	Code	Meaning
100	Continue	404	Not Found
101	Switching Protocols	405	Method Not Allowed
200	OK	406	Not Acceptable
201	Created	407	Proxy Authentication Required
202	Accepted	408	Request Time-Out
203	Non-Authoritative Information	409	Conflict
204	No Content	410	Gone
205	Reset Content	411	Length Required
206	Partial Content	412	Precondition Failed
300	Multiple Choices	413	Request Entity Too Large
301	Moved Permanently	414	Request-URL Too Large
302	Found	415	Unsupported Media Type
303	See Other	416	Requested range not satisfiable
304	Not Modified	417	Expectation Failed
305	Use Proxy	500	Internal Server Error
307	Temporary Redirect	501	Not Implemented
400	Bad Request	502	Bad Gateway
401	Unauthorized	503	Service Unavailable
402	Payment Required	504	Gateway Time-Out
403	Forbidden	505	HTTP Version Not Supported

Headers

Just like requests, HTTP responses can contain headers. To handle the extra information that is needed to handle an HTTP response, however, two new flavors are needed:

- Response headers—include `Accept-Ranges`, `Age`, `Etag`, `Location`, `Proxy-Authenticate`, `Retry-After`, `Server`, `Vary`, and `WWW-Authenticate`.
- Entity headers—include `Allow`, `Content-Encoding`, `Content-Language`, `Content-Length`, `Content-Location`, `Content-MD5`, `Content-Range`, `Content-Type`, `Expires`, `Last-Modified`, and `extension-header`.

Response headers are used to inform the client about server-specific processing details. Entity headers are used to inform the client about server-specific communication issues.

Working with response headers is just like working with request headers, except you set headers with a response object, and you get them with a request object. For example, to set the response headers to contain the server's name (which might be different than the original request due to a redirect or load-balancing feature), you would do the following:

```
response.setHeader("Server", "persistentjava.com") ;
```

Note that the JSP container does not check that the header name you specify as the first argument to this method is one of the official HTTP headers. This allows you to build on HTTP to provide additional functionality, which is what is done with the Simple Object Access Protocol (SOAP). You can also add a new header value to an already existing response header using the addHeader() method.

```
response.setHeader("MyHeader", "Value1") ;
response.addHeader("MyHeader", "Value2") ;
```

The response object has several additional, convenience methods that make it easier to place dates or integers into response headers. For example, to place the current date and the number of bytes in the response body into a response header, you can simplify things by using the setIntHeader() and setDateHeader() methods, as shown in this snippet:

```
response.setDateHeader("Date", new Date()) ;
response.setIntHeader("Content-Length", numBytes) ;
```

One last, but important, point about using response headers is that they must be set before the response body is committed. (When I say committed, I don't mean that the guys in white coats are going to come. In this case committed means finalized.) This is obvious when you think about it, as the response headers need to come before the response body so that the client can interpret the body of the response. Generally, the response body will just be HTML either from template text or the result of dynamic JSP processing.

It's really quite easy to see request headers (and status/error codes) in action. All you need to do is use the telnet program to talk to a web server. If you go to a command prompt (that is, a shell window) and type telnet www.mycompany.com 80 (the 80 tells the telnet program to connect to the machine using port 80, which is the default HTTP port number and not the default telnet port), you will get a listing of the response headers followed by the response body (which is generally just a bunch of HTML). For example, doing this for my persistentjava website, the telnet program connects to the web server running at persistentjava.com:

```
C:> telnet www.persistentjava.com 80
```

At this point, a connection is established and the screen is cleared. When I enter **GET /**, I get the following snippet:

```
HTTP/1.1 200 OK
Server: Microsoft-IIS/5.0
Date: Wed, 14 Nov 2001 05:43:12 GMT
Connection: Keep-Alive
Content-Length: 1270
Content-Type: text/html
Set-Cookie: ASPSESSIONIDGGGQQOBU=NLJDKJNAKPGPCFEAMKMPNAEN; path=/
Cache-control: private
```

By now, you can probably understand most of the response's header. First, the response indicates that the server understands version 1.1 of the HTTP protocol and that the request was successfully processed (that is, SC_OK). Afterward is a listing of several response headers, including the type of Server (in this case Microsoft IIS version 5.0), the data the response created, the length of the response body in bytes, and the content type.

One of the other headers is the Connection header, which has a value of Keep-Alive. This indicates to the client that the Server will keep this connection alive, which results in a persistent connection (one that stays open) between the client and the server. This produces significant performance gains, since the client and server don't need to continually reestablish connections every time the same client makes a new request.

Maintaining Information

As I have previously discussed, the HTTP protocol is stateless, which means that servers that use the HTTP protocol do not need to remember anything about a particular client or request once it has been processed. While this makes it considerably easier to write HTTP compliant servers, it makes it a lot harder to write useful applications that utilize HTTP compliant servers. For example, how useful would you find it if your favorite online store required you to keep track of all of the items that you have placed in your shopping cart? Talk about a dot-bomb!

Obviously, there are mechanisms that allow servers to "remember" information that is specific to a particular client. One of the simplest is the concept of a session, which is handled by yet another implicit object—you guessed it, the session object. Before jumping into a discussion about sessions, however, we need to talk about cookies, since sessions often use cookies to keep track of what you do.

Cookies

One of the headers in the server response from the last section that I did not mention was the Set-Cookie header. You may have heard of cookies—and no I am not talking about the kind your mom used to bake. This header is referring to the cookies sent from web servers to clients. The cookie is a small piece of data that allows the server to remember the client every time the client reconnects to the server. Whether you want to use them directly or not, cookies are important as they are often used to provide session management.

Formally, a browser is expected to handle 20 cookies for each web server, and 300 cookies in total, although they can and often do handle more. Also, a cookie should not be more than 4 kb in size, which is actually quite large considering their purpose. Whenever a browser reconnects to a particular server, it sends the cookies that were originally sent by that server. This allows the server to "remember" the client and personalize the web interaction. For example, this method can be used to keep shopping carts alive or to keep a secure login session alive.

Cookies, however, have gotten a bad rap from some pundits due to "Big Brother" fears. Unscrupulous websites have tried to monitor web surfers' habits by snooping on browsers' cookie jars. Ideally a website should only be able to "see" cookies that it sent to a browser, but due to insecure programming, some browsers allowed (and still allow) websites to view all of the cookies that a browser has received. Other potential problems arise from security holes in a browser that allow third parties to steal cookies, which might contain sensitive log-in information.

Politics aside, used properly, cookies provide an important and vital mechanism for persisting HTTP interactions. Cookies are sent to the browser using the response object, and they are retrieved from the browser via the request object. This is demonstrated in Listing 6.5, which first sets, and after a browser refresh, retrieves several cookies. To distinguish between the two cases, I use a global variable to count how many times a page has been viewed. I am cheating for simplicity and clarity in this example, as this is not what you would do in production code (which should allow multiple concurrent users) for a hit counter.

Listing 6.5   CookieCheck.jsp

```
<html>
<head><title>JSP Cookie Check Page</title></head>
<body>

<%!
  boolean cookieInit = false ;
%>

<%
  if(cookieInit == false){
%>
```

continues

Listing 6.5   CookieCheck.jsp   (continued)

```
<h2> Setting Cookies </h2>
<hr>
<h4>To see the Cookie List, refresh your browser window</h4>
<%
    response.addCookie(new Cookie("User", "Robert J. Brunner")) ;
    response.addCookie(new Cookie("User", "John A. Doe")) ;
    response.addCookie(new Cookie("Date", "June 21, 1904")) ;
    response.addCookie(new Cookie("Visits", Integer.toString(123))) ;
    response.addCookie(new Cookie("ABCD", "123456qwerty")) ;

    cookieInit = true ;

  } else{

    Cookie[] cookies = request.getCookies() ;
    Cookie cookie ;
%>

<h2> Displaying Cookies </h2>
<hr>
<table border="2">
  <tr>
    <th>Name</th>
    <th>Value</th>
  </tr>

<%
    for(int i = 0 ; i < cookies.length ; i++) {
       cookie = cookies[i] ;
%>

  <tr>
    <td> <%= cookie.getName() %> </td>
    <td> <%= cookie.getValue() %> </td>
  </tr>

<%   } %>

</table>

<% } %>

</body>
</html>
```

As you can see from this JSP page, working with cookies is very easy. One obvious point is that cookies are not implicit objects; you need to create them before using them. As you can see in the previous JSP page, we get an array of cookies from the request object. In order to find a particular cookie, you need to step through the array until you find the cookie of interest.

As is the case with this example, for most purposes, the only part of a cookie that you will be interested in is its name and its value. Cookies can also have associated comments, maximum ages, path information, URL domains where they are accessible, a security flag, and a version flag. Browsers do not always support these optional attributes, so you need to be careful when using them.

Figure 6.4

This figure shows the JSP Cookie check page after refreshing the browser window, displaying all the cookies that were added to the original HTTP Response.

Sessions

If you look carefully at the bottom of Figure 6.4, you will notice that an extra cookie is listed, called JSESSIONID. You may be wondering where it came from, since we never created it. The answer is that it is a special cookie created by the JSP container to allow the server to uniquely identify the client. This is the default mechanism used by a JSP or Servlet container to allow a server to track clients, or more formally, to provide session management.

In Chapter 7, I show you how to control whether sessions are used or not, but for now all you need to know is that by default, they are enabled. As long as the browser allows cookies, which most do unless the end user has explicitly turned them off, working with sessions is very easy. Even if cookies are turned off, things aren't much more difficult. In Listing 6.6, I show how easy it is to work with sessions. In this example, you have a simple shopping cart, and to show how the information is persisted (or saved) between client requests, you use the implicit session object.

Listing 6.6   SessionCheck.jsp

```
<%@page
    import="com.persistentjava.ShoppingCartBean, java.util.*"
%>
<html>
<head><title>JSP Session Page</title></head>
<body>

<%
  ArrayList sc = (ArrayList)session.getAttribute("sCart") ;
  ShoppingCartBean scb ;

  if(sc == null) {
    sc = new ArrayList() ;

    scb = new ShoppingCartBean() ;
    scb.setQuantity(10) ;
    scb.setItemName("CIG to JavaServer Pages") ;
    sc.add(scb) ;

    scb = new ShoppingCartBean() ;
    scb.setQuantity(3) ;
    scb.setItemName("Enterprise Java Database Programming") ;
    sc.add(scb) ;

    scb = new ShoppingCartBean() ;
    scb.setQuantity(8) ;
    scb.setItemName("Java Web Services Unleashed") ;
    sc.add(scb) ;

    session.setAttribute("sCart", sc) ;
%>

<h2> Filling Shopping Cart </h2>
<hr>
<h4>To see the Cookie List, refresh your browser window</h4>

<%
  } else {
%>

<h2> Displaying Shopping Cart </h2>
<hr>
<table border="2">
  <tr>
```

```
      <th>Name</th>
      <th>Quantity</th>
  </tr>

<%
    Iterator it = sc.iterator() ;
    while(it.hasNext()) {
       scb = (ShoppingCartBean)it.next() ;
%>

  <tr>
    <td> <%= scb.getItemName() %> </td>
    <td> <%= scb.getQuantity() %> </td>
  </tr>

<%  } %>

</table>

<%  } %>

</body>
</html>
```

The first thing you notice about this JSP is the page directive, which looks like this:

```
<%@page
    import="com.persistentjava.ShoppingCartBean, java.util.*"
%>
```

Don't worry, I talk about the page directive in Chapter 7. Right now, all you need to know is that it tells the JSP container to use the shopping cart JavaBean shown in Listing 6.7.

After that the page directive and some HTML, the JSP page checks whether the request already has an associated shopping cart (I use this to tell if the client is new or not):

```
ArrayList sc = (ArrayList)session.getAttribute("sCart") ;
```

If there is no shopping cart, create one:

```
if(sc == null) {
  sc = new ArrayList() ;
```

Next, fill the cart with wonderful books:

```
scb = new ShoppingCartBean() ;
scb.setQuantity(10) ;
scb.setItemName("CIG to JavaServer Pages") ;
sc.add(scb) ;
```

```
scb = new ShoppingCartBean() ;
scb.setQuantity(3) ;
scb.setItemName("Enterprise Java Database Programming") ;
sc.add(scb) ;

scb = new ShoppingCartBean() ;
scb.setQuantity(8) ;
scb.setItemName("Java Web Services Unleashed") ;
sc.add(scb) ;
```

Note that in a production environment you would have the user select these from a catalog.

Once the shopping cart is full, you add it to the session for safekeeping:

```
session.setAttribute("sCart", sc) ;
```

The next time the user returns to this web page, the session locates the shopping cart for you and displays the contents:

```
<%
    Iterator it = sc.iterator() ;
    while(it.hasNext()) {
       scb = (ShoppingCartBean)it.next() ;
%>

  <tr>
    <td> <%= scb.getItemName() %> </td>
    <td> <%= scb.getQuantity() %> </td>
  </tr>

<%  } %>
```

Figure 6.5 shows the results. If you are worried about the JavaBean you used for the shopping cart, don't fret; it is very simple, and I will cover JavaBeans in great detail in Chapter 14, "Brewing With Beans." Right now, it just simplifies the JSP page by having one object that holds everything. As you can see, working with sessions is rather easy.

Listing 6.7   ShoppingCartBean.java

```
package com.persistentjava;

public class ShoppingCartBean implements java.io.Serializable {

  private int quantity ;
  public String itemName ;
```

```
public int getQuantity() {
  return(quantity) ;
}

public String getItemName() {
  return(itemName) ;
}

public void setQuantity(int value) {
  quantity = value ;
}

public void setItemName(String name) {
  itemName = name ;
}
}
```

Figure 6.5

This figure shows the JSP Session check page after refreshing the browser window, displaying the books that were added to the shopping cart as part of this session.

All the Other Implicit Objects

So far I have only talked about three of the available implicit objects: the response, request, and session objects. There are six other implicit objects, which are not used as frequently in JSP pages, but you might find yourself needing to use them when we start talking about using JSPs with JavaBeans, Servlets, and tag libraries. These additional implicit objects are …

- pageContext object, which provides access to all of the implicit objects for the current JSP page. A JSP developer almost never uses the pageContext object.

- application object, which provides access to information specific to the current web application, including access to the web application log file for logging current server information. The application object is also used to store objects that have application scope.

- ◆ `out` object, which controls the writing of response output. Generally, you will let the JSP container automatically use the `out` object to write out all of your template text. If you are a glutton for punishment, you might use the print methods of the `out` object to print output directly, but generally that is to be avoided (otherwise, just use a Servlet).

- ◆ `config` object, which is used by the Servlet container to pass information to a Servlet during the Servlet's initialization stage. JSP authors almost never use the config object.

- ◆ `page` object, which is a reference to the current page; loosely this translates to the Java `this` object. A JSP author almost never uses the page object.

- ◆ `exception` object, which provides access to any runtime errors.

Now you've got some experience with implicit objects. Hurray! Next up are more details about the JSP container, which you start on in the very next chapter.

The Least You Need to Know

- ◆ Any object created with page scope is only accessible within the page where it is created.

- ◆ Any object created with request scope is accessible until the request processing is complete.

- ◆ Objects with session scope are valid throughout the duration of an entire session.

- ◆ In order to share information between sessions, you can use the application object, which provides a higher level of application scope and enables different sessions to share information.

- ◆ The request implicit object holds all information about a specific HTTP request.

- ◆ The response object is used to control the server's response to the client.

- ◆ A cookie is a small piece of data that allows the server to remember the client every time the client reconnects to the server.

Talking to the Container

In This Chapter

- ♦ Understanding language issues
- ♦ Generating error pages
- ♦ Understanding buffering

So far I've introduced you to JSP constructs that primarily are effective during the JSP execution phase, which occurs after the JSP page has been transformed into a Servlet. For example, scriptlets, expressions, and implicit objects are turned into Java code inside the _jspservice() method, which is executed whenever the JSP page is referenced. In this chapter, I discuss directives, which allow a JSP page to communicate with the JSP container during the page translation process. Directives provide the JSP author with basic control over the functionality of the generated Servlet.

The JSP specification details three different directives:

- ♦ The page directive
- ♦ The include directive
- ♦ The taglib directive

All of these directives follow the same syntax. First is the directive start tag ...

```
<%@
```

... followed by the directive name, any attributes, and finally, the directive end tag ...

```
%>
```

Optional white space (things like space characters and tabs) can follow the start tag or precede the end tag to improve the readability of the directive. The following list demonstrates the basic formats of the three different directives:

- ◆ `<%@ page info="The Page directive" %>`
- ◆ `<%@ include file="template.xml" %>`
- ◆ `<%@ taglib uri="http://www.persistentjava.com/dbtags" %>`

The first two directives can also be expressed in the more verbose XML syntax:

- ◆ `<jsp:directive.page info="The Page directive" />`
- ◆ `<jsp:directive.include file="template.xml" />`

Don't worry if this XML stuff seems as strange as Arnold Schwarzenegger in a tutu; you can't help it if you're dumb. Just kidding! I will talk more about XML syntax in Chapter 10, "Extending HTML."

The `taglib` directive is transformed into an attribute on the `jsp root` element in the XML syntax:

```
<jsp:root
  xmlns:jsp="http://java.sun.com/JSP/Page"
  xmlns:tagprefix="http://www.persistentjava.com/dbtags"
  version="1.2">
...
</jsp:root>
```

None of these directives produce output on the current out stream. (A stream is just a flow of data.) The rest of this chapter focuses on the `page` directive, which specifies the scripting language used in the JSP page, how errors are handled in the page, and controls different aspects of the JSP page that include the output mechanisms. I discuss the `include` directive in Chapter 8, "Mixing and Matching JSP Pages." The `taglib` directive is covered in Chapter 16, "Rolling Out Tags."

Specifying the Lingo

As a JSP author, you will use the `page` directive to first define specific page properties, and then communicate them to the JSP container. The `page` directive takes a number of optional attributes; some, such as the `import` attribute, you have already seen in previous chapters. For example, in Chapter 6, "Getting a Free Lunch," you saw the following snippet in Listing 6.1:

```
<%@
  page
  import="java.util.*"
%>
```

CAUTION

Hot Java _____

A JSP page can have multiple **page** directives, and they don't need to all be at the top of the page. You can have them anywhere, including in an included file, and the directives will still be effective. The only attribute that can be duplicated in multiple page directives within the same JSP translation unit is the **import** attribute, which becomes cumulative when duplicated. If any other attribute is duplicated, it is a fatal error. Likewise, including an undefined attribute is a fatal error.

In order to simplify the discussion, I have grouped the attributes into my own categories and will talk about the attributes in each category separately. The JSP specification does not use my categories, and some attributes overlap categories.

The first category is language-specific attributes, which has three members:

- ◆ The `language` attribute
- ◆ The `extends` attribute
- ◆ The `import` attribute

The `language` attribute is used to communicate the scripting language to the JSP container. In the current JSP specification, this attribute should be set to Java, as this is the only defined and required value for JSP containers to recognize. Different vendors can provide additional support for other scripting languages, such as JavaScript, but JSP pages using these nonstandard languages will not be usable with other JSP containers. In this book, I will always use the Java language, which is the default value.

The `extends` attribute is used to specify that the generated Servlet should extend (be based upon) a specific Java class. As a result, the value must be a fully qualified Java class name. This is clearly a very advanced topic, and I will not cover it in this book—for beginners, this can easily become more trouble than it is worth.

The `import` attribute is used to tell the JSP container what Java classes need to be imported (included) into the generated Servlet. By default, all of the classes in the javax.servlet, javax.servlet.http, and the javax.servlet.jsp packages are imported. As you have seen in previous chapters (like the aforementioned Listing 6.1), if you use classes from other Java packages, you need to import them before using the classes; otherwise, you will get a compiler error, which can be rather difficult to understand when working with JSP pages.

Coffee Break

You may be wondering why you need to import classes at all; after all, these classes are generally part of the Java runtime. The simple explanation is that the Java compiler needs to explicitly know that the Java classes are available. This allows it to distinguish between similarly named classes during compile-time type checking. (Type checking is when the compiler ensures that all the objects you use are of the correct data types.)

This is a very important technique for reducing errors in your program due to mistyping class names or using nonexistent methods. To do compile-time checking, the compiler needs to know the fully qualified Java class names of all classes. This includes the full package name. In order to simplify Java programs, you can import packages, which allows you to shortcut the lengthy name process in favor of just using the name of the class. For example, if you don't import the appropriate package, you need to refer to the class using its fully qualified name:

```
java.util.Vector vec = new java.util.Vector() ;
```

On the other hand, if you import the appropriate package, you only need to use the name of the class:

```
import java.util.* ;
...
Vector vec = new Vector() ;
```

Enough talking, how about an example showing what using a page directive actually does? Listing 7.1 shows a simple JSP page that consists entirely of multiple page directives. Notice that you can list the packages to import either one per import attribute, which means one per page directive, or you can list multiple packages per import attribute, by separating them with commas in the value of the import attribute.

Listing 7.1   paged.jsp

```
<%@
  page
  language="java"
  import="java.util.*"
%>


<%@ page import="java.sql.*" %>


<%@ page import="java.io.*,java.net.*, java.security.*" %>
```

When you look at the generated Servlet, you will notice that the appropriate import statements are now at the top of the Servlet. This is demonstrated in the following code snippet, where the new import statements are in boldface:

```
package org.apache.jsp;

import java.util.*;
import java.sql.*;
import java.io.*;
import java.net.*;
import  java.security.*;
import javax.servlet.*;
import javax.servlet.http.*;
import javax.servlet.jsp.*;
import org.apache.jasper.runtime.*;

public class paged$jsp extends HttpJspBase {
```

Next, check out how this example would look using the XML syntax, as opposed to the JSP syntax shown in Listing 7.1. First, in order to have a JSP page in XML syntax, you must enclose everything in the `jsp root` element. You cannot mix the two syntaxes, thus everything must now be in XML syntax. Instead of the JSP syntax using the `<%@` start tag and the `%>` end tag, you now use the empty `jsp:directive.page` elements. Other than that, everything is the same.

```
<jsp:root>
  <jsp:directive.page
    language="java"
    import="java.util.*"
  />
  <jsp:directive.page import="java.sql.*" />

  <jsp:directive.page
    import="java.io.*,java.net.*, java.security.*"
  />
</jsp:root>
```

Handling an Error

The page directive also enables the efficient handling of errors. In fact, you may have been wondering where all of the error handling has been in the previous sample JSP pages. The simple answer is that I've ignored error handling, which is allowed in the JSP framework. The truth is that I've decided error-handling is for wussies! Okay, not really.

The *real* truth is that ignoring errors is a bad programming practice and is not conducive to keeping one's job—unless, of course, you work at a job that doesn't involve computers, like … uh … taming lions at a circus. Instead, the JSP specification provides a very clean error-handling framework, which revolves around the use of two attributes of the page directive:

- The errorPage attribute
- The isErrorPage attribute

The errorPage attribute is used to indicate the URL of a Java resource that will handle all exceptions the JSP page doesn't handle. If the URL refers to another JSP page, that JSP page will have access to the exception implicit object that contains a reference to the original uncaught exception object. (An exception object contains information about the error that occurred.) In order to specify that a JSP page should handle error conditions, it needs to set the isErrorPage attribute to true.

To demonstrate this capability, take a look at the following two JSP pages. Listing 7.2 is a JSP page designed to throw an exception. The JSP page shown in Listing 7.3 catches the exception and provides a visual reference to the user.

Listing 7.2   divbyzero.jsp

```
<%@ page
   errorPage="firsterror.jsp"
%>

<html>
<head><title>The throw an exception JSP Page</title></head>
<body>

<%= 1/0 %>

</body>
</html>
```

Listing 7.3   firsterror.jsp

```
<%@ page
   isErrorPage="true"
%>

<html>
<head><title>JSP Error Page</title></head>
```

```
<body
 BGCOLOR="RED"
>
<h2> Warning an error has occurred during the processing of your request.
Please try your requst again </h2>
<hr/>

<%= exception.getMessage() %>

</body>
</html>
```

To run this example, first start up your copy of Tomcat. Then, type each listing and save each to your jakarta-tomcat-4.0.1\webapps\examples\jsp directory. Use the file names divbyzero.jsp and firsterror.jsp, respectively. Finally, start your web browser and give it the URL localhost:8080/examples/jsp/divbyzero.jsp.

Figure 7.1 shows the resulting web page after executing divbyzero.jsp. Clearly, you can get quite creative in presenting the error information to the user. Other possibilities that I will demonstrate later in this book include logging the error and forwarding the request back to a log-in page, and e-mailing an error report to a website administrator.

Figure 7.1

This figure shows how you can provide a simple error JSP page that reports relevant information to the client, or at least as relevant as the current JVM provides.

So how does this change the generated Servlet? This is easy to answer; just take a look at the Servlet that is generated for the divbyzero JSP page, or the relevant portion of it that is shown in Listing 7.4. First, notice that the creation of the pageContext object takes the name of the error handling JSP page as a parameter. Everything is the same, until it comes time to handle any exceptions. Inside the catch clause, the generating exception is passed onto the indicated error page for processing.

Listing 7.4   divbyzero$jsp.java

```
try {
  response.setContentType("text/html;charset=ISO-8859-1");
  pageContext = _jspxFactory.getPageContext(this, request, response,
  "firsterror.jsp", true, 8192, true);

  application = pageContext.getServletContext();
  config = pageContext.getServletConfig();
  session = pageContext.getSession();
  out = pageContext.getOut();

...

} catch (Throwable t) {
  if (out != null && out.getBufferSize() != 0)
    out.clearBuffer();
  if (pageContext != null) pageContext.handlePageException(t);
} finally {
  if (_jspxFactory != null) _jspxFactory.releasePageContext(pageContext);
}
```

Controlling Output

The final major function of the page directive is controlling output. There are four attributes in this category:

- ♦ The buffer attribute
- ♦ The autoFlush attribute
- ♦ The contentType attribute
- ♦ The pageEncoding attribute

The buffer attribute is used to tell the JSP container how to store the output from the JSP page. One possible value for this attribute is "none," which means that the container uses no buffer and writes all output directly to the client. All other possible values indicate the minimum size of the buffer, in kilobytes. The suffix "kb" is mandatory. By default, this attribute has a value of "8kb," indicating that all output is first placed in a buffer with a minimum size of eight kilobytes.

The autoFlush attribute tells the JSP container what to do when the buffer becomes full. When set to true, the buffer is flushed, which means written out to the client. On the other hand, when set to false, an exception is raised when the buffer becomes full and about to overflow. Since flushing makes no sense if buffering is not being used, this attribute can only be used when the `buffer` attribute is set to something other than "none."

The `contentType` attribute is used to indicate two things to the client. First, it specifies the MIME type of the content being sent to the client. Second, it specifies what character encoding is being used in the response to the client. The character encoding must be a value considered legal by the Internet Assigned Numbers Authority (IANA). By default, the `contentType` attribute has a value that specifies a MIME type of "text/html" and a character encoding of ISO-8859-1.

Tagged _____

Multipurpose Internet Mail Extensions (MIME) is a standard that allows Internet mail to support richer content. Early computer communications were limited to the ASCII set of characters, which meant no binary data and limited the number of languages that could be supported. The MIME standard extended the capabilities of Internet mail to allow messages in other character sets, binary data, multipart messages, and non-standard message headers.

Together, a type and a subtype heading are combined to form a particular MIME type. The primary type headers include `application`, `audio`, `image`, `message`, `model`, `multi-part`, `text`, and `video`. The number of specific subtypes is quite large, but is available online at the official content type repository maintained by IANA at

`www.isi.edu/in-notes/iana/assignments/media-types/media-types`

Specific examples that you will use include text/plain, text/html, text/xml.

The `pageEncoding` attribute is similar in spirit to the `contentType` attribute, except that it refers to the actual JSP page itself and not the character encoding of the response. As with the `contentType` attribute, allowed values must be legal IANA values for Internet character encodings. The default value of this attribute is the character encoding specified in the `contentType` attribute if it is present; otherwise, it is ISO-8859-1.

Once again, an example JSP page should prove helpful. Listing 7.5 shows a JSP page that indicates the output should be buffered using a buffer of size 4 kilobytes. The buffer should be flushed whenever it becomes full, and we explicitly set the content type of the response to be text/html.

Coffee Break

Character encodings are an important topic, and are expected to become more important with the worldwide growth of the Internet. If you think about it, the majority of the Internet content is currently in English. Most of the world, however, speaks other languages (duh!); and to reach these potential new customers, businesses will want to reach out to these people in their own language (double duh!). Ideally, we can write our JSP to seamlessly handle the specific languages the client chooses.

Formally, this process of developing your applications for international communities is known as Internationalization and Localization, which is discussed in Chapter 18, "Go Global, Stay Local." For now, the list of valid character encodings that you can use in a JSP page can be found at the IANA website www.iana.org/assignments/character-sets.

Listing 7.5   pageresponse.jsp

```
<%@ page
  contentType="text/html"
  buffer="4kb"
  autoFlush="true"
%>

<html>
<head><title>Page Response Test JSP Page</title></head>
<body>
<h2> Just Testing ... </h2>
</body>
</html>
```

These new directive attributes are reflected in the following snippet from the generated Servlet:

```
_jspxFactory = JspFactory.getDefaultFactory();
response.setContentType("text/html");
pageContext = _jspxFactory.getPageContext(this, request, response,
  "", true, 4096, true);

application = pageContext.getServletContext();
config = pageContext.getServletConfig();
session = pageContext.getSession();
out = pageContext.getOut();
```

As you can see, the implicit objects made available to you by the JSP container depend on the values assigned to specific attributes in the page directive. For example, the creation of the `pageContext` object, which provides the next four implicit objects, takes the buffer size and the value of the `autoFlush` attribute as parameters. You can contrast this example with the example in Listing 7.4, where the default values of the `contentType`, `buffer` and `autoFlush` attributes are demonstrated in the generated Servlet.

The Rest of the Story

At this point you may be wondering whether the discussion on the attributes of the `page` directive will ever end. Don't worry, there are only three more attributes, which don't nicely fit into any of the three previous categories. First, there is the `session` attribute, which is used to indicate whether the JSP page is participating in a HTTP session. If the value of the attribute is true, which is the default value, the session implicit object—as described in Chapter 6—is made available to the JSP page. If the value is false, then the session implicit object is not available.

The next attribute is the `info` attribute, which is used to provide an arbitrary string that is made available within the generated Servlet's `getServletInfo()` method. You won't use it very often. The last attribute is the `isThreadSafe` attribute, which, if true, tells the JSP container that the current JSP page can successfully handle multiple concurrent clients. If it is false, the JSP container must serialize all requests for the JSP page. In either case, however, the JSP author must be sure to properly synchronize access to any shared objects.

The Least You Need to Know

- ◆ The `page` directive is used to define page specific properties that are communicated to the JSP container during the JSP translation phase.
- ◆ The `page` directive is used to import necessary Java packages and classes.
- ◆ The `page` directive provides the error-handling framework within JSP documents.
- ◆ The `page` directive is used to control the output stream used to send the JSP content to the client.

Chapter 8

Mixing and Matching JSP Pages

In This Chapter

♦ Understanding the context path

♦ Using the `include` directive

♦ Using standard actions

In the previous chapter, I introduced error pages as part of the `page` directive. This separation of responsibilities is a good idea, allowing different JSP pages to be responsible for providing different functionality. You may be wondering if you can utilize this concept more generally in a JSP application, such as to handle a site-login or shipping calculations. Fortunately, the answer is yes—the JSP specification provides several mechanisms for both including content as well as forwarding requests as you'll see in this chapter.

Digging the Context

Before jumping into the fundamentals of mixing and matching JSP pages, you need to know how to actually indicate which page you are targeting. The problem is similar to getting driving directions. For example, suppose one of your friends recommends a new restaurant, and you need to know how to get there.

One option is to get complete step-by-step directions from your house to the restaurant. On the other hand, another option is to get directions that are relative to some place you already know, perhaps a different restaurant, cinema, or gas station.

These two alternatives are known as absolute and relative, and are the same two options you have when referencing external resources from a JSP page. You may already be familiar with this concept from HTML development, where you might have used an absolute reference to an image, as shown in this snippet:

```
<img src=http://www.persistentjava.com/cigjsp/image/banner.jpg/>
```

But what happens if the image is moved to a different directory, or even a different web server? To prevent breaking applications, you could also use a relative reference, where the resource location is specified relative to something else, such as the current web page:

```
<img src="image/banner.jpg"/>
```

Tagged

You may wonder what I mean by **contexts**. Basically, a web server might host multiple web applications. In order to distinguish between them, the web server needs a way of telling in what context (or environment) a specific resource should operate.

If the web server has predefined *contexts* (which might be done in an initialization or configuration script), you also can specify a resource relative to this context, which can serve as the root of a web application, such as the cigjsp resource:

```
<img src="/cigjsp/images/banner.jpg"/>
```

The obvious benefit of the two relative approaches is that the entire web application can be moved, without breaking the internal links. As you might have guessed, due to their flexibility, you will almost exclusively use relative references in JSP applications.

Directing the Include

Now that you know how to specify a particular resource from within a JSP page, you can start to do something with them. The first method I will discuss is include. As you may remember from Chapter 7, "Talking to the Container," directives allow a JSP page to communicate with the JSP container during the JSP page translation phase. Thus, the include directive is used to include content into the current JSP page while the implementation Servlet is being generated.

This implies that the included content is static (unchanging) in nature, as a JSP page is only translated once during its life cycle. As a result, the include directive is often used to build a more complex JSP implementation out of smaller and simpler JSP pages. Or in other words, you can now build template JSP pages, where content can be shared across a web application. To demonstrate this concept, take a look at the JSP page shown in Listing 8.1, which builds a new JSP page using a predefined header and footer JSP page.

Listing 8.1   included.jsp

```
<%@
  page
  contentType="text/html"
%>


<%@
  include
  file="header.jsp"
%>


<h4> Product Listing </h4>
<ul>
  <li> JDBC </li>
  <li> JDO </li>
  <li> JSP </li>
</ul>


<%@
  include
  file="footer.jsp"
%>
```

Notice how this JSP page is practically empty of content; the bulk of the work (including most of the HTML content) is in external resources that can be reused by other JSP pages. The header and footer JSP pages are shown in Listings 8.2 and 8.3, respectively. To see this example in action, type the listings and save each in your jakarta-tomcat-4.0.1\ webapps\examples\jsp under the names shown with each listing. Then start your version of Tomcat, load a browser, and go to localhost:8080/examples/jsp/included.jsp.

Listing 8.2   header.jsp

```
<html>
  <head>
    <title>
      A Demo Header Page
    </title>
  </head>
  <body>
    <h2> Persistent Java: </h2>
```

Listing 8.3 footer.jsp

```
<hr/>
&copy; Persistent Java:
WebMaster:
<a href="mailto:rjbrunner@pacbell.net">
  Robert J. Brunner
</a>
<p/>
Today is
<%= new java.util.Date() %>
</body>
</html>
```

As you might glean from Listing 8.3, footer.jsp is essentially a copyright indicator, and could easily be shared among all of the JSP pages in a particular web application. Likewise, header.jsp might be shared among multiple JSP pages, although it should be beefed up, possibly incorporating a corporate logo. Figure 8.1 shows the entire template web application. If you reload this JSP page, you will notice that the date never changes. This demonstrates the static nature of resources that are included using the include directive.

Figure 8.1

A template web application, built using the include directive.

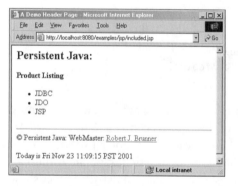

Remember, the include directive content is included while the JSP page is being translated. Thus, the included content is parsed (checked for correct syntax) along with the main JSP content while generating the implementing Servlet. This has two additional consequences.

First, all content is treated as a static resource. What does this mean? The answer is easy to show; just reload the included.jsp page. The date at the bottom of the page never changes. Since the date is evaluated only when the implementation class is generated, it is never updated.

Second, if you change the header or footer JSP pages, the changes are not reflected in the included.jsp page (note that this is true for the Tomcat reference implementation; other

JSP containers may interpret the JSP specification differently). Again, this shows that the included content is treated as a static resource.

One last issue concerns the nature of the context used to indicate the included material. The functionality of the `include` directive occurs during page translation. Thus, the context is considered to be relative to the current JSP file, not the JSP page. While a minor point, this demonstrates that if you precompile your web application, you can ship a completed web application without the header.jsp and footer.jsp pages and not incur any errors.

Executing Standard Actions

By now, you probably grasp the concept that a developer can use JSP directives to communicate with a container during page translation. But how can a developer communicate with the container during the processing of a page request? After all, if you want to perform dynamic processing (creating web content on the fly), you need to do it while a request is being processed, not when a page is being translated.

In a JSP page, besides scriptlets and expressions, dynamic capability is provided by actions. Actions follow XML syntax and come in two flavors: standard and custom. Standard actions are predefined elements and are listed in Table 8.1. Custom actions, also known as tags, are developed outside the JSP specification.

Table 8.1   Standard Actions

Name	Description
UseBean	Allows a JSP page to use a JavaBean.
setProperty	Sets a property value for a JavaBean.
getProperty	Gets a property value from a JavaBean.
include	Includes a resource into the current page.
forward	Forwards a request to a new resource.
param	Adds a parameter key/value pair to the current request.
plugin	Instructs the JSP page to use the Java Plugin.
params	Adds parameters to be used by the Java plugin.
fallback	Instructs the browser what to do in lieu of the Java plugin.

To use an action, you first write the start tag ...

```
<jsp:actionName>
```

... for the action element including any attributes. Most standard actions do not have any body content; the major exception to this is the use of param actions. To conclude the action, you write out the action end tag ...

```
</jsp:actionName>
```

Thus to use the include action without adding any parameters to the current request, you would use the following syntax:

```
<jsp:include page=header.jsp"/>
```

On the other hand, if you want to pass a new parameter to a forwarded page, you would use the following syntax:

```
<jsp:forward page="badlogin.jsp">
  <jsp:param name="loginName" value=badValue/>
</jsp:forward>
```

In the rest of this chapter, I will work with the include, forward and param actions.

Dynamic Includes

One of the problems with the include directive is that the content remains static, which is sometimes the intended result, but can also be limiting. Using the include action, however, enables you to include dynamic (changing) content. To see how this works, take a look at Listing 8.4, which shows a modified version of the original included.jsp page that includes the header and footer JSP pages using the include action. As a result, the date that is displayed in the footer of the generated web page changes with each new request, as shown in Figure 8.2.

To run this example, type the listing and save it in your jakarta-tomcat-4.0.1\webapps\ examples\jsp under the name newIncluded.jsp. Then start your version of Tomcat, load a browser, and browse to localhost:8080/examples/jsp/newIncluded.jsp.

Listing 8.4 newIncluded.jsp

```
<%@
  page
  contentType="text/html"
%>

<jsp:include
  page="header.jsp"
/>

<h4> Product Listing </h4>
```

```
<ul>
  <li> JDBC </li>
  <li> JDO </li>
  <li> JSP </li>
</ul>

<jsp:include
  page="footer.jsp"
/>
```

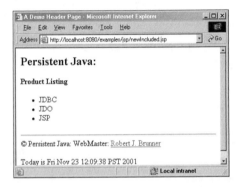

Figure 8.2

This figure shows the revised template web application built using the include action.

One of the other benefits of using the include action is that you can pass parameters to an included resource for dynamic processing. For example, in Listing 8.5, you have a hit counter that is passed to the footer for displaying. While this method does work in a limited sense, a better example would be to use JavaBeans. You also need to modify the footer.jsp page to display the new parameter, which is shown in Listing 8.6.

To run this example, type the listings and save each in your jakarta-tomcat-4.0.1\webapps\examples\jsp under the names shown with each listing. Then start your version of Tomcat, load a browser, and browse to localhost:8080/examples/jsp/hcIncluded.jsp.

Listing 8.5   hcIncluded.jsp

```
<%@
  page
  contentType="text/html"
%>

<%! int hitCounter = 0 ; %>

<%@
  include
  file="header.jsp"
```

continues

Listing 8.5   hcIncluded.jsp   (continued)

```
%>

<h4> Product Listing </h4>
<ul>
  <li> JDBC </li>
  <li> JDO </li>
  <li> JSP </li>
</ul>

<jsp:include page="hcFooter.jsp">
  <jsp:param name="HC" value="<%= hitCounter++%>" />
</jsp:include>
```

Listing 8.6   hcFooter.jsp

```
  <hr/>
  &copy; Persistent Java:
  WebMaster:
  <a href="mailto:rjbrunner@pacbell.net">
    Robert J. Brunner
  </a>
  <p/>
  This page has been viewed <%= request.getParameter("HC") %> times.
  </body>
</html>
```

Notice how the main JSP page includes the header, which is static using the include *directive*, and it includes the footer, which is dynamic, using the include *action*. This sort of include style mixing is perfectly legal, and even a good idea. In order to minimize the load on your web server, you should handle all static content using the include directive. The resulting web page is shown in Figure 8.3, after the page has been viewed 10 times.

Figure 8.3

This figure shows a template web application where a parameter is passed to the included resource.

Before concluding this section, two more comments are warranted. First, because the resource included with the `include` action is processed at request time, the locator for it is *page relative* (as opposed to the `include` directive, which was *file relative*). This is easy to remember, because the name of the attribute that indicates the included resource is `file` for the `include` directive and `page` for the `include` action.

Second, the `include` action takes an optional attribute, named `flush`, which affects the response output whenever it is buffered. In order to provide maximum flexibility, the `flush` attribute allows a JSP developer to send all output to the client before the indicated resource is included. The default value for this attribute is `false`, allowing the included content complete control over the response buffer.

Being Forward

So far, I have shown you included external resources. However, JSP developers have another option—the `forward` action. Unlike an include operation where the included resource is processed and control is returned to the original JSP page, a `forward` action drops everything and passes complete control over the current request to the new resource. The new resource can be a static file, a JSP page, or even a Servlet.

A good example for using the `forward` action is a login page, shown in Listing 8.7. If the login is successful, the user is forwarded on to the desired resource, such as a bank account, an e-commerce checkout, or an online mail account. Since all processing of the current page is terminated prior to forwarding the request, any buffered output is cleared prior to the forward. By now, you should know how to run an example like this in your browser. If you've forgotten, check back with a previous example. If you sort of remember, here's a hint: You need both Listings 8.7 and 8.8, and the URL is localhost:8080/ examples/jsp/loginforward.jsp.

CAUTION

Hot Java

If any content has been sent to the client, an attempt to forward a request will result in an error, specifically an `IllegalStateException`. There are two potential scenarios where this might arise. First, if the output is buffered, the buffer must not have been flushed. Second, if the output is not buffered, nothing must have been written to the output stream.

Listing 8.7   loginforward.jsp

```
<%@
  page
  contentType="text/html"
%>

<html>
<head><title>Login JSP Page</title></head>
```

continues

Listing 8.7   loginforward.jsp   (continued)

```
<body>

<%
  String user = request.getParameter("user") ;
  if(user != null) {
    if(user.equals("java")) {
%>

    <jsp:forward page="process.jsp" />

<%
    } else {
%>

<h2> Invalid User. Please try again. </h2>

<%
    }
  } else {
%>

<h2> Please Login. </h2>

<%
  }
%>

<form method="post">
  <input type="text" name="user" value="" />
  <p/>
  <input type="password" name="passwd" value="" />
  <p/>
  <input type="submit" value="submit" />
</form>

</body>
</html>
```

The overall process involved in this JSP page is quite simple. First, you check whether the user has tried to log in yet. If not, you simply ask the user to login and provide the appropriate form, as shown in Figure 8.4. (I will discuss forms more thoroughly in Chapter 10, "Extending HTML.") If the user has tried to log in (which you can tell because a parameter named user has been submitted as part of the current HTTP request), you check to see if the name is "java." If it is, you forward the request appropriately; otherwise, you print out an error message and allow the user to try again.

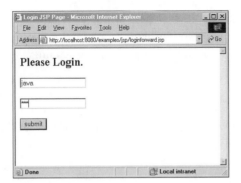

Figure 8.4

This figure shows the main login page.

Note that this is a simple login page. A more realistic example would have the verification in a separate page, and the user credentials would be attached to any forwarded pages to prevent user spoofing. In the process JSP page, you just print out a simple message as shown in Figure 8.5, but it could easily be modified to perform more advanced processing.

Listing 8.8   process.jsp

```
<%@
   page
   contentType="text/html"
%>

<html>
<head><title>Login Success JSP Page</title></head>
<body>

<h2> Congratulations, you have been successfully confirmed </h2>

</body>
</html>
```

Figure 8.5

This figure demonstrates a successful login.

The forward action takes place on the server; the client will not see any changes and will not need to issue a separate request. On the other hand, sometimes it is useful to inform the client that a resource has been moved, which is best done by sending a redirect header to the client:

```
response.sendRedirect() ;
```

Now, you're ready to put your newly gained knowledge to work. In the next chapter, you'll put together a real, albeit simple, web application.

The Least You Need to Know

- ◆ Resources can be specified using either absolute or relative references. Relative references simplify the development of web applications, since absolute paths can break when moving content.
- ◆ The `include` directive allows for the inclusion of static content during the JSP page translation phase.
- ◆ The `include` action allows for the inclusion of either static or dynamic content during the JSP page request processing phase.
- ◆ The `forward` action allows a JSP page to forward a request to another resource.

Wrapping It Up!

In This Chapter

♦ Creating web applications

♦ Exploring directory structures

♦ Understanding deployment descriptors

Up until now, I have placed all JSP pages in the examples/jsp directory under the Apache Tomcat 4.0 directory structure. I did this because it was the easiest way to make everything work. However, this is obviously not a practical solution—after all, developers typically don't want their hot new killer web application to always be under the examples/jsp context.

Fortunately, there is a standard way to package web applications. In this chapter, I will first discuss exactly what constitutes a web application. I then continue with the specific nature of a deployment descriptor. I recognize that you haven't really built any "real-world" web applications; after all, at best we have only linked three or four (if you include the error page) JSP pages together. As a result, in this chapter, I will use simple, previously developed JSP pages to demonstrate the basics, and, as I introduce more complex examples, I will show you how to add them to our ongoing web application.

Creating a Web Application

Throughout this book, I have casually referred to web applications, without really defining what they are. Fundamentally, a web application is a collection of

JavaServer Pages, Servlets, HTML pages, and other resources—such as images, audio content, video content, XHTML, XML—and even enterprise content—such as database connections and EJBs (although these can also be hosted on separate servers that are interfaced to the web application). This collection of resources forms a complete application that is made accessible to clients from a web server. A web application can be packaged into a single entity, known as a web application archive (WAR) file, and executed on multiple, possibly different, containers.

In order to provide access to the web application, it is rooted at a particular context within the web server. For example, if your website is www.persistentjava.com, you could root your web application at www.persistentjava.com/cigjsp, in which case, your context for this web application is /cigjsp. The context information is encapsulated within the web application by a ServletContext implicit object.

Sifting Through the Parts

Web applications may consist of the following elements:

- **JavaServer Pages,** which are used to handle client requests and generate dynamic content as part of the server's response. This can also include any custom actions that are defined by tag libraries.

- **Servlets,** which also are used to handle client requests and generate dynamic content as part of the server's response.

- **JavaBeans,** which provide server-side support for processing client requests and generating dynamic content.

- **Static textual content** in the form of HTML, XHTML, or XML pages.

- **Static content** in the form of images, audio, video, or similar binary data.

- **Resource files,** which are used by Java classes to process requests and generate responses, including configuration information.

- **Java classes,** which operate on the client-side, including Java Applets and JavaBeans. This can also include a Java Runtime Environment (JRE) that is obtained via the Plugin or Java Web Start.

In order to make sense of all of this potential information, a web application utilizes a standard directory structure, and also employs a standardized deployment descriptor that defines the interrelationship between all of the components.

Defining a Web Application

Okay, now that you can recognize a web application, how do you tell a web server about it? Basically, all you need to do is modify the server's configuration file to define a new context, and associate your web application with the new context. Normally, this would be done by a system (or website) administrator, but why not give it a try yourself? This process is somewhat server dependent, but since you have been using Apache Tomcat, I will show you how to register a new context using this server.

First, you will need to open the Apache Tomcat configuration file, which is called server.xml. It is located in the $TOMCAT_HOME/conf directory, where $TOMCAT_ HOME, refers to the installation directory for your Tomcat installation. For example, I installed Tomcat on my D: drive under the Program Files directory. Thus my $TOMCAT_HOME variable has the value "D:\Program Files\Apache Tomcat 4.0." If you look at Figure 9.1, this should be easy to understand.

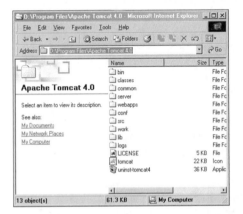

Figure 9.1

This figure shows the installation hierarchy of the Apache Tomcat server. Your installation might appear slightly different (maybe very different if you are working on Linux), but the basics will be the same.

If you open the server.xml configuration file in a standard text editor such as Notepad, you will notice a lot of XML elements and XML comments. Taken together, these provide the initial configuration for the Tomcat server, which is actually quite powerful. Be careful what you change—these settings control all aspects of Tomcat's behavior, including what ports it listens to (in this example, the port is 8080). If you change the wrong thing, Tomcat may cease to function properly. Worse, the Tomcat police will knock down your door and take away all your computer equipment. If you believe that last one, shall we talk about a bridge I have for sale?

If you scroll down near the bottom of the file, you see where the contexts are defined. As you can see from the root context definition (which is actually commented out in the standard server.xml file), the basic format is rather simple. Here's what it looks like in the file:

```
<!-- Tomcat Root Context -->
<!--
  <Context path="" docBase="ROOT" debug="0"/>
-->
```

If you look at the examples context definition, however, you can see how complicated they can quickly become:

```
<!-- Tomcat Examples Context -->
<Context path="/examples" docBase="examples" debug="0"
         reloadable="true">
  <Logger className="org.apache.catalina.logger.FileLogger"
            prefix="localhost_examples_log." suffix=".txt"
    timestamp="true"/>
  <Ejb   name="ejb/EmplRecord" type="Entity"
         home="com.wombat.empl.EmployeeRecordHome"
        remote="com.wombat.empl.EmployeeRecord"/>
  <!-- PersistentManager: Uncomment the section below to test Persistent
        Sessions.

        saveOnRestart: If true, all active sessions will be saved
          to the Store when Catalina is shutdown, regardless of
          other settings. All Sessions found in the Store will be
          loaded on startup. Sessions past their expiration are
          ignored in both cases.
        maxActiveSessions: If 0 or greater, having too many active
          sessions will result in some being swapped out. minIdleSwap
          limits this. -1 means unlimited sessions are allowed.
          0 means sessions will almost always be swapped out after
          use - this will be noticeably slow for your users.
        minIdleSwap: Sessions must be idle for at least this long
          (in seconds) before they will be swapped out due to
        maxActiveSessions. This avoids thrashing when the site is
          highly active. -1 or 0 means there is no minimum - sessions
          can be swapped out at any time.
        maxIdleSwap: Sessions will be swapped out if idle for this
          long (in seconds). If minIdleSwap is higher, then it will
          override this. This isn't exact: it is checked periodically.
          -1 means sessions won't be swapped out for this reason,
          although they may be swapped out for maxActiveSessions.
            If set to >= 0, guarantees that all sessions found in the
            Store will be loaded on startup.
        maxIdleBackup: Sessions will be backed up (saved to the Store,
            but left in active memory) if idle for this long (in seconds),
            and all sessions found in the Store will be loaded on startup.
            If set to -1 sessions will not be backed up, 0 means they
            should be backed up shortly after being used.

        To clear sessions from the Store, set maxActiveSessions, maxIdleSwap,
        and minIdleBackup all to -1, saveOnRestart to false, then restart
        Catalina.
  -->
```

For your first attempt at creating a context, you can start simple. Assume that you want to build your first web application, and root it at the /cigjsp context. To do so, all you need to do is add the following entry to the server.xml file (add it right after the root context):

```
<Context
  path="/cigjsp"
  docBase="cigjsp"
  debug="0"
  reloadable="true"/>
```

Once you have added this line, save the file, stop the Tomcat server, and then restart it. Congratulations, you have successfully created a new context.

Understanding what the previous snippet tells the Tomcat server is rather easy. First, the path attribute tells Tomcat that your web application will be rooted at /cigjsp. Second, the docBase attribute tells the Tomcat server that the web application is stored under the $TOMCAT_HOME/webapps directory in the cigjsp directory. Finally, the debug attribute merely indicates that we are working in a production environment (okay, stop laughing now), and the reloadable attribute indicates that we want to allow JSP pages to be dynamically reloaded.

Exploring the Directory Structure

Since you are probably very eager to test out your first web application, I will quickly cut to the chase. The simplest web application is a single JSP page. For this example, reuse your first JSP page, hello.jsp, which is shown (again) in Listing 9.1. All you need to do is place this JSP page in the cigjsp directory, and voilà, you have your first web application.

Listing 9.1   hello.jsp

```
<html>
    <head>
        <title> Hello World Example </title>
    </head>
    <body>
        <h1> Hello World! </h1>
    </body>
</html>
```

Assuming you did everything correctly, including changing the server.xml file to add the new context, restarting the Tomcat server, creating the cigjsp directory under the $TOMCAT_HOME/webapps directory, and pointing your web browser to the URL localhost:8080/cigjsp/hello.jsp, you should see the web page shown in Figure 9.2.

Figure 9.2

This figure shows the hello.jsp page deployed as your first web application.

Obviously, I skimmed over a lot of details; however, given a few extra twists, the overall process really is this easy. To demonstrate, take a look at Figure 9.3, which shows the directory structure for the examples context that comes with the Tomcat server.

Figure 9.3

This figure shows the examples web application directory structure that comes with the Tomcat server.

The first thing to notice from this directory structure is the WEB-INF directory. This directory holds information needed by the web application, but is not supposed to be visible to the client. Thus, it is a great place to put configuration and resource information. In fact, this is where the web application deployment descriptor is stored. (As you'll see later in this chapter, the deployment descriptor provides such information as security configurations and session configurations.)

You also can place helper classes in the WEB-INF\classes directory, including any JavaBeans or precompiled JSP pages. The only caveat is that the directory structure inside the classes directory must match the package naming hierarchy.

Another useful directory is the WEB-INF\lib directory, where you can place any jar files that contain classes you may need, such as JDBC drivers or Java 2 standard extension jar files. (Jar files are compressed data.) The amazing fact about these two subdirectories, classes and lib, is that any classes stored either directly in these directories, or in a jar file that is stored in these directories, are automatically added to the Java Virtual Machine (JVM) that executes your JSP pages. This can really make life easy.

One last item concerning the example web application is the use of a JSP and Servlets subdirectory. In practice, this is not necessary, but subdirectories are a good idea, if only to organize your content. For example, it is often wise to place images in an images subdirectory, likewise with any audio or video files, JavaScript files, and even XHTML files. This simplifies the reuse of the code, and makes it easier to debug your web application.

Exploring the Deployment Descriptor

So far, you've looked at the server configuration file, which for Tomcat is called server.xml. This file tells the web server, or in this case the Servlet container, the context for your web application. All other information regarding your web application is contained in the deployment descriptor. The type of information recorded in this file includes the following:

♦ Security configurations

♦ Session configurations

♦ Servlet and JSP definitions

♦ Servlet and JSP mappings

♦ MIME type mappings

♦ The welcome file list

♦ Error pages

All of this information is stored in the web.xml file, which provides a repository for all of the deployment information necessary for your web application. To be effective, this file should be stored in the WEB-INF directory of your web application directory structure. Because this file is an XML document, it needs to have something called a Document Type Declaration (DTD), which is defined as part of the Servlet specification, shown in this example:

```
<?xml version="1.0" encoding="ISO-8859-1"?>

<!DOCTYPE web-app
    PUBLIC "-//Sun Microsystems, Inc.//DTD Web Application 2.3//EN"
    "http://java.sun.com/dtd/web-app_2_3.dtd">

<web-app>
...
</web-app>
```

Mapping JSP Pages

Perhaps the most useful feature of the deployment descriptor is the way knowing this stuff attracts people of the opposite sex. Er … my mistake. This stuff actually makes those folks run screaming in the opposite direction. Some people just don't know how to have fun. The feature I'm really talking about here is the ability to first define and then *map* a Servlet (or JSP) to a specific URL, or name—mapping is when you associate a more understandable name with the Servlet; not a name like "Joe," but rather a name that better describes the Servlet.

For example, you may want to have a Servlet provide a catalog listing whenever the user first enters your web application. You can do this by defining a mapping between the name you want to use (such as "catalog") and the name of the Servlet (which might be much longer or in a complicated directory structure).

You can demonstrate this using your simple hello JSP. First you need to define the Servlet name for the container, which involves naming the Servlet, and indicating where the implementation exists, like this:

```
<servlet>
  <servlet-name>helloworld</servlet-name>
  <jsp-file>/hello.jsp</jsp-file>
</servlet>
```

This sequence of XML elements first defines a new Servlet called "helloworld," and indicates that it's implemented by a JSP page called hello.jsp, which is rooted at the base of your web application (in other words in the cigjsp directory). The next step is to map the Servlet name to the URL you want to use:

```
<servlet-mapping>
  <servlet-name>helloworld</servlet-name>
  <url-pattern>/hello</url-pattern>
</servlet-mapping>
```

To see this example in action, follow these steps:

1. Create a folder inside your cigjsp folder. Name this new folder WEB-INF.

2. Start Notepad, and create your web.xml file, which should look like this:

```
<?xml version="1.0" encoding="ISO-8859-1"?>

<!DOCTYPE web-app
    PUBLIC "-//Sun Microsystems, Inc.//DTD Web Application 2.3//EN"
    "http://java.sun.com/dtd/web-app_2_3.dtd">

<web-app>
```

```
<servlet>
  <servlet-name>helloworld</servlet-name>
  <jsp-file>/hello.jsp</jsp-file>
</servlet>

<servlet-mapping>
  <servlet-name>helloworld</servlet-name>
  <url-pattern>/hello</url-pattern>
</servlet-mapping>

</web-app>
```

3. Save the file you created in Step 2 to your new WEB-INF folder, using the file name web.xml.

4. Start Tomcat. (If it's already running, shut it down and restart it.)

5. Start your browser and go to localhost:8080/cigjsp/hello.

As you can see, after the Tomcat server processes your new deployment descriptor, you will be able to refer to the hello.jsp resource using /hello, as shown in Figure 9.4.

Figure 9.4

This figure shows the result of mapping your hello.jsp page to the /hello URL. Notice the address bar of the web server.

Bits and Pieces

The last two items deserve a little more discussion. First, there's something called a *welcome file list* that enables a developer to specify a particular file or list of files that the server should provide to a client when the server receives a valid partial request. For example, you could use the welcome file list to tell the server that, whenever it receives a request for www.persistentjava.com/cigjsp/, the server should map the request to the hello.jsp resource:

```
<welcome-file-list>
  <welcome-file>hello.jsp</welcome-file>
</welcome-file-list>
```

If you add this to your deployment desciptor for your simple web application, any attempt to open the /cigjsp URL, including both /cigjsp and /cigjsp/, converts automatically to the URL /cigjsp/hello.jsp resource. Go ahead and try it:

1. Add the previous lines to your web.xml file, so that the complete file looks like this (the new lines are in bold):

```
<?xml version="1.0" encoding="ISO-8859-1"?>

<!DOCTYPE web-app
    PUBLIC "-//Sun Microsystems, Inc.//DTD Web Application 2.3//EN"
    "http://java.sun.com/dtd/web-app_2_3.dtd">

<web-app>

<servlet>
  <servlet-name>helloworld</servlet-name>
  <jsp-file>/hello.jsp</jsp-file>
</servlet>

<servlet-mapping>
  <servlet-name>helloworld</servlet-name>
  <url-pattern>/hello</url-pattern>
</servlet-mapping>

<welcome-file-list>
  <welcome-file>hello.jsp</welcome-file>
</welcome-file-list>

</web-app>
```

2. Shut down and restart Tomcat.

3. Use your browser to go to localhost:8080/cigjsp.

How cool is that?

The error page's information supplements the page directive's error-handling mechanism. Using the error page elements in a deployment descriptor, a developer can customize the error information that the server returns to the client. For example, this technique enables you to return a custom error page whenever a Servlet either explicitly sets a status code that signifies an error, or generates an error condition that is sent to the Servlet container. Assuming you have created an error page, error.html, that is rooted at the base of our context (that is, in the cigjsp directory), the following error-page element would tell the Servlet container that any request for nonexistent content (for example, response status code 404) should be forwarded to the error.html page.

```
<error-page>
  <error-code>404</error-code>
  <location>/error.html</location>
</error-page>
```

If you add this to the deployment descriptor for your simple web application, any attempt to retrieve nonexistent resources results in the return of the /error.html file, which is shown in Listing 9.2, to the client.

Listing 9.2 error.html

```html
<html>
    <head>
        <title> ERROR Example </title>
    </head>
    <body>
        <h1> ERROR!!!!! </h1>
    </body>
</html>
```

For example, if you try to retrieve the resource /cigjsp/HelloWorld, you will get the response shown in Figure 9.5.

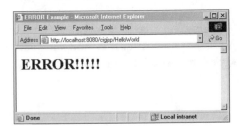

Figure 9.5

This figure shows the custom error page that is returned whenever a user requests a nonexistent resource from the sample web application.

Ready to try this out? Follow these steps:

1. Start Notepad, and type Listing 9.2. Save the file to your cigjsp folder under the file name error.html.

2. Add the error page information to your web.xml file. The complete file should now look like this (the new stuff is in bold type):

```xml
<?xml version="1.0" encoding="ISO-8859-1"?>

<!DOCTYPE web-app
    PUBLIC "-//Sun Microsystems, Inc.//DTD Web Application 2.3//EN"
    "http://java.sun.com/dtd/web-app_2_3.dtd">

<web-app>

  <servlet>
    <servlet-name>helloworld</servlet-name>
    <jsp-file>/hello.jsp</jsp-file>
  </servlet>
```

```
<servlet-mapping>
  <servlet-name>helloworld</servlet-name>
  <url-pattern>/hello</url-pattern>
</servlet-mapping>

<welcome-file-list>
  <welcome-file>hello.jsp</welcome-file>
</welcome-file-list>

<error-page>
  <error-code>404</error-code>
  <location>/error.html</location>
</error-page>

</web-app>
```

3. Shut down and restart Tomcat.

4. Use your browser to go to the nonexistent page localhost:8080/cigjsp/HelloWorld.

You're really cooking now. Set this book down and go brag to your friends and family that you know how to use web deployment descriptors. After they nod and smile, pretending that they know what you're talking about, come back to this book. In the next chapter, you'll learn even more amazing stuff.

The Least You Need to Know

◆ Fundamentally, a web application is a collection of JavaServer Pages, Servlets, HTML pages, JavaBeans, and other resources—such as images, audio content, video content, XHTML, XML—and even enterprise content—such as database connections and EJBs.

◆ A web application utilizes a standard directory structure, and also employs a standardized deployment descriptor that defines the interrelationship between all of the components.

◆ The server.xml file, located in the $TOMCAT_HOME/conf directory, contains configuration information about a web application.

◆ The WEB-INF directory holds information needed by the web application and is a great place to put configuration and resource information.

◆ The deployment descriptor, which is stored in the web.xml file, provides such information as security configurations, session configurations, Servlet and JSP definitions, Servlet and JSP mappings, MIME type mappings, the welcome file list, and error pages.

◆ The web.xml file should be stored in the WEB-INF directory of your web application directory structure.

◆ You can associate a more understandable name with a Servlet, a process called mapping.

◆ A welcome file list enables a developer to specify a particular file or list of files that the server should provide to a client when the server receives a valid partial URL.

◆ Using the error page elements in a deployment descriptor, a developer can customize the error information that the server returns to the client.

Part 3

Working on the Client

JSP pages are a server-side technology, but when building your website, sometimes you need to control how things look and feel on your client's turf. In this part, you'll learn how to do this and make it work from JSP pages.

Extending HTML

In This Chapter

♦ Introducing XHTML

♦ Extending HTML

♦ Exploring links, lists, and tables

♦ Using XHTML forms

Up to this point, I have focused solely on using JSP technology to generate a response to a client's request. As a result, I haven't spent much time actually discussing the format of the response. You may have noticed that so far I have only shown you how to send textual responses using JSP; in particular, the text has always been in the form of HyperText Markup Language (HTML).

As I discussed in Chapter 7, "Talking to the Container," by default, the contentType attribute of the page directive is set to text/html. This tells the client to expect an HTML encoded response. Clearly, you can set this to other values, such as text/plain for plain text, or even text/xml to indicate the response is an Extensible Markup Language (XML) document. Due to its extensible nature, XML provides significant benefits over HTML.

In order to simplify the adoption of XML, the W3C created Extensible HTML (XHTML). XHTML is a relatively new markup language that uses almost all of the familiar HTML elements, while enforcing the rules of XML. Although not a complete tutorial on the subject, this chapter is designed to help you get started using XHTML, and in particular, the XHTML elements that are important for developing dynamic websites.

Coffee Break

You may wonder about nontextual responses from JSP pages (for example, images). While it might seem possible, it is actually illegal (no, you can't actually go to jail). In the Javadoc for the `ServletResponse` object, the Servlet specification states that character data should be sent to a client using a `PrintWriter` object, which is obtained by calling the `ServletResponse.getWriter()` method. For binary, or mixed character and binary data, however, the specification states that a `ServletOutputStream` object should be used, which is obtained by calling the `ServletResponse.getOutputStream()` method.

Furthermore, the specification also states that a Servlet can call either the `getWriter()` method, or the `getOutputStream()` method, but not both. Since a JSP page is compiled into a Servlet, all JSP pages must follow the guidelines in the Servlet specification. As you may recall from the discussion on implicit objects, the `out` object, which is automatically used to send template data to the client is an instance of `JspWriter`, which implements the `PrintWriter` interface. Thus a JSP already has effectively called the `getWriter()` method and can only send textual content as part of the response. To send nontextual data, the request must be forwarded to an appropriate Servlet.

Venturing Beyond HTML

If you are familiar with HTML—or just by nature the type that likes to challenge authority—you may wonder why we even need a new markup language. After all, HTML is the lingua franca of the web. Simply put, while this is true, HTML is not a rigid, consistent standard; instead, there are multiple different versions with varying degrees of compliance among the different browsers. As a result, developing websites that are interesting and informative has become increasingly difficult as developers attempt to stretch the limits of what can be done while still supporting most browsers.

Fresh Brew

XML, like its ancestor Standard Generalized Markup Language (SGML), is a actually a meta language. That is you do not use XML to markup a document; instead, you create a new markup language, like XHTML, that obeys the rules of XML and defines the types of data that can be encoded in the new markup language. This new language is called an XML application.

Out of this mess, the W3C community developed the XHTML recommendation, which is an XML application that has all of the functionality of HTML, while imposing the rules of XML. This enables a developer to separate the presentation of a document from its content. Formally this is accomplished by encoding the content of a document using an XML language, while describing the presentation of the document using a style language like cascading style sheets (CSS) or extensible style language (XSL). Since XHTML is an XML application, it can be extended with new, custom elements and tags. Even more important, by adopting XHTML now, developers can move to other, more complex XML applications in the future.

Declaring XML

The first item that any XML application needs to address is the XML declaration. While it is an optional element, including it is a recommended practice. If you are going to include the XML declaration in your document, it must be first. The XML declaration element is enclosed in a <? start tag and a ?> end tag.

Two optional attributes that can be applied to an XML declaration are the version and encoding attributes. The version attribute should have the value of 1.0, since there is only one version of XML, although this may eventually change. The encoding attribute indicates the character encoding that is used by the XML document. Like Java, XML is Unicode aware, thus you can support any language and character that is supported by Unicode. The default encoding is UTF-8.

Fresh Brew

The W3C maintains the XHTML recommendation, which is available at www.w3.org/TR/xhtml1/. This is the reference for understanding the details of the XHTML specification.

Putting it all together, you have the full XML declaration element:

```
<?xml version="1.0" encoding="UTF-8" ?>
```

Which DTD?

Since XML is a meta-language, developers must explicitly define the new elements that actually are used in an XML application. In order to harness the full power of XML, it is desirable for developers to share these definitions, so that clients and servers can communicate effectively. These definitions can be encoded in two different ways:

◆ Document Type Declarations (DTDs)
◆ XML Schemas

Schemas provide a very powerful way to completely describe the data within a document; however, a full discussion of schemas is way beyond the scope of this book.

Fortunately, XHTML is defined using a DTD; in fact, there are three different versions of XHTML, which are distinguished by three different DTDs:

◆ Strict DTDs
◆ Transitional DTDs
◆ Frameset DTDs

After the XML declaration, the next item in an XHTML document is the DTD specification.

If you want to use a clean markup language that follows the most restrictive rules of XHTML, you should choose the strict DTD. This DTD does not allow a developer to use either deprecated (old-style) elements, like center, or obsolete elements. The following snippet shows the strict DTD:

```
<!DOCTYPE html
   PUBLIC "-//W3C//DTD XHTML 1.0 Strict//EN"
   "http://www.w3.org/TR/xhtml1/DTD/xhtml1-strict.dtd">
```

The transitional DTD, on the other hand, is more lenient and allows a developer to use deprecated elements, like center, but not obsolete elements. The transitional DTD is often used when a developer needs to support older client applications that might not understand CSS, and must rely on the presentation capabilities of HTML. The following snippet shows the transitional DTD:

```
<!DOCTYPE html
   PUBLIC "-//W3C//DTD XHTML 1.0 Transitional//EN"
   "http://www.w3.org/TR/xhtml1/DTD/xhtml1-transitional.dtd">
```

The last DTD is the frameset DTD and is used for documents that are framesets, which is a document that defines frames that are filled with other XHTML documents. The frameset document must use the frameset DTD, but the XHTML documents that are used in the actual frames can use either the strict or the transitional DTD. The following snippet shows the frameset DTD:

```
<!DOCTYPE html
   PUBLIC "-//W3C//DTD XHTML 1.0 Frameset//EN"
   "http://www.w3.org/TR/xhtml1/DTD/xhtml1-frameset.dtd">
```

Being Well-Formed

After the DTD, an XHTML document starts to look nearly identical to an HTML document. The differences that remain are often hard to notice, and all revolve around making the XHTML document well-formed. Well-formed is a term used to describe a document that obeys the rules of XML. First, a well-formed document must have a root element, which for XHTML is <html>, with the caveat that you can explicitly state that you are using the XHTML namespace:

```
<html xmlns="http://www.w3.org/1999/xhtml">
```

If you have developed HTML applications, you may know that HTML is case-insensitive, thus <HTML>, <html> and <Html> are all treated in the same manner. XML, and therefore XHTML, on the other hand, is case-sensitive. By that I mean, all XHTML elements and attributes must be named the same way on your opening and closing tags, thus if you open your tag as <HTML> you must close it as <HTML>, not <html>.

The next requirement is that all attribute values must be properly quoted, either using single or double quotes. While HTML clients are rather forgiving, XML applications must follow the rules, thus all attribute values, such as the namespace declaration above, must be properly quoted.

The rest of the rules specify how elements must be used. First, all elements must have both a start and an end tag. An end tag is identical to the start tag, but the name is preceded by a forward slash. Thus our XHTML applications will start with <html> and end with </html>. Likewise, all other elements must be properly terminated, such as the following list, where the list item elements are properly terminated:

```
<ul>
   <li> Item One </li>
   <li> Item Two </li>
   <li> Item Three </li>
</ul>
```

Sometimes, an element does not have any body content, as it may only use attributes, in which case it is said to be empty. Rather than adding a terminating end tag to an empty element, a shorthand notation was developed, where the start and end tags were combined. Thus rather than adding an end tag to the image elements, as in this example ...

```
<img src="banner.jpg"></img>
```

... you can use the following shorthand:

```
<img src="banner.jpg"/>
```

Fresh Brew

Some browsers may not understand the canonical empty element declaration. As a result, an alternative declaration was introduced which allows extra whitespace before the forward slash character. For example, to indicate a horizontal rule, you can use the standard form, <hr/>, or the alternative form <hr />. If your document is not displayed properly, try the alternative declaration.

One last rule that deals with elements is the requirement for their proper nesting. For example, if you want to specify that a text block should be both bold and italicized, you could use the following HTML markup:

```
<b><i> This is very important text </b></i>
```

and many browsers will render the text correctly. This is not legal XML, however, because XML requires that any nested elements be properly nested. Thus the previous example must be converted so that the italicized element is completely contained inside the boldface element, as shown in this example:

```
<b><i> This is very important text </i></b>
```

If you put all of these rules together, you have created your first XHTML document, as shown in Listing 10.1.

Listing 10.1   first.xhtml

```
<?xml version="1.0" encoding="UTF-8" ?>
<!DOCTYPE html
    PUBLIC "-//W3C//DTD XHTML 1.0 Strict//EN"
    "http://www.w3.org/TR/xhtml1/DTD/xhtml1-strict.dtd">
<html xmlns="http://www.w3.org/1999/xhtml">
    <head>
        <title> First XHTML </title>
    </head>
    <body>
        <hr/>
        <ul>
            <li> Item One </li>
            <li> Item Two </li>
            <li> Item Three </li>
        </ul>
        <b><i> This is very important text </i></b>
    </body>
</html>
```

Fresh Brew

The W3C provides an XHTML validation service at validator.w3.org/. Simply visit this page and enter a website, or, alternatively, upload your XHTML page and it will check the content to see if it is well-formed.

To see what this file looks like, save it to your cigjsp context (remember, this is a subdirectory of the Apache Tomcat webapps directory). If you browse to localhost:8080/cigjsp/first.xhtml, you should see your first XHTML file rendered. If you display first.xhtml in Internet Explorer, it will validate your XHTML and verify that it is well-formed, as shown in Figure 10.1. That wasn't so hard, now was it?

Figure 10.1

This figure shows how Internet Explorer 6.0 renders the sample XHTML document. First the document is checked to see if it is well-formed, and then the document is rendered.

Adding Static Interactions

Now that you have the basics of XHTML down, how about adding some interactive elements? The easiest way to do this is to use XHTML links, which are just like links in regular old HTML. For example, if you want to link to the home page for the White House, you would use the following element:

```
<a href="http://www.whitehouse.gov/"> The White House </a>
```

This might seem mundane, but remember that you can generate an XHTML page dynamically, building up a series of links from within a JSP page. These links can be determined from user input (as part of a search request), or generated out of a database. Right now, you shouldn't worry about the technique so much as how to do it. Listing 10.2 shows how to generate an XHTML list of links to bookstores.

Listing 10.2   bookstores.jsp

```
<%@
  page
  contentType="text/xhtml"
%>
<?xml version="1.0" encoding="UTF-8" ?>
<!DOCTYPE html
  PUBLIC "-//W3C//DTD XHTML 1.0 Strict//EN"
  "http://www.w3.org/TR/xhtml1/DTD/xhtml1-strict.dtd">

<%!
  String[] bookstores =
    {   "http://www.amazon.com/",
        "http://www.bn.com/",
        "http://www.bookpool.com/",
        "http://www.a1books.com/"
        } ;
%>

<html xmlns="http://www.w3.org/1999/xhtml">
<head>
  <title> A List of Links </title>
</head>
  <body>
    <h1> Where to buy this book? </h1>
    <hr/>
    <ul>
<% for(int i = 0 ; i < bookstores.length ; i++) { %>
      <li>
```

continues

Listing 10.2 bookstores.jsp (continued)

```
      <a href="<%= bookstores[i] %>">
      <%= bookstores[i] %>
      </a>
    </li>
<% } %>
   </ul>
  </body>
</html>
```

If you create this JSP page in the cigjsp context, you can view its output by viewing local-host:8080/cigjsp/bookstore.jsp, as shown in Figure 10.2.

Figure 10.2

This figure shows how the XHTML output from the bookstores.jsp page is rendered.

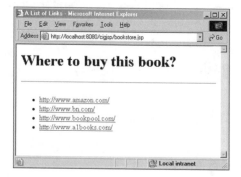

While lists can be useful, sometimes you want to generate a table of links and associated information. As you can see from Listing 10.3, with a few minor tweaks, you can change the bookstore JSP page to list the name of the bookstore along with a link to the appropriate website. Figure 10.3 shows the output from this page.

Listing 10.3 newbookstores.jsp

```
<%@
  page
  contentType="text/xhtml"
%>
<?xml version="1.0" encoding="UTF-8" ?>
<!DOCTYPE html
  PUBLIC "-//W3C//DTD XHTML 1.0 Strict//EN"
  "http://www.w3.org/TR/xhtml1/DTD/xhtml1-strict.dtd">

<%!
    String[] storenames =
    {  "Amazon",
       "Barnes & Noble",
       "BookPool",
```

```
            "A1 Books"
    } ;

    String[] bookstores =
    {   "http://www.amazon.com/",
        "http://www.bn.com/",
        "http://www.bookpool.com/",
        "http://www.a1books.com/"
    } ;
%>

<html xmlns="http://www.w3.org/1999/xhtml">
<head>
  <title> A Table of Links </title>
</head>
  <body>
    <h1> Where to buy this book? </h1>
    <hr/>
    <table border="4" width="100%">
      <tr>
        <th>Book Store</th>
        <th>Web Site</th>
      </tr>
<% for(int i = 0 ; i < bookstores.length ; i++) { %>
      <tr>
        <td> <%= storenames[i] %> </td>
        <td>
          <a href="<%= bookstores[i] %>">
          <%= bookstores[i] %>
          </a>
        </td>
      </tr>
<% } %>
    </table>
  </body>
</html>
```

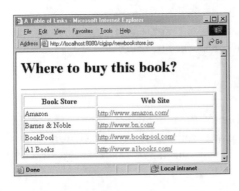

Figure 10.3

This figure shows how the XHTML output from the newbookstores.jsp page is rendered.

Adding Dynamic Interactions

The static interactions discussed in the previous section can certainly help improve the usability of a website; but how about letting the client actually send information to the server? After all, how else are you going to let a user log in to a site or enter search criteria? You can enable this type of dynamic interaction using the form element. First, however, you need to understand some of the basic syntactical components of this element.

Forming the Request

As you can probably imagine, obtaining input from a user opens up a lot of possibilities. However, with this new power come new responsibilities. In order to properly establish communication, you will need to master a few new, and possibly unfamiliar, elements.

First, the form element encompasses the entire act of obtaining information from a user. The form element accepts a large number of attributes, but the two most commonly used attributes are action and method. The action attribute specifies a Uniform Resource Indicator (URI), where the data should be sent when the form is submitted (which occurs when the user clicks the Submit button). In a JSP page, the action attribute will default to the current page.

The method attribute specifies the HTTP method for sending the data to the server. This attribute can either be set to GET, in which case the data is appended to the URL, or it can be set to POST, in which case the data is sent to the server in the body of the request. GET requests can be bookmarked, but if the data contains non-ASCII characters, or is very large, you must use POST.

Three other optional attributes—accept-charset, enctype, accept—control the character encoding and MIME types in which the input data can be encoded and sent to the server. Likewise, the optional target attribute indicates where the server response should be displayed, and can specify a frame, or even a new window.

The standard XHTML attributes can also be utilized, including the id, class, title, style, dir, and lang attributes. Finally, the form element also supports event attributes, which specify an action that should be performed whenever a specific user interface event occurs. These attributes include onsubmit, onreset, onclick, ondblclick, onmousedown, onmouseup, onmouseover, onmousemove, onmouseout, onkeypress, onkeydown, and onkeyup.

Specifying the Input

While the form element may control how the input data is sent to the server, the real heavy lifting is done by elements that are explicitly designed to control how the user enters information. These elements include the input, textarea, label, button, option, `select`, `fieldset`, and `legend` elements. A full description of each of these elements is beyond the scope of this book, but the `input` element deserves more discussion as it is heavily used.

The `input` element has several attributes that are most often used, including `type`, `name`, and `value`. The `name` attribute specifies a name by which the input data is known, while the `value` attribute either specifies a default value, or a name to be displayed for a button. The `type` attribute determines what type of input control the browser displays and can take one of the following values:

- ◆ `text`, to create a text field control.
- ◆ `checkbox`, to create a checkbox control.
- ◆ `radio`, to create a radio button control.
- ◆ `password`, to create a text field where the input is not displayed directly, but hidden by an asterisk character.
- ◆ `hidden`, to create a hidden control. This is often used to provide a crude session management capability.
- ◆ `submit`, to create a button that when clicked sends the input data to the server. The actual name displayed on the button can be specified using the value attribute.
- ◆ `reset`, to create a rest button that reinitializes the form to all default values.
- ◆ `button`, to create a standard button control.
- ◆ `file`, to create a file upload control.
- ◆ `image`, to create an image control.

Action Forms

Enough with the legalese, how about some examples? In Chapter 8, "Mixing and Matching JSP Pages," you have already used forms to enter login information. Listing 10.4 builds on the previous login example to show several different input controls used together.

Listing 10.4   controls.jsp

```
<?xml version="1.0" encoding="UTF-8" ?>
<!DOCTYPE html
   PUBLIC "-//W3C//DTD XHTML 1.0 Strict//EN"
   "http://www.w3.org/TR/xhtml1/DTD/xhtml1-strict.dtd">

<html xmlns="http://www.w3.org/1999/xhtml">
  <head>
```

continues

Listing 10.4   controls.jsp   (continued)

```
    <title> Input Controls </title>
  </head>
  <body>

<%
  String user = request.getParameter("user") ;
  if(user != null) {
%>

    <h2> Greetings User </h2>
    <hr/>
    <h4> Username: <%= user %> </h4>
    <h4> Password: <%= request.getParameter("passwd") %> </h4>
    <h4> Email: <%= request.getParameter("email") %> </h4>
    <h4> Sex: <%= request.getParameter("sex") %> </h4>
    <hr/>

<%
  } else {
%>

    <h2> Please Login. </h2>

    <form method="post">
      Username <input type="text" name="user" value="" />
      <p/>
      Password <input type="password" name="passwd" value="" />
      <p/>
      Email <input type="text" name="email" value="" />
      <p/>
      Sex
        <input type="radio" name="sex" value="Male" />   M
        <input type="radio" name="sex" value="Female" />   F
      <p/>
      <input type="submit" value="submit" />
    </form>

<%
  }
%>

  </body>
</html>
```

This example JSP page demonstrates several important things in regard to using input controls. First, the input data can be retrieved from the request using the `request.getParameter()` method. The name of the parameter is the same as the name of the input control. Second, the default action for a form element is the same URL as the current page. Thus you can have one JSP page that performs double duty.

Finally, no verification of the data is performed. Ideally, this would be done at the client in order to minimize the work on the server. In Chapter 12, "Controlling the Client," I present a solution to this problem using JavaScript. Figures 10.4 and 10.5 show this JSP page in action—first when the user is entering the information, and then when the information is being displayed.

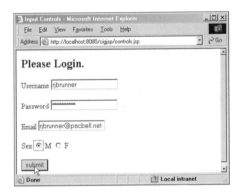

Figure 10.4

This figure shows several input controls being used in an XHTML page to gather information from the user.

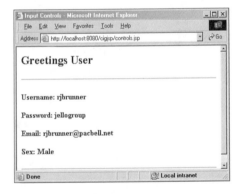

Figure 10.5

This figure shows the information entered in the previous figure being displayed back to the user.

The Least You Need to Know

◆ XHTML is a powerful markup language that is very similar to HTML.

◆ XHTML links can be generated dynamically using JSPs.

◆ Forms provide a simple way for a client to communicate information back to the server.

11

Using Cascading Style Sheets

In This Chapter

♦ Understanding the basics of CSS

♦ Using CSS selectors

♦ Working with CSS properties

In the previous chapter, I explored XHTML, which, being an XML application, provides a powerful method for describing the content of the data in a document. But the presentation of the data is left to the discretion of the browser. In order to provide developers with greater control over the appearance of their documents, the W3C has produced the cascading style sheets (CSS) recommendations.

In this chapter, I will go over the basics of CSS Level One (CSS1), which is currently supported by most browsers. More advanced style control is available with CSS Level 2 and CSS Level 3, which are not as widely supported. For more information, visit the CSS homepage at www.w3.org/Style/CSS/.

I will work with several examples that combine XHTML and CSS. Since the full power of CSS relates to the appearance of an XHTML document, I strongly suggest you follow along by trying the examples out for yourself. The figures in this book, which are limited to static grayscale, don't demonstrate the full power of the combination of CSS and XHTML.

Cascading What?

When HTML was first created, it was designed to describe the content of the data in a document. For example, the `<p>` element was used to mark up a paragraph, and the `<ul>` and `<ol>` elements were used to denote unordered and ordered lists. Eventually, however, different vendors began to add more elements, such as the `<font>` element, or attributes to existing elements in a desire to allow greater flexibility to developers in describing the style of the document.

Fresh Brew

You may be wondering what the big deal is about separating presentation markup from the document. Basically, once the description for how to present a document to a client is separated from the content, it becomes trivially simple to generate different views of the document, each with their own presentation style. For example, you can generate a view using larger fonts for clients who prefer large type, or you could generate an aural, or audio, view of the document for those who prefer to hear the document.

In the end, HTML became more about describing the presentation of a document rather than describing the content of a document. In order to clean up the resulting mess, the W3C introduced CSS as a way to separate the presentation of a document from the document itself. By using CSS, a developer can easily control the appearance of large numbers of XHTML documents. In addition, if the appearance of a website needs to be changed—imagine what happens when you get a new boss who likes green instead of blue—the tasks of presentation modifications is greatly simplified if all of the presentation markup is encoded in a small number of style sheets.

Fresh Brew

If you are familiar with Extensible Style Language (XSL), you may wonder why someone would use CSS to control the presentation of an XML application like XHTML. First, unlike XSL, a wide range of browsers supports CSS today. Second, XSL is a transformation language, in which a document is transformed into a different document. While this might seem natural to programmers, it can be difficult for some web developers to grasp.

Instead, CSS is more like an annotative language, in which developers can easily control the presentation style of different XHTML elements. Eventually, XSL support may become more widespread, at which time you may feel more comfortable using it. In the end, all that matters is that you get the job done!

But why are they called cascading? Simply put, a given XHTML document can have multiple style sheets attached to it. There are four different techniques for specifying a particular style element:

♦ A style can be attached to a particular XHTML element.

♦ A style can be encoded inside the head element.

♦ The style can be listed in an external style sheet.

♦ The style reverts to the browser's default style.

To determine what style to apply, the browser cascades down this list until it finds the appropriate style. The basic syntax for CSS elements is …

```
selector {property1: value1;
          property2: value2;
          ... }
```

… where `selector` is a particular XHTML element, `property` is a specific style property and `value` is the desired style value. For example, to set all h2 elements to be displayed in green (which has a hexadecimal representation of #008000), you would use the following CSS:

```
p {color: #008000}
```

To attach a particular style to a specific XHTML element, you can use the style attribute:

```
<p style="color=#008000"> Here is a paragraph that is green. </p>
```

On the other hand, you can also collect styles together inside the head element:

```
<head>
  <style type="text/css">
    p {color: #008000}
  </style>
</head>
<p> Here is another green paragraph. </p>
```

The best technique, however, is to place the style elements in an external style sheet. This maximizes reusability, while also providing the greatest flexibility. First, the external style sheet, which I will name style.css, would simply have the following line:

```
p {color: #008000}
```

> **CAUTION**
>
> **Hot Java**
>
> You might be wondering why you have to use hexadecimal values, why not just use the name of the color. While many browsers support a large number of names, the W3C does not, and according to the CSS specification, only the hexadecimal representations are allowed. In order to support the widest possible array of clients, you had better do what the W3C says.

This simple style sheet isn't going to scare anyone, but once you have built up large numbers of selectors and properties, you may want to quickly check that everything is kosher. The W3C provides a CSS validation service at jigsaw.w3.org/css-validator/, where you can download the validator to use at your own site, upload a CSS file, refer to a style sheet by its URL, or even enter the CSS in a text area.

In the sample XHTML document, I refer to this CSS file inside the head element:

CAUTION

Hot Java _____

While CSS provides many benefits, you should be very careful about securing any external style sheets. If a hacker can gain access to your style sheets, they can change the entire look of your website. Probably not a good idea!

```
<head>
  <link
    rel="stylesheet"
    type="text/css"
    href="style.css" />
</head>
<p> Here is yet another green paragraph </p>
```

For simplicity, I suggest you place all style sheets inside a separate directory, aptly named css, inside your web application. This makes it easier to quickly change styles that will modify an entire website.

Selecting Selectors

The rules governing selectors are slightly more complicated than what was shown in the previous section. For example, sometimes you might want a specific style to apply to multiple XHTML elements. You can group elements together to form a single selector by separating them with commas. In order to have header levels one through four centered on the page, you can either use multiple selectors:

```
h1 {text-align: center}
h2 {text-align: center}
h3 {text-align: center}
h4 {text-align: center}
```

Or else use a single selector:

```
h1,h2,h3,h4 {text-align: center}
```

You can also specify a selector for nested elements. For example, to set bold face elements to be red, italicized elements in green, and boldfaced and italicized elements to be blue, you can use the following selector.

```
b {color: #FF0000}
i {color: #00FF00}
b i {color: #0000FF}
```

If you apply this style to the XHTML in Listing 11.1, you should end up with the XHTML document shown in Figure 11.1.

Listing 11.1   styled.xhtml

```xml
<?xml version="1.0" encoding="UTF-8" ?>

<!DOCTYPE html
  PUBLIC "-//W3C//DTD XHTML 1.0 Strict//EN"
  "http://www.w3.org/TR/xhtml1/DTD/xhtml1-strict.dtd">

<html xmlns="http://www.w3.org/1999/xhtml">
  <head>
    <link
      rel="stylesheet"
      type="text/css"
      href="css/style.css" />
    <title> A styled XHTML page. </title>
  </head>
  <body>
    <b> Here is Bold Face type </b>
    <p/>
    <i> Here is Italicized type </i>
    <p/>
    <b> <i> Here is Bold Face, Italicized type </i> <b>
  </body>
</html>
```

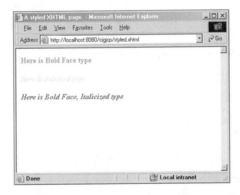

Figure 11.1

This figure shows how Internet Explorer 6.0 renders the styled XHTML document using a simple CSS page.

Both CSS2 and CSS3 provide more powerful selectors, including finer control over inheritance, selecting sibling elements, and selecting elements based on what the user is doing. We still have two more ways in CSS1 to control the selection of elements, however, both of which make use of special attributes that are attached to XHTML elements.

The class Attribute

Sometimes you will want an XHTML element to have different styles, which are determined by where the element is used within a document. The CSS1 specification enables you to do this by specifying the element, a decimal point, followed by a value. Essentially this creates new elements to use in your XHTML document. For example, to specify green and blue paragraphs, you would use the following CSS statements:

```
p.green {color: #00FF00}
p.blue {color: #0000FF}
```

To specify that a paragraph should be green or blue, you set the class attribute appropriately, as shown in this example:

```
<p class="green"> This is a green paragraph. </p>
<p class="blue"> This is a blue paragraph. </p>
```

You can also omit the element part of the class selector, which will then be applied to any element that has a class attribute with the appropriate value. For example, to set all elements to blue that have the class attribute set to blue, you would use the following CSS statement.

```
.blue {color: #0000FF}
```

This can be applied to the following XHTML snippet to turn items blue:

```
<body>

  <h1 class="blue"> Here is a blue heading. </h1>

  <p> Here is normal text </p>

  <p class="blue"> This is a blue paragraph. </p>

</body>
```

The id Attribute

The class attribute approach shown in the previous section provided a technique for developing XHTML documents that utilize specific CSS functionality for multiple elements. Sometimes, however, you want to target a specific instance of an element. To do this, you can use the id selector, which is very similar to the class selector, with the exception that a given id can only be used once within an XHTML document. In other words, values for the id attribute must be unique within an XHTML document.

For example, if you want to highlight important text in a document, you could use the following selector:

```
#highlight {color: #FF0000}
```

In your XHTML document, you pick the important text by setting the `id` attribute on the desired element:

```
<p> Here is a dull paragraph </p>
<p> Here is another dull paragraph </p>
<p id="highlight"> This is an important paragraph. </p>
```

The first two paragraphs appear in normal style, while the last paragraph is changed to appear in red. This method for selecting an element will select any element that has an id attribute whose value is highlight. If you want to only select paragraph elements, you can restrict the selector appropriately by placing the element type before the hash symbol.

```
p#highlight {color: #FF0000}
```

Choosing Properties

Now that you know all about selecting elements, you need to learn all of the different style properties that you can use to control the appearance of your document. In short, if you want to do it, there is probably a property that controls it. For example, you can explicitly control the text layout, apply borders, specify the font, and control the layout of lists and tables.

Text Properties

The text properties that you can specify include colors, transformations to different cases, and decorations using lines. These are demonstrated in Listing 11.2, which defines four selectors.

Listing 11.2   textstyle.css

```
.uc {text-transform: uppercase}

.over {text-decoration: overline}

.lt {text-decoration: line-through}

p#special {
  text-transform: capitalize;
  color: #FF0000
}
```

To demonstrate these styles, an XHTML document is needed—such as the one in Listing 11.3—that utilizes the selectors in Listing 11.2.

Listing 11.3 textstyle.xhtml

```
<?xml version="1.0" encoding="UTF-8" ?>
<!DOCTYPE html
  PUBLIC "-//W3C//DTD XHTML 1.0 Strict//EN"
  "http://www.w3.org/TR/xhtml1/DTD/xhtml1-strict.dtd">

<html xmlns="http://www.w3.org/1999/xhtml">
  <head>
    <link
      rel="stylesheet"
      type="text/css"
      href="css/textstyle.css" />
    <title> A styled XHTML page. </title>
  </head>
  <body>

    <p class="uc"> Here is an all caps paragraph </p>

    <p class="lt"> Can you read this? </p>

    <p class="over"> This text wears a hat. </p>

    <p> Just a plain, old paragraph. </p>

    <p id="special"> Here is a special paragraph </p>


  </body>
</html>
```

If you place these files appropriately in the cigjsp context, you can view the end result, which is shown in Figure 11.2.

Figure 11.2

The XHTML document shown in Listing 11.3 rendered with the style sheet shown in Listing 11.2.

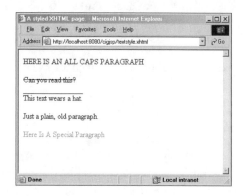

Selecting Fonts

With the font styles, you can change the actual font used to display your document, as well as control the size, weight, style, and variant of the selected font. If a given browser does not support a particular font, the default font will be substituted. Alternatively, you can list multiple fonts for a selector, separated by commas, and the browser will select the first one it recognizes. To demonstrate using font style properties, the style sheet shown in Listing 11.4 specifies different fonts to use for different selectors.

Listing 11.4   fontstyle.css

```
.one {
  font-family: arial, garamond, times;
  font-size: 24pt;
  font-variant: small-caps
}

.two {
  font-family: garamond;
  font-weight: bolder;
  font-size: xx-large
}

.three {
  font-family: courier;
  font-style: oblique;
  font-size: large
}
```

To demonstrate these styles, the XHTML in Listing 11.5 uses these selectors to generate the XHTML document shown in Figure 11.3.

Listing 11.5   fontstyle.xhtml

```
<?xml version="1.0" encoding="UTF-8" ?>
<!DOCTYPE html
  PUBLIC "-//W3C//DTD XHTML 1.0 Strict//EN"
  "http://www.w3.org/TR/xhtml1/DTD/xhtml1-strict.dtd">

<html xmlns="http://www.w3.org/1999/xhtml">
  <head>
    <link
      rel="stylesheet"
      type="text/css"
```

continues

Listing 11.5 fontstyle.xhtml (continued)

```
      href="css/fontstyle.css" />
   <title> A styled XHTML page. </title>
 </head>
 <body>

   <p class="one"> Here is an all caps paragraph </p>

   <p class="two"> Can you read this? </p>

   <p class="three"> This text wears a hat. </p>

   <p> Just a plain, old paragraph. </p>

 </body>
</html>
```

Figure 11.3

The XHTML document shown in Listing 11.5 rendered with the style sheet shown in Listing 11.4.

Making Borders

You can also place borders around any element. The type of borders includes dotted lines, dashed lines, grooves, solid lines, and many more. You can also specify the width and color of a border. If you are rather adventurous, you can even control the four different parts of the border independently, as shown in the style sheet shown in Listing 11.6.

Listing 11.6 borderstyle.css

```
.one {
  border-style: solid;
  border-width: thick
}
```

```
.two {
  border-top-style: groove;
  border-bottom-style: dashed;
  border-left-style: inset;
  border-right-style: outset
}

.three {
  border-left: thick groove;
  border-right: thin dotted
}
```

To demonstrate these styles, the XHTML in Listing 11.7 uses these selectors to build a document that shows how borders can be placed around different elements as shown in Figure 11.4.

Listing 11.7   borderstyle.xhtml

```
<?xml version="1.0" encoding="UTF-8" ?>
<!DOCTYPE html
   PUBLIC "-//W3C//DTD XHTML 1.0 Strict//EN"
   "http://www.w3.org/TR/xhtml1/DTD/xhtml1-strict.dtd">

<html xmlns="http://www.w3.org/1999/xhtml">
  <head>
    <link
      rel="stylesheet"
      type="text/css"
      href="css/borderstyle.css" />
    <title> A styled XHTML page. </title>
  </head>
  <body>

    <p class="one"> Here is a surrounded paragraph </p>

    <p class="two"> This is too much! </p>

    <p class="three"> This paragraph is bounded. </p>

    <p> Just a plain, old paragraph. </p>

  </body>
</html>
```

Figure 11.4

The XHTML document shown in Listing 11.7 rendered with the style sheet shown in Listing 11.6.

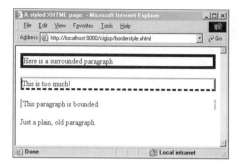

Lists and Tables

Apart from placing borders around elements, and controlling the text and font properties, you can also explicitly control the appearance of lists and tables. For example, you can specify the type of bullet to be used to display a list, and also the type of padding to use within a table, as shown in Listing 11.8.

Listing 11.8   ltstyle.css

```
ol.order {
list-style-type: lower-roman
}

ul.unorder {
  list-style-type: square;
  list-style-position: outside;
  list-style-image:none
}


td {
  padding-bottom: 0.1cm;
  padding-top: 0.1in;
  padding-right: 12pt;
  passing-left: 10%
}

th {
  padding: 1em 2em 3em 4em
}
```

To demonstrate these styles, the XHTML in Listing 11.9 uses these selectors to generate a table that holds an ordered and an unordered list, as shown in Figure 11.5. Notice how the different units of measure can be mixed within the same selector.

Listing 11.9   ltstyle.xhtml

```
<?xml version="1.0" encoding="UTF-8" ?>
<!DOCTYPE html
  PUBLIC "-//W3C//DTD XHTML 1.0 Strict//EN"
  "http://www.w3.org/TR/xhtml1/DTD/xhtml1-strict.dtd">

<html xmlns="http://www.w3.org/1999/xhtml">
  <head>
    <link
      rel="stylesheet"
      type="text/css"
      href="css/ltstyle.css" />
    <title> A styled XHTML page. </title>
  </head>
  <body>

    <table border="4">
      <tr>
        <th> Ordered List </th>
        <th> Unordered List </th>
      </tr>
      <tr>
        <td>
          <ol class="order">
            <li> Item One </li>
            <li> Item Two</li>
            <li> Item Three </li>
          </ol>
        </td>
        <td>
          <ul class="unorder">
            <li> Item One </li>
            <li> Item Two</li>
            <li> Item Three </li>
          </ul>
        </td>
      </tr>
    </table>

    <p> Just a plain, old paragraph. </p>

  </body>
</html>
```

Figure 11.5

Here is the XHTML docu-ment shown in Listing 11.9 rendered with the style sheet shown in Listing 11.8.

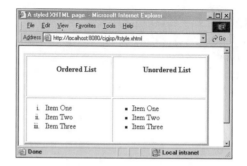

With CSS, you can create pretty amazing websites. In this chapter, I only scratched the surface. You can control the individual positioning of every element on the page, specify the margins for a page, and control the layouts of images; and this is only CSS Level One. CSS Levels Two and Three provide even greater support for both selecting elements, as well as the properties that can be assigned to those elements.

The Least You Need to Know

◆ Using CSS is simple—all you need to do is link the style sheet to your XHTML document and see the result in your browser.

◆ Using CSS, you can quickly change the appearance of an entire document.

◆ To choose the XHTML elements to modify, you use a CSS selector.

◆ The properties available in CSS1 enable you to control the text, fonts, borders, and list and table appearances.

Controlling the Client

In This Chapter

- ◆ Understanding the basics of JavaScript
- ◆ Combining JavaScript with XHTML
- ◆ Using JavaScript event handlers
- ◆ Implementing client-side verification

Right now, you are probably wondering what is going on here. This book is supposed to be about JSP technology, and now he is talking about JavaScript, after a chapter on CSS and another one on XHTML. Don't worry; I haven't lost my marbles. XHTML, CSS, and JavaScript are important technologies for controlling how your pages appear to your clients.

While XHTML and CSS control how your website appears to the client, JavaScript—or more properly, any scripting language that adheres to the ECMAScript standard—enables you to provide custom interactions with your client, without taxing the load on your server. You can also perform client-side verification of form data, and make a website visit more interactive. Fortunately, the JavaScript syntax is very similar to Java, thus it is easy to pick up the basics. This chapter is not a thorough tutorial on JavaScript; instead, it introduces important concepts and demonstrates how to perform tasks that might be useful to JSP developers.

Fresh Brew

What is ECMAScript? Well, as part of the original browser wars (remember the days when Netscape Navigator was the dominant web browser?), the Netscape team, who invented JavaScript, and the Microsoft team, who created the similar JScript, tweaked their browsers and scripting languages slightly, to the net effect that JavaScript programs were not as portable as one would like.

To simplify matters, the European Computer Manufacturers Association (ECMA) provided a forum where a JavaScript standard was developed. In order to minimize confusion, the standard is known as ECMAScript. You can freely browse the standard online at www.ecma.ch/ecma1/STAND/ECMA-262.HTM.

Individual vendors' offerings continue to be known by their original monikers (in other words, JavaScript and JScript), but they can now adhere to a standard to improve script portability. Nevertheless, certain software companies continue to offer "extensions" making it difficult to write completely portable scripts.

Using JavaScript

JavaScript is a portable scripting language that was invented by Netscape to simplify dynamic website development. Originally introduced with version 2 of the Netscape web browser, the popularity of JavaScript spread and quickly became a popular technique for generating dynamic content, verifying form data, and customizing appearance based on the browser's properties.

Hot Java

As with many web technologies, different browsers have different levels of support for JavaScript. In part, this is a direct result of browser innovations—each new browser version adds more bells and whistles. Before JavaScript was standardized by the ECAM, different versions of the Microsoft Internet Explorer and Netscape browsers were not 100 percent compatible, to say nothing of cross-vendor compatibility. The modern versions of these browsers, however, are starting to show very good compatibility, at least in the area of JavaScript support.

This does not help, however, when you need to support customers who may be using older browsers. A common approach to solving this problem is to wrap any special functionality in a conditional statement that tests whether a feature is supported by the browser before using the functionality. For example, before using dynamic image loading, you could test the document images property. If it is nonzero, you know that your

With all of the warnings about cross-platform portability and lack of support, you may be wondering, "Why even use JavaScript?" Basically, all is not doom-and-gloom, and in the near future, browser compliance within your client base will increase significantly. Also, the ability to perform dynamic processing on the client, which can make your website more interactive, can't be simulated with server-side processing. Perhaps the most important reason, however, is that it can be a lot of fun! If you want a good introduction to JavaScript, I suggest you visit the Netscape developer central JavaScript website at developer.netscape.com/docs/manuals/javascript.html, where you can freely browse, or even download, the JavaScript manuals.

Combining JavaScript and XHTML

Okay, now you are convinced that learning at least a little JavaScript is a good thing—you *are* convinced, aren't you? The first thing you need to know is how to add it to your XHTML documents. As was the case with CSS, you can either place your JavaScript directly into the web page, or you can place it in a separate file that you include into your web page. When developing new scripts, it is often easier to just place the script inline; however, when you place scripts in their own file, reusing and maintaining them across multiple web pages becomes considerably easier.

To include a script in your web page, you embed it inside a `script` element. To indicate that you are using JavaScript, be sure to set the `type` attribute to text/javascript as shown in this snippet:

```
<script type="text/javascript">
  // JavaScript code goes here
</script>
```

This sort of declaration can go anywhere, but if you are defining functions or variables that you will use later in your web page, you should place their definitions in a script block inside the XHTML head element. On the other hand, if you want to generate dynamic content in the current web page, you should place your script inside the XHTML body element. This ensures that your script is called when the page is loaded into the user's browser.

The alternative, of course is to place them in a separate file, which customarily has a .js file extension. To include the JavaScript file in an XHTML file, you use the XHTML script element with the `src` (source) attribute set to the location of your JavaScript. For example, to tell the web page to load a JavaScript file named csquare.js from the scripts subdirectory of the current context, you set the `src` attribute appropriately, and remember that the script element is now empty:

```
<script src="scripts/csquare.js"/>
```

Hot Java

What do you do if a browser doesn't support JavaScript at all? If you aren't careful, the browser will ignore the script elements, and complain about the JavaScript code inside. The simple solution is to wrap the body of the script element in an XHTML comment. JavaScript will ignore the opening XHTML comment tag (`<!--`), but you need to prefix the end XHTML comment tag (`-->`) with a JavaScript single line comment indicator, which is easy since it is the same as Java's single line comment indicator (`//`).

```
<script type="text/javascript">
<!--
// JavaScript code goes here
// -->
</script>
```

You can also place template data inside a special XHTML element called noscript that should only be processed if the browser cannot process scripts. For example, you could have a message informing users they should upgrade their browsers if necessary.

```
<script type="text/javascript">
  // JavaScript code goes here
</script>
<noscript>
  <h1> You need a JavaScript compliant browser </h1>
</noscript>
```

Since you already have a solid grasp of Java, and you are also an eager coder (and you thought I couldn't hear all that panting!), this chapter will be heavily example driven. In order to make your life easier, however, a quick overview of the basics of JavaScript is warranted.

First, JavaScript is not (yet) an object-oriented language. But objects are simulated, and the difference is mostly semantics, especially for JavaScript novices like us. JavaScript variables are dynamically typed, which is a major departure from Java, which has statically typed variables. What this means is that all variables are of type var, and you can assign an integer to a variable, change the variable to a string, and later to an object.

In JavaScript, you can create new objects, which have properties and methods. The language provides built-in objects (such as Date, String, and Math), and web browsers provide extra built-in objects. The browser built-in objects include the window and document. In fact, using the built-in browser objects, you can dynamically generate a table of contents for any web page.

You can also define functions in JavaScript, which are just like functions or procedures in other languages. Since variables are dynamically typed in JavaScript, you can pass and return them from a function without specifying their type. Perhaps the most important reason for learning JavaScript is that you can bind JavaScript functions to XHTML events, like moving the mouse or clicking a button. Most of the examples in this chapter utilize this functionality to make a web page more dynamic.

JavaScript also provides the customary conditional statements and basic operators that are common in other languages. One additional important item is that code blocks must be enclosed in curly braces, even if the block is only one line.

Enough of the jabbering, it's time to start writing some scripts. The first one is shown in Listing 12.1. This web page shows a blue square image, followed by a caption (which tells you it is a blue square), followed by a button, as shown in Figure 12.1. When the user clicks the button, a new window appears that shows an image of a red square. The new window is undecorated, meaning it has no toolbar and no menu bar.

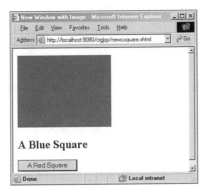

Figure 12.1

The initial display of newcsquare.xhtml in Internet Explorer 6.0.

Listing 12.1   newcsquare.xhtml

```
<?xml version="1.0" encoding="UTF-8" ?>
<!DOCTYPE html
  PUBLIC "-//W3C//DTD XHTML 1.0 Strict//EN"
  "http://www.w3.org/TR/xhtml1/DTD/xhtml1-strict.dtd">

<html xmlns="http://www.w3.org/1999/xhtml">
  <head>
    <title> New Window with Image</title>

    <script type="text/javascript">

      function newsquare() {
        csquare = window.open("", "",
                        "height=220,width=220,menubar=no,toolbar=no")
;
```

continues

Listing 12.1   newcsquare.xhtml   (continued)

```
        csquare.document.open() ;
        csquare.document.write("<html><head><title>A Red
Square</title></head>") ;
        csquare.document.write("<body><img src=\"images/red-
square.jpg\"/><p/>") ;
        csquare.document.write("<h2 align=\"center\">A Red
Square</h2></body></html>") ;
      }
    </script>

  </head>

  <body>

    <img src="images/blue-square.jpg"/> <p/>
    <h2>A Blue Square</h2>
    <p/>
    <form align="center">
      <input type="button" onclick="newsquare()" value="A Red Square"/>
    </form>

  </body>
</html>
```

The script is fairly easy to understand. First, you define a new function called
`newsquare()` that takes no arguments:

```
    function newsquare() {
```

This function first creates a new window, using the `open()` method on the window object.
Remember how JSP has implicit objects such as `request` and `out`? Well JavaScript has a
similar concept. There are certain objects that are just available to you. You don't have to
create them but you are able to access them within your scripts. The `window` objects are an
example of this. As parameters, you indicate the size for the new window, and specify that
it should be undecorated:

```
        csquare = window.open("", "",
                          "height=220,width=220,menubar=no,toolbar=no")
;
```

After you create the window, you generate the HTML that should go into the new window, which includes the image, as shown in Figure 12.2:

```
        csquare.document.open() ;
        csquare.document.write("<html><head><title>A Red
Square</title></head>") ;
```

```
        csquare.document.write("<body><img src=\"images/red-
square.jpg\"/><p/>") ;
        csquare.document.write("<h2 align=\"center\">A Red
Square</h2></body></html>") ;
```

Okay, so what's the big deal about blue and red squares, even if they appear in a new window? Simple. Imagine that the blue square is a small image showing one of your products, and the red square is a larger version of the same image. This script shows you how to allow the web client to get a close-up picture of your product.

Figure 12.2

After clicking the button, a new window opens up with no decoration that displays a red square, appropriately labeled, in Internet Explorer 6.0.

The next example, shown in Listing 12.2, is very similar; except that instead of showing a different image in a new window, this script changes the image that is displayed in the current web page, as shown in Figure 12.3.

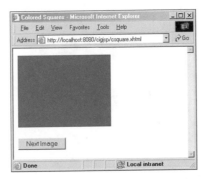

Figure 12.3

The initial display of csquare.xhtml in Internet Explorer 6.0. Clicking the button changes the color of the square. In actuality, an entirely different image is being displayed.

Listing 12.2   csquares.xhtml

```
<?xml version="1.0" encoding="UTF-8" ?>
<!DOCTYPE html
   PUBLIC "-//W3C//DTD XHTML 1.0 Strict//EN"
   "http://www.w3.org/TR/xhtml1/DTD/xhtml1-strict.dtd">

<html xmlns="http://www.w3.org/1999/xhtml">
  <head>
    <title>Colored Squares</title>

    <script type="text/javascript">
```

continues

Listing 12.2   csquares.xhtml   (continued)

```
var current = 0 ;
var squares = Array(5) ;
var colors = new Array("blue",
                       "green",
                       "yellow",
                       "orange",
                       "red") ;

for(i = 0 ; i < colors.length ; i++) {
  squares[i] = new Image ;
  squares[i].src = "images/" + colors[i] + "-square.jpg" ;
}

function next() {
  if(current == 4) {
    current = 0 ;
  }else {
    current++ ;
  }

  document.square.src = squares[current].src ;
}
</script>

</head>

<body>

  <img name="square" src="images/blue-square.jpg" />

  <form>
    <input type="button" onclick="next()" value="Next Image"/>
  </form>

</body>
</html>
```

This script is very similar to the previous one, with a few minor changes. First, the images are preloaded—this improves the performance of the web page, as the user does not need to reload them every time a new image is selected. We preload the images by creating an image object and setting the src attribute for the image to the image source file, which in this case is in the images subdirectory of the current context:

```
for(i = 0 ; i < colors.length ; i++) {
  squares[i] = new Image ;
  squares[i].src = "images/" + colors[i] + "-square.jpg" ;
}
```

After this, you define a new function called `next()` that changes the `src` attribute for the current image, which we reference using the image elements name attribute. You do this by referencing the `src` property of the image named square of the current document:

```
function next() {
   if(current == 4) {
      current = 0 ;
   }else {
      current++ ;
   }

   document.square.src =
squares[current].src ;
   }
```

Fresh Brew _____

You can use JSP technology to overcome differences in web browsers, by using a JSP page to either dynamically generate your JavaScript or dynamically change the script filename to support multiple browsers.

The script becomes dynamic when you bind the `next()` function to the `onclick()` method of the button.

As before, maybe you are wondering what all of the fuss is about. After all, clicking the button just changes the color of the square. Ah, but that is the point—you are dynamically changing which image is displayed; in this case, all that changes is the color. You might do something similar for online shopping where you want to allow a customer to dynamically change the color of a particular item to see what it looks like.

Handling Events

As you saw in Listing 12.1 and Listing 12.2, linking JavaScript methods to XHTML events is easy, making JavaScript a natural choice for developing event handlers. But what events are generated, and by what XHTML elements? To answer this question, all 18 "official W3C" events are listed in Table 12.1, with the following caution from the W3C: that these events, their handlers, and the elements that can be affected by these events are subject to change. Some browsers support additional events, but these are the most common.

Table 12.1   Intrinsic Events

Event	Event Handler	XHTML Elements
Finish loading page or all frames.	onload	BODY, FRAMESET
Finish removing document from a page or frame.	onunload	BODY, FRAMESET
Pointing device button is clicked over an element.	onclick	Most elements

continues

Table 12.1 Intrinsic Events (continued)

Event	Event Handler	XHTML Elements
Pointing device button is double-clicked over an element.	ondblclick	Most elements
Pointing device button is pressed over an element.	onmousedown	Most elements
Pointing device button is released over an element.	onmouseup	Most elements
Pointing device is moved onto an element.	onmouseover	Most elements
Pointing device is moved while over an element.	onmousemove	Most elements
Pointing device is moved away from an element.	onmouseout	Most elements
Focus is received either from a pointing device or from tabbing navigation.	onfocus	LABEL, INPUT, SELECT, BUTTON, and TEXTAREA
Focus is lost either from a pointing device or from tabbing navigation.	onblur	LABEL, INPUT, SELECT, BUTTON, and TEXTAREA
Key is pressed and released over an element.	onkeypress	Most elements
Key is pressed down over an element.	onkeydown	Most elements
Key is released over an element.	onkeyup	Most elements
Form is submitted.	onsubmit	FORM
Form is reset.	onreset	FORM
Text is selected in a text field.	onselect	INPUT and TEXTAREA
Control loses focus and its value was modified since it gained focus.	onchange	INPUT, SELECT, and TEXTAREA

The event handler is the name of the attribute that is used within the start tag of an XHTML element to link the *event* to the script that should be invoked to handle the event. If you recall from the previous examples, you had the onclick attribute linked to the next() method. The next() function call is just a small piece of JavaScript; you could actually replace the function call with an entire scriptlet, as in the following example.

```
<input type="text" onfocus="window.status = 'Enter Something Important'"/>
```

This input control creates a text field with an onfocus event handler that creates a message in the browser's status bar, in this case "Enter Something Important." You might think that you could dynamically write to the current XHTML document in an event handler using the `document.write` method. However, once the document has been loaded, this method will only write to a new document, and not modify the current one.

Tagged

An **event** is a programmatic term that refers to the notification that a specific action, or event, has occurred. The browser keeps track of what the user is doing with the keyboard and any pointing devices, and communicates this information to scripting languages via events. This simplifies the programming requirements on the script developer, and allows you to write dynamic XHTML documents with very little effort.

Listing 12.3 shows another example of using JavaScript directly inside an event handler. It shows a simple XHTML document that loads a blue square image. When the mouse is moved over the image, a red square image is loaded and replaces the blue square. When the mouse moves off the image element, a yellow square image is loaded and replaces the red square. Again, this is not the sexiest example of using events—but you should still see the power of using JavaScript for handling events.

Listing 12.3   event-color.xhtml

```
<?xml version="1.0" encoding="UTF-8" ?>
<!DOCTYPE html
  PUBLIC "-//W3C//DTD XHTML 1.0 Strict//EN"
  "http://www.w3.org/TR/xhtml1/DTD/xhtml1-strict.dtd">

<html xmlns="http://www.w3.org/1999/xhtml">
  <head>
    <title>Colored Squares</title>
  </head>

  <body>

    <img name="square" src="images/blue-square.jpg"
      onmouseover="document.square.src='images/red-square.jpg'"
      onmouseout="document.square.src='images/yellow-square.jpg'"/>

  </body>
</html>
```

In the following code snippet (shown earlier):

```
<input type="text" onfocus="window.status = 'Enter Something Important'"/>
```

You saw how to print a message inside the browser's status bar. This was done by setting the window.status. While sort of neat, it's something that can be easily missed by a user. On the other hand, you don't always want to go to the length of creating a new window and generating new XHTML documents just to communicate some piece of information with the user. In short, there has to be a better way of alerting the user to an important event.

The good news is that there are three easy ways to do this, using the alert(), confirm(), or prompt() methods.

The alert() method displays a dialog box that alerts the user with an optional user-supplied message. For example, the following JavaScript will create the alert dialog box, with the message "What Happened." In order to remove the dialog box, as shown in Figure 12.4, the user must click the OK button.

```
<script type="text/javascript"/> alert("What Happened") </script>
```

Figure 12.4

*The alert dialog box
generated by the sample
JavaScript.*

The confirm() method displays a confirmation dialog box with an OK and a Cancel button and an optional user-supplied message, shown in Figure 12.5. This method returns true if the user clicks OK, and false if the user clicks Cancel.

```
<script type="text/javascript"/>
  var result = confirm("Would you like to continue?")
  // Do something
</script>
```

Figure 12.5

*The confirmation dialog
box generated by the sample
JavaScript.*

The prompt() method displays a dialog box that prompts the user with an optional message along with an input text box (see Figure 12.6). An optional second argument for this method provides a default value for the input field. This method returns the value entered by the user, either as a String or an Integer, depending on what was entered by the user.

```
<script type="text/javascript"/>
  var result = prompt("Enter your UserName:", "rjbrunner")
  // Do Something
</script>
```

Figure 12.6

The prompt dialog box generated by the sample JavaScript.

Verifying the Client

As you have seen, including JavaScript code in your XHTML files is easy, as is linking JavaScript functions to XHTML events. Perhaps the most useful capability this provides is allowing you to validate the user input before it is sent to the server. The simple code examples in this section demonstrate three different types of data validation. You can actually use JavaScript to perform Regular Expression matching (checking strings for specific patterns), allowing very complicated data validation, such as checking that an e-mail is of the form john@doe.com, or that a U.S. Social Security number is of the form XXX-XX-XXXX. You also can use JavaScript to quickly reformat data to a particular format. For example, you could reformat U.S. telephone numbers to take the form (XXX) XXX-XXXX.

Listing 12.4 shows an XHTML document that requests a user enter their age. The validation here checks that the entered value is not less than 0 and not greater than 125 (the upper limit is arbitrary here; you can always set it to something else).

Listing 12.4   age.xhtml

```
<?xml version="1.0" encoding="UTF-8" ?>
<!DOCTYPE html
   PUBLIC "-//W3C//DTD XHTML 1.0 Strict//EN"
   "http://www.w3.org/TR/xhtml1/DTD/xhtml1-strict.dtd">

<html xmlns="http://www.w3.org/1999/xhtml">
  <head>
    <title> Age Verification </title>

    <script type="text/javascript">

      function validateAge() {
        var age = document.ageForm.ageInput.value ;
        if((age < 0)||(age > 125)) {
            alert("Please enter a valid age.") ;
        }
      }
    </script>

  </head>
```

continues

Listing 12.4   age.xhtml   (continued)

```
<body>

    <form name="ageForm" onsubmit="validateAge()">

        <h2> Please enter your age: </h2>

        <input type="text" name="ageInput">

        <input type="submit" value="Submit">

    </form>

    </body>
</html>
```

The JavaScript here is rather simple—I did forewarn you it was easy. All you need to do is tie the JavaScript function that validates the input to the proper event handler, in this case, form submission, but it could be a different event if you decide to pursue a different path. The validation method does the range checking, first obtaining the appropriate value via the object property hierarchy:

```
var age = document.ageForm.ageInput.value ;
if((age < 0)||(age > 125)) {
    alert("Please enter a valid age.") ;
```

The example shown in Listing 12.5 is very similar, except that this time the program checks that the user enters a valid name, with the major validation being that the name has less than 80 characters and is nonzero in length.

Listing 12.5   name.xhtml

```
<?xml version="1.0" encoding="UTF-8" ?>
<!DOCTYPE html
   PUBLIC "-//W3C//DTD XHTML 1.0 Strict//EN"
   "http://www.w3.org/TR/xhtml1/DTD/xhtml1-strict.dtd">

<html xmlns="http://www.w3.org/1999/xhtml">
    <head>
       <title> Name Verification </title>

       <script type="text/javascript">

          function validateName() {
             var length = document.nameForm.name.value.length ;
             if(length < 1){
                alert("Please enter a valid name.") ;
```

```
            }else if(length > 80) {
                alert("Please limit your name to less than 80 characters.") ;
            }
        }
    </script>

  </head>

  <body>

    <form name="nameForm" onsubmit="validateName()">

        <h2> Please enter your name: </h2>

        <input type="text" name="name">

        (Limit of 80 Characters) <p/>

        <input type="submit" value="Submit">

    </form>

  </body>
</html>
```

The example shown in Listing 12.6 checks that the user entered a valid e-mail. In a production environment, you would probably make the validation more complex, but this simple check verifies that the email address has more than four characters and that it has the at (@) symbol somewhere in the string.

Listing 12.6   email.xhtml

```
<?xml version="1.0" encoding="UTF-8" ?>
<!DOCTYPE html
   PUBLIC "-//W3C//DTD XHTML 1.0 Strict//EN"
   "http://www.w3.org/TR/xhtml1/DTD/xhtml1-strict.dtd">

<html xmlns="http://www.w3.org/1999/xhtml">
  <head>
    <title> Email Verification </title>

    <script type="text/javascript">

      function validateEmail() {
        var email = document.emailForm.email.value ;
        var length = email.length ;
```

continues

Listing 12.6   email.xhtml   (continued)

```
      if((email.indexOf("@") == -1)||(length < 5)) {
        alert("Please enter a valid email.") ;
      }
    }

  </script>

</head>

<body>

  <form name="emailForm" onsubmit="validateEmail()">

      <h2> Please enter your email: </h2>

      <input type="text" name="email">

      <input type="submit" value="Submit">

  </form>

</body>
</html>
```

These simple validation JavaScript examples will hopefully inspire you to roll your own. For simplicity, I have neglected to use HTML comments and the noscript elements, which ensure maximal portability. In addition, I would strongly suggest that you place your scripts in external files, preferably in a subdirectory named scripts within your web application context, and link them into your XHTML documents. This will greatly simplify maintenance as well as simplify their reuse.

The Least You Need to Know

♦ JavaScript is a scripting language that you can embed in web pages, which have a Java-similar appearance.

♦ JavaScript can be embedded directly in a web page, or stored in a separate file to simplify the sharing of scripts across a website.

♦ JavaScript provides an easy, yet powerful technique for handling events that are generated when a client views an XHTML document.

♦ JavaScript provides an elegant solution for performing client-side verification.

Using Forms and Applets

In This Chapter

◆ Introducing static HTML forms

◆ Using Java applets with JSP pages

In this chapter, I'll introduce you to rich clients, and I don't mean the types who play golf all day. A rich client provides a more interactive experience than is available with a typical web browser. Whether it be the result of animation, dynamic editing, or multimedia, rich client interfaces often allow users to accomplish more complex tasks in a shorter period of time, because they seem more intuitive. While rich clients can be developed in a variety of fashions, in this chapter, I will look at building rich client interfaces using Java.

Using a Static HTML Login

There are a variety of ways to spice up your client interface, but for the most part everything you need you can do with HTML and a good graphic artist. I'll look at a simple static HTML login form and then show how you can add some JSP flavor to it.

If you are really interested in building some "wow" applications, you can look further into Java Swing. Swing is used for building advanced graphical user interfaces (GUI), but you'd better be prepared to spend some serious time learning it. It's beyond the scope of this book, so I won't be going into the details, but you'll surely find bookshelves full of books on the topic at your local bookstore.

Coffee Break

The Java Swing–based interface is a fancy term for a Graphical User Interface (GUI) for compiled Java code. If you are working in Java, there are a whole slew of packages that are associated with Swing. You can do some pretty fancy GUI when using Swing, but it takes a good amount of time to learn. However, you will have a much prettier-looking application for the user if you use Swing.

An HTML login is accomplished by using the FORM element, as shown in Listing 13.1. First, you define the form, state that you will use the POST method (so that your password is not written in clear text on the browser URL), and define the input controls. Two of the input controls are for entering the username and password, while the third control is to send the information to the server. Note that you could have JavaScript methods that validate the data on the client end, but that would not change the overall appearance of the HTML form, which is shown in Figure 13.1.

Listing 13.1   login.html

```html
<html>
  <head>
    <title>Static HTML Login Demo</title>
  </head>

  <body>

    <h1>Please Login</h1>
    <hr>
    <form method="post" name="login" action="">
      User Name: <input type="text" name="username"/> <p/>
      Password : <input type="password" name="password"/> <p/>
      <input type="submit" value="Login""/>
    </form>

  </body>
</html>
```

While functional, this approach is rather boring; it still serves its purpose in that it enables a user to log in.

While it's possible to do everything in JSP that you can do in HTML, sometimes you want to have an application already bundled that can perform the actions you are looking for. There's a special type of application in Java called Applets. Applets are just what they sound like, little applications. Applets can't do everything that a regular application can do. I'll talk about what they can and can't do in the following section.

Figure 13.1

The HTML Login web page, requesting the user name and password.

Connecting Applets and JSP Pages

You know that JSP pages can generate HTML that is directly displayed in the browser. However, JSP pages can generate any type of text, which can be sent to a client. This includes HTML, but also XML and plain text as well. While you are able to use Java-Script to make a more interactive website, support for JavaScript is not uniform across browsers, and JavaScript has its own limitations.

What would be great is if we could combine Java programs with JSP pages to provide a rich client interface. Fortunately, this can be easily done with Applets, as the rest of this section demonstrates.

> **⚠ CAUTION**
>
> ### Hot Java
>
> For security reasons, Java Applets are limited in what they can do. Formally this restriction is known as the sandbox. Imagine you are only allowed to play in a specific sandbox. You can't see or communicate with anything outside the sandbox without explicit permission. Pretty restrictive, isn't it?
>
> For an Applet, this means that it cannot interact with the local file system, and it can't connect to arbitrary URL's, among other things. When writing an Applet, you need to keep these things in mind. There are ways to get around these restrictions, primarily through the use of certificates, and digital signatures, but they are beyond the scope of this discussion.

Rich client interfaces can be tied to JSP pages in a variety of ways, but the simplest is using the JSP plugin action. The plugin action allows you to specify another program within the JSP page. A program such as an Applet. Think of a plugin as a program that runs within your browser and that allows other programs to run. In order to work its magic, the browser needs to know how and when to run the plugin. This is done by specfic HTML code. The plugin action directs the JSP container to automatically gener-ate the appropriate HTML directives to inform the browser that an Applet is part of the web page. In and of itself, this is not a tricky issue. However, when the Applet requires more recent features from the Java language, as the examples in this chapter do, the task becomes more challenging.

This is due to the fact that Microsoft only provides an older version of the Java Virtual Machine in Internet Explorer browser versions (several years old actually). In order to get around this, Sun Microsystems developed the Java plugin, which allows Applets to utilize newer JVMs. Before an Applet that uses these newer features can run, however, the Java plugin has to be downloaded. The primary benefit of using the JSP plugin action is that the necessary directions are automatically generated and placed in the HTML page. These directions are read by the browser, which can then acquire and install the appropriate Java plugin.

Remember, plugins define programs that will be run. When you're running a program, chances are you have to give it some information or attributes so it knows how to run correctly. The plugin action takes a number of attributes, three of which are required.

◆ `type`, which specifies whether the included component is an applet or a bean.

◆ `code`, which specifies the class that implements the Applet, or Japplet, interface.

◆ `codebase`, which specifies the HTML context in which the applet is located.

Other, optional attributes can also be included, such as the `archive` attribute, which is used to name an archive file that contains the Applet, and `jreversion`, which specifies the minimum version of the Java Runtime Environment that is needed to run the Applet. The rest of the optional attributes are HTML attributes that control the appearance and layout of the Applet on the HTML page. These include the `align`, `height`, `width`, `hspace`, and `name` attributes. These layout attributes determine how much space in the browser window the Applet has to run.

Fresh Brew

Applet and Japplet are two peas in a pod. All Applets written in Java must implement either the Applet or Japplet interface. If you are writing a Java Swing application, with the fancy GUI, and you want to make an Applet, you must implement the Japplet interface. Otherwise, you use the Applet interface. They both accomplish the same thing.

Applets can also accept parameters that are provided to it by the browser. To submit attributes, you use the `param` action. Unlike the `include` and `forward` actions, when submitting parameters to an Applet, the individual `param` actions must be wrapped inside a single `params` action. For example, to set the default username to "java" you would use the following `params` action.

```
<jsp:params>
  <jsp:param
    name="username"
    value="java"/>
<jsp:params>
```

The plugin action takes one additional, optional action element, the fallback action. This is used to specify a message to clients who cannot run the Applet for some reason. This might be due to the fact that they do not want to install the Java plugin, or the browser does not understand the `object` or `embed` HTML elements. Putting all of these actions together, you can create a plugin action that tells the JSP container to include the necessary HTML for a Login Applet.

The following code sample does this: It includes an Applet that will run the Login.class. This class can be found in the /cigjsp directory of the document root of the web server. Any additional classes needed are found in the Login.jar. This Applet takes a parameter called "username" that will have the value "java". If the Applet fails to run for any reason, then the message "Unable to start Applet, please upgrade your browser" will be displayed in the browser window.

```
<jsp:plugin type="applet" code="Login.class" codebase="/cigjsp"
archive="Login.jar">
  <jsp:params>
    <jsp:param
      name="username"
      value="java"/>
  <jsp:params>
  <jsp:fallback>
    <p> Unable to start Applet. Please
upgrade your browser </p>
  </jsp:fallback>
<jsp:plugin>
```

One of the main reasons for using Applets is to keep complex code out of the JSP pages. As you can see, there is no Java-specific code included in this page.

Fresh Brew

The jar file archives the files using the same zip file format as popular zip utilities. This means that you can open a jar file with a zip utility like WinZip.

The Least You Need to Know

- ◆ Rich client interfaces support greater interaction between the client and the application. This often makes them easier for users to interact with since actions may seem more natural.
- ◆ JSP simplifies the task of deploying Java Applets through the use of the plugin action.
- ◆ Applets can be packaged into an archive file using the jar tool.

Part 4

Working on the Server

So you've mastered the basics, and your web pages will impress just about anyone. If you're serious about Java web applications, you'll need to master the topics in this part. With JavaBeans, Servlets, and custom actions, you'll look like a pro. But best of all, your website will work great, and you won't have to pull all-nighters.

Brewing With Beans

In This Chapter

- ◆ JavaBeans
- ◆ JavaBeans and JSP
- ◆ XHTML Forms and JavaBeans
- ◆ Passing data with JavaBeans

JSP technology provides built-in support for JavaBeans. This support simplifies several tasks detailed in earlier chapters, including the interaction with XHTML forms, as well as the sharing of data between different JSP pages and Servlets. In fact, you have already used JavaBeans in Chapter 10, "Extending HTML," when you built the shopping cart demonstration. This chapter formally introduces the concept of JavaBeans, and details how this technology can simplify tasks when used with a JSP page.

Grinding Beans

In an object-oriented programming language, like Java, you deal with objects, which are collections of attributes and associated methods. These attributes encapsulate the state of an object, while the methods enable you to change the state, or behavior, of an object. These objects form components that are pieced together to solve a problem. When you move to the next problem, ideally you would be able to reuse preexisting components to solve your new problem.

In order to reuse a component, specific characteristics of a component, known as properties, may need to be modified. Likewise, sometimes a behavior, or the response to an external event, needs to be modified. Through proper object-oriented techniques, you can facilitate greater code reuse. However, the ability to reuse code is further increased if your code follows a component object model, which allows objects to be shared more easily. The component object model for Java is JavaBeans, simply known as Beans.

To be a proper Bean, a Java class doesn't need to do much; in fact, you can even retrofit existing classes, even if you don't have the source code. Basically, you just need to follow a simple naming convention, and a few other simple rules of thumb.

Fresh Brew

The JavaBean specification is available online, along with a wealth of other information on JavaBeans at the JavaBeans homepage at java.sun.com/beans/.

Primarily, this convention requires that given a property, you need to have two public methods, one called getProperty(), which provides access to the property, and one called setProperty(), which changes the value of the property. For example, if you have a property named password, you would have a getPassword method and a setPassword method. These methods are known as getters and setters, respectively.

Two important points relating to these methods remain. First, the actual property datatype does not need to be exposed. For example the password may be encoded in double precision floating-point number, but the getPassword method might return a String, while the setPassword method could take a String argument. A String is a basic Java object that represents a string of characters. For example, all of the characters that make up the word "example" would be considered a String object. Second, the method naming convention is to append the property name to get and set to form the method name, with the first letter of the property type capitalized, thus we have getPassword.

If the datatype for a particular property is a Boolean, you can either use the "get" and "set" naming scheme, or you can use "is" instead of "get". For example, if you have a property called valid that is a Boolean type, you would have a setValid method, and either a getValid or an isValid method.

In order to use a JavaBean within a JSP page, one item remains. When any object in Java is created, there is a special method called a constructor. The constructor is called—you guessed it—construct the object. When something is constructed, or built, anything that needs to be initialized for that object can be done in the constructor. The Bean must have a default constructor; that is a constructor that takes no arguments. If you put this all together, you can write your first JavaBean, shown in Listing 14.1.

Listing 14.1   LoginBean.java

```java
import java.beans.* ;
import java.io.Serializable ;

public class LoginBean  implements Serializable {

  private String username ;
  private String password ;

  public LoginBean() {
  }

  public String getUsername() {
    return(username) ;
  }

  public void setUsername(String name) {
    username = name;
  }

  public String getPassword() {
    return(password) ;
  }

  public void setPassword(String passwd) {
    password = passwd;
  }
}
```

You can see that all of the requirements that a Bean needs to adhere to are put into practice. The null constructor LoginBean() is provided, along with the get and set methods for each of the properties.

The formal JavaBean specification has a few additional requirements, which are always applicable when using JavaBeans with JSP pages. One of these is the requirement that a JavaBean implement the Serializable interface. The LoginBean implements a special interface called Serializable but there are no methods to support it. The reason why it's necessary for a JavaBean to implement Serializable is so that it can be passed between a client and a server or so it can maintain information between web server restarts. Serializing allows the Bean to

Fresh Brew

While not required, it is a good, and strongly recommended, practice, to always end the name of your JavaBean class with "Bean". Thus, you have LoginBean instead of just Login. This enables other developers to immediately know that the Login class is a JavaBean.

write its complete state to an output stream and then recreate that object at some later time by reading its serialized state from an input stream. By requiring that JavaBeans implement the `Serializable` interface, the Beans can be saved to disk whenever the server is shut down, and can be recreated when the server starts up again.

Coffee Break

Its not that the other JavaBean requirements aren't applicable within a JSP environment, it's that they are rarely—if ever—needed. After implementing the `Serializable` interface, the only other major JavaBean requirement relates to events and implementing listener objects. Since JSP does not provide explicit support for these, a JSP developer needs to provide all event-handling code. As a result, they aren't generally used, and, thus, rarely mentioned within the context of JavaBeans and JSPs.

Using JavaBeans in JavaServer Pages

The JSP specification provides for a tight integration between JSP pages and JavaBeans. In order to take advantage of this integration, however, you need to explicitly tell the JSP container that you want to use a JavaBean. This task is accomplished by using the `useBean` JSP action. This action takes a number of attributes, including the following:

- `id`, which indicates the name that is used to identify the Bean instance
- `scope`, which specifies the scope in which the Bean is visible
- `class`, which is the fully qualified name for the class that actually implements the JavaBean
- `beanName`, which is the name of a Bean that can be used by the JavaBean class instantiation method
- `type`, which defines the type of scripting variable used in the JSP page

Of these, the first three are the most common. As discussed in Chapter 6, "Getting a Free Lunch," an object can have four different scopes: `page`, `request`, `session`, and `application`. Basically, the `useBean` action creates a new scripting variable with a name given by the `id` attribute. The new variable is an instance of the specified class, and has a specific scope. This means that the JSP page can access the Bean and use any methods it provides for the defined scope.

For example, to use the LoginBean with request scope, you could use the following action:

```
<jsp:useBean id="login" class="LoginBean" scope="request" />
```

After this, you can access the methods of this Bean just as if you had explicitly created the login object.

```
<%
    login.setUsername("java") ;
    login.setPassword("sun") ;
%>
```

Two other JSP actions simplify calling the get and set methods for a JavaBean. The first action is getProperty, which, as its name suggests, is used to retrieve the value of a property. The getProperty action takes two attributes: name and property. The name attribute is used to indicate which Bean should be used, and must correspond to the id attribute of a JavaBean object created by a useBean action. The property attribute is used to specify which property value should be accessed.

Coffee Break

The two attributes: beanName and type, are less obvious to understand. JavaBeans can be automatically instantiated by using the instantiation method within the java.beans.Beans class. The type attribute, on the other hand, enables a developer to treat the JavaBean instance created in the JSP page to be a different type, as opposed to of type classname, which is specified by the class attribute. You can't arbitrarily choose a type. However, the type must be either the actual class itself, a superclass of the class, or an interface that is implemented by the class. Remember, I warned you these weren't that common!

The second action is setProperty, which is used—drumroll please—to set a property. The setProperty action has four attributes: name, property, param, and value. The name and property attributes are the same as for the getProperty action. A setProperty action can either have a param attribute, or a value attribute, but not both.

The param attribute is used to match a request parameter to a Bean property. A request parameter is one that is included in the HTTP request. Usually this is a result of an input type on a form being set. The value attribute, on the other hand, is used to explicitly indicate the new value for the property. If no param or value attribute is specified, the JSP container will try to find a matching parameter with the same name as the property. If no param or value attribute is specified, the JSP container will try to find a matching parameter with the same name as the property.

Once a Bean is created, you can use these two actions in a JSP page to interact with a JavaBean. For example, you can set the password property, and print out the username property when creating a HTML page.

```
<jsp:setProperty name="login" property="password" value="sun"/>
User Name = <jsp:getProperty name="login" property="username"/>
```

The useBean action can also have a body, in which case the body content is invoked only if the Bean is created. Often, the body contains setProperty actions that initialize the new Bean; but the contents of the useBean body are not restricted. For example, you could create and initialize our LoginBean all at once.

```
<jsp:useBean id="login" class="LoginBean" scope="request" />
  <jsp:setProperty name="login" property="username" value="java"/>
  <jsp:setProperty name="login" property="password" value="sun"/>
</jsp:useBean>
```

You can shorten this by taking advantage of the tight integration between JSP pages and JavaBeans. A beautiful and useful shorthand exists for the case where a Bean is completely matched to an XHTML form element. In this case, the setProperty action is called with the name attribute set properly, but the property attribute is set to the wildcard character (*). For example, if a login form exists that has username and password input controls, you can automatically bind them to your LoginBean as shown in this example:

```
<jsp:useBean id="login" class="LoginBean" scope="request" />
<jsp:setProperty name="login" property="*"/>
```

While this is useful for this small Bean, it is extremely powerful when you start working with large XHTML form elements.

Mixing Beans with Forms

As you just saw, grabbing data out of an XHTML form is much easier using a JavaBean than it is with a horde of request.getParameter statements. To demonstrate this, rewrite your previous login form from Chapter 10 explicitly, controls.jsp shown in Listing 10.7. This time, use the JavaBean shown in Listing 14.2.

Listing 14.2   LoginBean.java

```
import java.beans.* ;
import java.io.Serializable ;

public class LoginBean  implements Serializable {

  private String username ;
  private String password ;
  private String email ;
  private String sex ;
```

```
public LoginBean() {
}

public String getUsername() {
  return(username) ;
}

public void setUsername(String name) {
  username = name;
}

public String getPassword() {
  return(password) ;
}

public void setPassword(String passwd) {
  password = passwd;
}

public String getEmail() {
  return(email) ;
}

public void setEmail(String value) {
  email = value;
}

public String getSex() {
  return(sex) ;
}

public void setSex(String value) {
  sex = value;
}
}
```

Hot Java

The LoginBean and the beancontrols.jsp page are for demonstration purposes. You should never place any password in an unsecured form, as any packet-sniffing program will be able to steal it. In Chapter 17, "Locking It Down," I will revisit security, and discuss alternative techniques that are more secure.

Using this JavaBean, you can rewrite controls.jsp, as shown in Listing 14.3. The result after entering the requested information is shown in Figure 14.1.

Listing 14.3   beancontrols.jsp

```
<%@page language="java" contentType="text/html"%>
<html>
<head><title>Forms and Beans</title></head>
<body>
```

continues

Listing 14.3   beancontrols.jsp   (continued)

```
<jsp:useBean id="login" class="com.persistentjava.LoginBean" scope="session"/>
<jsp:setProperty name="login" property="*"/>

<%
  if(login.getUsername() != null) {
%>

    <h2> Greetings User </h2>
    <hr/>
    <h4> Username: <jsp:getProperty name="login" property="username"/> </h4>
    <h4> Password: <jsp:getProperty name="login" property="password"/> </h4>
    <h4> Email: <jsp:getProperty name="login" property="email"/> </h4>
    <h4> Sex: <jsp:getProperty name="login" property="sex"/> </h4>
    <hr/>

<%
  } else {
%>

    <h2> Please Login. </h2>

    <form action="beancontrols.jsp" method="post">
      Username <input type="text" name="username"/>
      <p/>
      Password <input type="password" name="password"/>
      <p/>
      Email <input type="text" name="email"/>
      <p/>
      Sex
        <input type="radio" name="sex" value="Male" />   M
        <input type="radio" name="sex" value="Female" />   F
      <p/>
      <input type="submit" value="submit" />
    </form>

<%
  }
%>

</body>
</html>
```

Notice that the setProperty action is not inside the body of the useBean action. If it were, it would only be called once, when the Bean is created. Since the Bean is created when the page is first loaded, the form data is null, thus you would initialize your Bean to have all null values—not what you want. Instead, you want the Bean properties to be updated whenever the form is submitted.

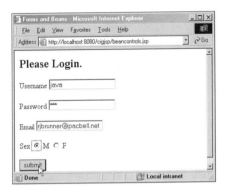

You also might have noticed that the LoginBean is inside the com.persistentjava package. This is used to demonstrate using a fully qualified class name, which must include the full package name. Remember that in a web application, Java classes are loaded from the WEB-INF\classes directory. Since the LoginBean is in the com.persistentjava package, you actually need to place the LoginBean in the WEB-INF\classes\com\persistentjava\ directory under the cigjsp context in order for Tomcat to find and use it.

The context of a web application is provided in the configuration files of the web server. It is common to have a directory called WEB-INF (short for web information) that has the class file structure and other necessary configuration files that are specific to that application.

Forwarding Data

In the beancontrols.jsp page, everything was handled inside the same JSP page. In production code, you will most likely have several JSP pages, across which you will want to share information. JavaBeans are also useful in this capacity, as you can pass a JavaBean using the param action inside the forward action. Listing 14.4 shows a modified version of the beancontrols JSP page that forwards the login information to a second JSP page, shown in Listing 14.5. Figure 14.2 shows the result.

Listing 14.4   newbeancontrols.jsp

```
<%@page language="java" contentType="text/html"%>
<html>
<head><title>More Forms and Beans</title></head>
<body>

<jsp:useBean id="login" class="com.persistentjava.LoginBean" scope="session"/>
<jsp:setProperty name="login" property="*"/>
```

continues

Listing 14.4 newbeancontrols.jsp (continued)

```
<%
  if(login.getUsername() != null) {
%>

<jsp:forward page="/beandisplay.jsp"/>

<%
  } else {
%>

    <h2> Please Login. </h2>

    <form action="newbeancontrols.jsp" method="post">
      Username <input type="text" name="username"/>
      <p/>
      Password <input type="password" name="password"/>
      <p/>
      Email <input type="text" name="email"/>
      <p/>
      Sex
        <input type="radio" name="sex" value="Male" />   M
        <input type="radio" name="sex" value="Female" />   F
      <p/>
      <input type="submit" value="submit" />
    </form>

<%
  }
%>

</body>
</html>
```

Figure 14.2

Using Beans and Forms together simplifies development; here you fill in a form that automatically populates the LoginBean.

Listing 14.5   beandisplay.jsp

```
<%@page contentType="text/html"%>
<html>
<head><title>Bean Display</title></head>
<body>

    <h2> Greetings User </h2>
    <hr/>
    <h4> Username: <jsp:getProperty name="login" property="username"/> </h4>
    <h4> Password: <jsp:getProperty name="login" property="password"/> </h4>
    <h4> Email: <jsp:getProperty name="login" property="email"/> </h4>
    <h4> Sex: <jsp:getProperty name="login" property="sex"/> </h4>
    <hr/>

</body>
</html>
```

As you can see, newbeancontrols is very similar to beancontrols, except that the request is forwarded to beandisplay after the user has entered information into the form. In the beandisplay JSP page, you just output the data from the LoginBean, as shown in Figure 14.3. Notice that this figure shows the output from the beandisplay.jsp page, yet the browser still displays the newbeancontrols.jsp URL. This demonstrates how the forward action hides the processing details from the user.

Figure 14.3

While this web page looks very similar to Figure 14.1, there is one minor difference—the browser URL does not reflect the actual JSP processing page.

Wait a minute, how can you use the LoginBean named login inside beandisplay.jsp? The secret is the scope of the LoginBean. When you created the Bean, you specified that it had session scope. Thus any other JSP page participating in the session has implicit access to the login Bean—nice, huh? The combination of JavaBeans and JSP pages actually has a name—Model One JSP development. In the following two chapters, I will introduce you to other powerful techniques for improving your JSP development skills.

The Least You Need to Know

◆ JavaBeans are a useful component model in Java.

◆ JSP pages and JavaBeans are tightly integrated, with three JSP actions used to integrate JavaBeans into a JSP page.

◆ JavaBeans can be automatically populated from an XHTML form.

◆ JavaBeans provide an elegant technique for passing data between JSP pages.

Chapter 15

Introducing Servlets

In This Chapter

- Using Servlets
- Building filters
- Understanding Model 2 web development

Servlets shouldn't really be a totally new concept to you. Because JSP pages must be compiled into Servlets before they process a request, you have been working with Servlets implicitly for most of the book. If your memory is sharp, you may recall that you already looked at Servlets in Chapter 1, "The Backgrounder," where I discussed the Servlet life cycle and demonstrated a simple "Hello World" Servlet. Likewise, in Chapter 3, "Building Your First JSP," I examined the generated Servlet of the "Hello World" JSP. In this chapter, however, you will actually start using Servlets, which provide a great deal of power to developing web applications.

And in This Corner—Servlets

So what is a Servlet? Put simply, a Servlet is a Java class used to build dynamic web applications and which is managed by a web server extension, known as a container. This container is often referred to as the Servlet container, or Servlet engine, to emphasize that the container deals with Servlets, as opposed to a different type of web component.

The Servlet container can be built into a web server or a web application server, or it can be an add-on component. All Servlet containers must support the HTTP protocol, which is the dominant web protocol. Other protocols, such as HTTP over Secure Sockets (HTTPS), are optional, but are generally supported because security is such an important feature. I will continue to use the Apache Software Foundation's Tomcat Servlet container.

The Servlet container provides the framework in which Servlets operate. As with any framework, many of the routine tasks are performed for you. For a Servlet container, these tasks include handling network communication and handling MIME processing as well as managing Servlets throughout their life cycle. (MIME stands for Multipurpose Internet Mail Extension and is a way for providing e-mail with media content other than text. MIME can also be used by applications other than mail. MIME is also something you do in the park in order to coax quarters from strangers, but that really has nothing to do with this book.)

The Servlet Life Cycle

The Servlet life cycle is very simple and consists of:

+ An initialization phase
+ A service phase
+ A destruction phase

This life cycle is one of the main reasons for the Servlet model's success. Before any of this can occur, however, the Servlet must be instantiated (which means to create an object from a class), just like any other Java class. Instantiation consists of loading the Servlet into the container and creating it. This phase can either occur when the container itself is started, or it can be delayed until the first request for the Servlet arrives.

After instantiation, a Servlet needs to be initialized before it can handle client requests. The initialization phase occurs only once, allowing a Servlet to obtain configuration information and initialize any resources required for the Servlet to properly function. The initialization phase is handled by the Servlet's `init()` method.

If the `init()` method for a Servlet generates an exception (that's a fancy word for an error, remember?), the Servlet container releases the instantiated Servlet object. The `destroy()` method will not be called, because the Servlet wasn't successfully initialized, and no requests will be passed to the `service()` method. After a failed initialization, the Servlet container can create and initialize a new Servlet instance.

Once a Servlet has been initialized, it is ready to process requests. This phase in a Servlet's life cycle is called the service phase. The Servlet's task is to process one or more client requests, dynamically (in real time) generating responses to these requests. This processing occurs in the `service()` method. Requests and responses are handled in the

ServletRequest and ServletResponse objects, respectively, and are provided as method parameters to the service() method.

Coffee Break

When working with Servlets, you need to be aware that most Servlet containers are multithreaded to improve performance. As a result, a service() method may be sent concurrent requests. In other words, you need to make your service() method thread-safe. For simple tasks like generating an HTML web page, this is generally not an issue. On the other, hand, if you are sharing data or resources across requests, like a page hit counter or application objects, you need to properly synchronize their access, or risk corrupted data or inconsistent program state.

A Servlet container can remove a Servlet from service when deemed necessary. This action can occur either when the container process itself terminates, or perhaps when the container needs to conserve resources. When the container needs to remove a Servlet, it calls the Servlet's destroy() method. This allows a Servlet to release any resources that were acquired during the initialization phase or to save relevant information. Once the destruction phase is complete, the Servlet is available for garbage collection (which means that the system can delete the Servlet from memory).

Coffee Break

I can hear you now—whoa, Robert, where is the service() method? The class that defines the basic Servlet functionality is GenericServlet. To write a protocol-independent Servlet, you create a new class from GenericServlet and override the service() method to provide whatever functionality you need.

On the other hand, when you want to write an HTTP protocol-dependent Servlet, which is almost always the case, you create a new class from the HTTPServlet class, which provides a service() method that interprets the HTTP Request. If you remember from Chapter 1, an HTTP request can be GET, PUT, POST, DELETE, OPTIONS, and TRACE. The HTTPServlet service() method dispatches the HTTP request to the appropriate method. For example, the service() method dispatches GET requests to the doGet() method, while it dispatches POST requests to the doPost() method.

As a result, when working with Servlets that extend the HTTPServlet class, you get the service() method for free, and implement the appropriate do methods.

Hello World, Servlet Style

Enough talk, you want action! In Listing 15.1 you have a simple "Hello World" Servlet. This Servlet demonstrates the complete Servlet life cycle, showing the initialization phase, the service phase, and the destruction phase. When this Servlet is deployed and called for the first time, it displays "Hello World" and informs the client that it has been accessed one time.

Listing 15.1 HelloWorldServlet.java

```java
import java.io.* ;

import javax.servlet.*;
import javax.servlet.http.*;

public class HelloWorldServlet extends HttpServlet {

  private final static String filename = "hit-counter.txt" ;
  private int count ;

  public void init(ServletConfig config) throws ServletException {
    super.init(config);

    try{
      File file = new File(filename) ;

      if(file.exists()){
        FileReader hits = new FileReader(file) ;
        count = hits.read() ;
        hits.close() ;
      }else {
        file.createNewFile() ;
        count = 0 ;
      }
    }catch(IOException ioe){
      throw new ServletException(ioe.getMessage()) ;
    }
  }

  public void destroy() {
    try{
      FileReader hits = new FileReader(new File(filename)) ;
      count = hits.read() ;
      hits.close() ;
    }catch(IOException ioe){
      ; // DO nothing as Servlet is being destroyed anyway.
    }
  }
```

```
  protected void processRequest(HttpServletRequest request, HttpServletResponse
response)
    throws ServletException, java.io.IOException {
      response.setContentType("text/html");
      java.io.PrintWriter out = response.getWriter();

      count++ ;

      out.println("<html>");
      out.println("<head>");
      out.println("<title>HelloWorldServlet</title>");
      out.println("</head>");
      out.println("<body>");
      out.println("<h1>Hello World!</h1>");
      out.println("<hr/>");
      out.println("<h2>This page accessed " + count + " times.</h2>");
      out.println("</body>");
      out.println("</html>");

      out.close();
  }

  public void doGet(HttpServletRequest request, HttpServletResponse response)
    throws ServletException, java.io.IOException {
      processRequest(request, response);
  }

  public void doPost(HttpServletRequest request, HttpServletResponse response)
    throws ServletException, java.io.IOException {
      processRequest(request, response);
  }

  public String getServletInfo() {
      return "Hello World, Servlet Style!";
  }
}
```

As you can see in the `init()` and `destroy()` methods, the hit counter is retrieved from a file, which allows the hit count to be saved across server, or Servlet, shutdowns. For example, here's what the `init()` version of this code looks like:

```
try{
  File file = new File(filename) ;
```

Fresh Brew

As is the case with Java-Beans, you don't need to end the name of your Servlet with Servlet, as in `HelloWorldServlet`. However, doing so is a good practice, as it makes the role of the class obvious to anyone looking at it.

```
  if(file.exists()){
    FileReader hits = new FileReader(file) ;
    count = hits.read() ;
    hits.close() ;
  }else {
    file.createNewFile() ;
    count = 0 ;
  }
}catch(IOException ioe){
  throw new ServletException(ioe.getMessage()) ;
}
```

The main complication is that the init() method must support file creation when the "hit-counter.txt" file doesn't exist. After that, all requests are processed identically, whether they be HTTP GET or PUT requests. All that is done as the hit counter is incremented, an HTML page is generated, and the hit counter is displayed.

This simple Servlet is not thread-safe—intentionally, I can assure you. The service() method shares a single instance of the count variable across service calls, as required in order to implement the concept of a hit counter. However, the accesses to the count variable are not synchronized (controlled so that two threads can't access the variable simultaneously), thus one service thread can update the count variable after a different thread has accessed the count value, but before the count value is added to the response. In this fictitious scenario, both responses would have the same value for the hit counter.

In this simple example, such a result is not devastating, but many situations exist where you must properly synchronize access to any shared data or resource. The simple solution is to first minimize shared access, and after that, be sure to synchronize any shared data access.

Saying Hello

While this example is simple, and perhaps a bit contrived, it also demonstrates how to actually use Servlets. Since Servlets are Java classes, they must be compiled before they can be used. In addition, before a container can serve them up, the Servlet must be properly deployed. For simplicity, place this Servlet in the cigjsp context that you have been using in the last few chapters. Here's how to get this puppy compiled:

1. Save Listing 15.1 as HelloWorldServlet.java in the folder cigjsp\WEB-INF\classes directory. (You'll need to create this directory yourself.)

2. Start a DOS command-prompt window, and enter **set PATH=X:\Java\bin**, where *X* is the drive on which you installed the Java SDK, and *Java* is the folder into which you installed the SDK. For example, you might type **set PATH=C:\j2sdk1.4.0-beta3\bin**. This tells your system where to find the Java compiler.

3. Now, type **set CLASSPATH=X:\\Jakarta\\common\\lib\\Servlet.jar**, where X is the drive on which you installed Tomcat, and *Jakarta* is the folder into which you installed Tomcat. For example, you might type **C:\\jakarta-tomcat-4.0.1\\ common\\lib\\Servlet.jar**. This tells Java where to find the javax.Servlet and javax.Servlet.http packages that the Servlet imports.

4. Move to the directory in which you stored the HelloWorldServlet.java file. To do this, you might type **cd C:\\jakarta-tomcat-4.0.1\\webapps\\cigjsp\\WEB-INF\\classes.** (Whew! All these long path names are why the Powers That Be invented batch files! Then, you only have to type the paths once and run the batch file to set them.)

5. Type **javac HelloWorldServlet.java** to compile the Servlet. You'll then end up with a file named HelloWorldServlet.class, which is the compiled form of HelloWorldServlet.java.

At this point, you should have successfully compiled the Servlet. Now all you need to do is tell the Servlet container that you have a new Servlet to deploy. You do this using the deployment descriptor for the web application that contains the new Servlet—web.xml. Remember when you created that file? You may also remember that you stored it in the WEB-INF subdirectory of the cigjsp context. The first step in deploying the Servlet is to add a servlet element to the deployment descriptor, as shown in this example:

```
<servlet>
  <servlet-name>hi-serve</servlet-name>
  <description>The Hello World Servlet.</description>
  <servlet-class>HelloWorldServlet</servlet-class>
</servlet>
```

This maps HelloWorldServlet to the name hi-serve. The next step is to map this name to a URL so that the Servlet container knows when to invoke your Servlet:

```
<servlet-mapping>
  <servlet-name>hi-serve</servlet-name>
  <url-pattern>/Hello</url-pattern>
</servlet-mapping>
```

Putting it all together, you have the full deployment descriptor shown in Listing 15.2, ignoring any previous mappings you added in other chapters.

Listing 15.2   The Deployment Descriptor

```
<?xml version="1.0" encoding="ISO-8859-1"?>
<!DOCTYPE web-app
    PUBLIC "-//Sun Microsystems, Inc.//DTD Web Application 2.3//EN"
    "http://java.sun.com/dtd/web-app_2_3.dtd">
```

continues

Listing 15.2   The Deployment Descriptor   (continued)

```
<web-app>
  <servlet>
    <servlet-name>hi-serve</servlet-name>
    <description>The Hello World Servlet.</description>
    <servlet-class>HelloWorldServlet</servlet-class>
  </servlet>
  <servlet-mapping>
    <servlet-name>hi-serve</servlet-name>
    <url-pattern>/Hello</url-pattern>
  </servlet-mapping>
</web-app>
```

Now all you need to do is start up the Tomcat server (or, if it's already running, shut it down and restart it), and browse to localhost:8080/cigjsp/Hello, and you see the fruits of your labors, shown in Figure 15.1.

Figure 15.1

The first invocation of HelloWorldServlet shows that the page has been accessed one time. Every time you reload the page, the counter is updated.

Fresh Brew

If you are thinking, "Talk about a lot of work for a simple result!" you are right. When developing web pages, JSP pages are much simpler to work with than Servlets, since the work of compiling and deploying is taken care of automatically. Furthermore, you don't need to stop and restart the server every time you make a change, as you do with Servlets, because the container needs to reload the new Servlet class.

Servlets are very useful, however, when you have a lot of processing, because they allow you to remove the Java code from your JSP pages, simplifying code development and maintenance, as well as promoting code reuse.

Filtering Servlets

Servlets provide a powerful solution for handling complex processing, but with the recent 2.3 Servlet specification, they also provide another useful function—dynamically filtering requests and responses. Filters can provide a variety of functions, including the following:

- Authentication
- Logging specific requests
- Auditing resource requests
- Image conversions

- Response compression
- Encryption
- Localization

Building a Filter

The Filter API is defined in the Servlet specification and is composed of three interfaces:

- `Filter`
- `FilterChain`
- `FilterConfig`

To build a Filter, you need to write a Java class that implements the Filter interface. The `FilterChain` interface is used to—surprise, surprise—chain filters together, and `FilterConfig` contains initialization data.

Usually, when building a Filter, all you need to do is write three methods: `init()`, `destroy()`, and `doFilter()`. The `init()` and `destroy()` methods are identical in functionality to the equivalent methods in the Servlet interface. The most important method in the `Filter` interface is the `doFilter()` method. In this method, you can …

- Access resources before a request is processed.
- Preprocess a request.
- Modify request headers and data.
- Modify response headers and data.
- Access resources after a request is processed.

So what does a Filter look like? Listing 15.3 contains a Filter that blocks access to a resource unless the request includes the user header with a value of java.

Listing 15.3   BlockFilter.java

```
import javax.servlet.*;
import javax.servlet.http.*;

public class BlockFilter implements Filter {
```

continues

Listing 15.3   BlockFilter.java   (continued)

```
private ServletContext ctx ;
private final static String msg = "Sorry, we don't like Microsoft" ;

public void init(FilterConfig config) throws ServletException {
  ctx = config.getServletContext() ;
  ctx.log("Initializing BlockFilter") ;
}

public void destroy() {
  ctx.log("Destroying BlockFilter") ;
}

public void doFilter(ServletRequest request,
ServletResponse response,
FilterChain chain) throws ServletException, java.io.IOException {

  HttpServletRequest req = (HttpServletRequest)request ;

  if(req.getHeader("User-Agent").indexOf("MSIE") != -1){
    HttpServletResponse res = (HttpServletResponse)response ;
    res.sendError(res.SC_SERVICE_UNAVAILABLE, msg) ;
  }
 }
}
```

The init() and destroy() methods just print messages in the log file, in this case just to demonstrate a nonempty method. The doFilter() method, on the other hand, is where the real action is located. First, you need to cast (convert) the request and response objects that are passed in to the doFilter() method to their HTTP representations—this is legal since they really are HTTP Requests and Responses. The filter then tests to see if the "User-Agent" header contains the string "MSIE," which is used by Internet Explorer to indicate the browser's presence. If the filter finds a Microsoft web browser, it stops the request processing and returns an appropriate error and message to the browser.

Deploying a Filter

Okay, now that you have built the Filter (don't forget to compile it, using the same procedure you used previously), you need to deploy it. Just as was the case with HelloWorldServlet, you need to modify the web.xml deployment descriptor, located in the WEB-INF subdirectory of the cigjsp context. In this case, you need to name your filter using the filter-name element; associate the name with an implementation or Java class file with the filter-class element; and specify either a Servlet name with the Servlet-class element or a URL with the url-pattern element for which the Filter should be applied. In order to only apply the BlockFilter to your HelloWorldServlet, you can use the deployment descriptor shown in Listing 15.4.

Listing 15.4   web.xml

```xml
<?xml version="1.0" encoding="ISO-8859-1"?>
<!DOCTYPE web-app
    PUBLIC "-//Sun Microsystems, Inc.//DTD Web Application 2.3//EN"
    "http://java.sun.com/dtd/web-app_2_3.dtd">
<web-app>

<filter>
  <filter-name>BadBill</filter-name>
  <filter-class>BlockFilter</filter-class>
</filter>
<filter-mapping>
  <filter-name>BadBill</filter-name>
  <url-pattern>/Hello</url-pattern>
</filter-mapping>
<servlet>
  <servlet-name>hi-serve</servlet-name>
  <servlet-class>HelloWorldServlet</servlet-class>
</servlet>
<servlet-mapping>
  <servlet-name>hi-serve</servlet-name>
  <url-pattern>/Hello</url-pattern>
</servlet-mapping>
</web-app>
```

Once you have completed the deployment descriptor, restart your Tomcat server, and browse to the HelloWorldServlet URL, localhost:8080/cigjsp/Hello.

JSPs, Beans, and Servlets, Oh My!

In Chapter 14, "Brewing With Beans," you saw how easy it was to use JavaBeans together with JSP pages. The result simplified the development of your web application, and promoted code reuse. You can now add Servlets into the mix, and move from Model 1 web application development, which combines with JSP pages, to Model 2, which combines Servlets, Beans, and JSP pages.

JSP, Beans, and Servlet—what are you supposed to do with them all? The answer arises when you utilize the Model-View-Controller (MVC) design pattern, mentioned earlier in the book. In this pattern, the model is populated with the relevant data, the controller handles the interaction with the model, and the view controls how the model is presented. In Model 2 development, you use Servlets to implement the controller components, JavaBeans implement the model, and JSP pages provide the view.

A simple example will demonstrate how this all fits together. If you remember from Chapter 14, you used the LoginBean to encapsulate the login information for a client. Instead of a single JSP page that handles everything, you can have separate JSP pages for every view, and a single controller Servlet that handles the requests.

First, you need a JSP page that provides the login form, which will simply be a modified version of beancontrols.jsp shown in Listing 14.3. Second, you need a JSP page that presents the data back to the client. The model will be encapsulated within the LoginBean shown in Listing 14.2; and finally, you need a controlling Servlet to manage the incoming requests. The two JSP pages and the controlling Servlet are shown in Listings 15.5, 15.6, and 15.7.

Listing 15.5   mvclogin.jsp

```
<%@page contentType="text/html"%>
<html>
<head><title>MVC Login</title></head>
<body>

    <h2> Please Login. </h2>

    <form action="Welcome" method="post">
      Username <input type="text" name="username"/>
      <p/>
      Password <input type="password" name="password"/>
      <p/>
      Email <input type="text" name="email"/>
      <p/>
      Sex
        <input type="radio" name="sex" value="Male" />  M
        <input type="radio" name="sex" value="Female" />  F
      <p/>
      <input type="submit" value="submit" />
    </form>

</body>
</html>
```

Listing 15.6   mvcdisplay.jsp

```
<%@page language="java" contentType="text/html"%>
<html>
<head><title>MVC Display</title></head>
<body>

<jsp:useBean id="login" class="com.persistentjava.LoginBean" scope="session"/>
<jsp:setProperty name="login" property="*"/>

    <h2> Greetings User </h2>
    <hr/>
    <h4> Username: <jsp:getProperty name="login" property="username"/> </h4>
    <h4> Password: <jsp:getProperty name="login" property="password"/> </h4>
    <h4> Email: <jsp:getProperty name="login" property="email"/> </h4>
    <h4> Sex: <jsp:getProperty name="login" property="sex"/> </h4>
    <hr/>

</body>
</html>
```

Listing 15.7   MvcServlet.jsp

```
import javax.servlet.*;
import javax.servlet.http.*;

public class MvcServlet extends HttpServlet {

  public void processRequest(HttpServletRequest request, HttpServletResponse
response)
  throws ServletException, java.io.IOException {

    String dispatch ;

    if(request.getParameter("username") != null){
      dispatch ="mvcdisplay.jsp" ;
    }else {
      dispatch = "mvclogin.jsp" ;
    }

    RequestDispatcher dispatcher = request.getRequestDispatcher(dispatch) ;
    dispatcher.forward(request, response) ;
  }
```

continues

Listing 15.7   MvcServlet.jsp   (continued)

```
  protected void doGet(HttpServletRequest request, HttpServletResponse
response)
  throws ServletException, java.io.IOException {
    processRequest(request, response);
  }

  protected void doPost(HttpServletRequest request, HttpServletResponse
response)
  throws ServletException, java.io.IOException {
    processRequest(request, response);
  }
}
```

If you take a look through these listings, you notice how clean this design appears. Each JSP page and Servlet has a single task. In addition, each component is isolated from the others, making it easy to change one component without causing problems in other components. You also may notice that there is no Java code in the JSP pages. Anyone familiar with writing web pages could write these JSP pages, showing how you have effectively separated out responsibilities by using the Model 2 development approach.

The only real new item in this example is the forwarding of requests from the Servlet to the appropriate JSP pages. In order to keep the request parameters around, you need to tell the Servlet container to forward the entire request; thus you can't just forward the request yourself. This requires obtaining a RequestDispatcher and using it to forward your request to the appropriate JSP page.

Compile MvcServlet, and place it in the WEB_INF\classes directory, and place the two JSP pages in the cigjsp directory. Because you are just reusing the LoginBean, it is already in the proper directory. The last step in the process is to deploy this application. As before, you need to modify the deployment descriptor so that the Servlet container knows about your new Servlet. An example deployment descriptor is shown in Listing 15.8.

Listing 15.8   web.xml

```
<?xml version="1.0" encoding="ISO-8859-1"?>

<!DOCTYPE web-app
    PUBLIC "-//Sun Microsystems, Inc.//DTD Web Application 2.3//EN"
    "http://java.sun.com/dtd/web-app_2_3.dtd">

<web-app>
```

```
<servlet>
  <servlet-name>mvc</servlet-name>
  <servlet-class>MvcServlet</servlet-class>
</servlet>

<servlet-mapping>
  <servlet-name>mvc</servlet-name>
  <url-pattern>/Welcome</url-pattern>
</servlet-mapping>

</web-app>
```

With your new deployment descriptor in place, you will need to restart your Servlet container and open a browser window to localhost:8080/cigjsp/Welcome, as shown in Figure 15.2.

Figure 15.2

The login screen for your web application. Notice how the browser's URL displays the Welcome page, even though you are seeing the output from mvclogin.jsp.

After filling out the form as shown and clicking on the Submit button, you will be presented with the information you just entered, as seen in Figure 15.3. While nothing seems to have changed from previous examples, you might notice that the URL in the browser's window never changes. This is because it never does change; all communication between the client and our web application passes through the controller Servlet.

This is both a blessing and a curse. It can be a curse, because the controlling Servlet can become a bottleneck for high traffic sites if not developed properly; and it can be a blessing, because you explicitly control all requests.

Figure 15.3

Here is the display screen for your web application. Notice how the browser's URL still displays the Welcome page, even though we are seeing the output from mvcdisplay.jsp.

The Least You Need to Know

- ◆ Servlets are better at processing data than JSP pages.
- ◆ JSP pages are better at generating HTML output than Servlets.
- ◆ Filters are a powerful technique for preprocessing of requests and post processing of responses.
- ◆ Model 2 web development uses Servlets to implement the controller, JSP pages to implement the view, and JavaBeans to implement the model from the MVC design pattern.

Chapter 16

Rolling Out Tags

In This Chapter

◆ Introducing custom tags

◆ Building tags

◆ Deploying tags

◆ Working with Tag Libraries

If you ask 10 different JSP developers how to best design a user interface, you will probably get 10 different answers (okay, maybe 12). If you ask the same 10 developers, however, what is the most powerful feature in the JSP specification, you will probably only get one answer—custom tags. Custom tags, also known as custom actions, enable a developer to remove Java code from the JSP page, replacing it with new JSP tags that look, feel, and work just like the JSP tags that provide the support for JSP standard actions.

In this chapter, I will first explain the JSP tag extension architecture. After that, I'll show you how to build, deploy, and test two custom tags, an empty tag, and a tag that uses attributes and processes its body content. Finally, we will work with the current release of the JSP standard Tag Library.

Introducing Custom Tags

In Chapter 8, "Mixing and Matching JSP Pages," you started working with standard actions. These actions are written using valid XML and can include attributes and sometimes other elements. As you have seen, you can use a standard action to forward a request, dynamically include content, and use JavaBeans and Applets from within a JSP page. Essentially, you use an action within a JSP page to work with Java, without actually doing so—a powerful concept that allows web developers who do not know Java to write dynamic web applications using JSP. This makes JSP pages easier to read and write.

The tag extension API extends the ability of a JSP developer to utilize not only standard actions, but also custom actions, that can do just about anything you might want to do. Basically, if you so desire, you can remove all scriptlets, declarations, and expressions from your JSP page. By using tags, you can write a JSP page that is a well-formed, valid XML document, allowing you to dynamically pass JSP pages to be used by different servers.

A custom action is used in a JSP page just like a standard action. They can have no attributes, like the `fallback` and `params` action; they can take attributes and have empty bodies, like the `include`, `forward` actions or `useBean` actions; or they can take attributes and have body content, like the `plugin` action. You can use tags to generate HTML, or any other content type that is supported by the JSP specification. You gather custom tags together into a Tag Library, which allows you to group related custom actions together for easier deployment.

Here are some tag examples. You can have an empty tag …

```
<cig:hi/>
```

Or a tag that takes an attribute …

```
<cig:hi name"Robert"/>
```

Or a tag that has no attributes, but has a nonempty body …

```
<cig:hi>Brunner</cig:hi>
```

Or, lastly, a tag that takes an attribute and has a nonempty body …

```
<cig:hi name="Robert">Brunner</cig:hi>
```

Unlike standard actions, however, custom actions need to be defined before they can be used. The next section will walk you through this whole process; right now I will just review the process.

First, you need to write the Java class that implements the tag. The next step is to add the tag to a Tag Library descriptor, which is an XML document that, among other things, allows the JSP container to map a tag name to the implementing class. You tell the JSP container about your new tags by adding an entry to your application's deployment descriptor.

At this point, you are ready to use your tag in a JSP page. In order to tell the JSP container that you will use custom tags in your JSP page, you use the `taglib` directive. This directive uniquely identifies the Tag Library, and associates a tag prefix that distinguishes the new custom actions in your JSP page. For example, the following directive introduces a new tag library and associates a prefix with it:

```
<%@ taglib uri="http://www.persistentjava.com/tags/cigjsptags" prefix="cig" />
```

The JSP container loads the appropriate Tag Library by mapping the `uri` attribute in the `taglib` directive to the classes that implement the tags using the information stored in the Tag Library descriptor (tld) file. The actual mapping between the uri and the tld file is what you place in your web application deployment descriptor, which is named web.xml. I don't know about you, but sometimes a good example is the best way to comprehend something complex.

> what Information do tld is used?

Hello World, Tag Style

In order to show you how easy it is to build, deploy, and use a custom tag, the following simple example builds a custom tag that generates the familiar "Hello World" web page. The first step is to write the Java class that provides the functionality for the custom tag. In Listing 16.1, I used HelloTag.java.

Because this tag will be empty—that is, it has no body content—we will extend the `TagSupport` class. The `TagSupport` class is a helper class that implements the `Tag` interface. The other alternative is to extend (create a new class from) the `BodyTagSupport` class, which implements the `BodyTag` interface. The `BodyTagSupport` class provides the extra functionality that is required to process a tag that is not empty.

The `Tag` interface defines how the JSP container interacts with the tag. First, the tag is created and any properties are initialized. When the JSP container encounters the tag in the JSP page, it calls the `doStartTag()` method, which allows you to associate specific functionality with the custom action start tag. This method returns one of three enumerated values:

- ♦ `EVAL_BODY_INCLUDE` to indicate that the JSP container should include any body content directly into the JSP page output
- ♦ `EVAL_BODY_BUFFERED` to indicate that any body content should be buffered for evaluation by the tag
- ♦ `SKIP_BODY` to indicate that any body content should not be evaluated

In this case, you are working with an empty tag, thus you return `SKIP_BODY`, and the JSP container will immediately call the `doEndTag()` method. In this method, you can finish any processing associated with the occurrence of the tag. This method returns one of two possible values:

◆ `EVAL_PGE` to tell the JSP container to continue processing the rest of the JSP page,

◆ `SKIP_PAGE` to tell the JSP container to stop processing the JSP page.

Because this tag generates the desired response all on its own, you don't need to do anything else after the tag has been processed, so you return `SKIP_PAGE`. The last method that you can implement is the `release()` method, which allows a tag class to clean up any resources that were acquired, like the `destroy()` method of a Servlet. You can just use the default implementation in the TagSupport class, because you didn't acquire any resources with this tag.

Because this tag class is in the com.persistentjava.tags package, the class file needs to be placed in the WEB-INF\classes\com\persistentjava\tags subdirectory of the web application. In order to keep things straight, I suggest you create a new context, called tags, to hold our custom tag JSP pages. Here's the listing:

Listing 16.1 HelloTag.java

```java
package com.persistentjava.tags;

import javax.servlet.jsp.tagext.TagSupport ;
import javax.servlet.jsp.* ;
import javax.servlet.ServletRequest ;
import java.io.* ;

public class HelloWorldTag extends TagSupport {

  public int doStartTag() throws JspException {
    try{
      pageContext.getOut().print("<html>");
      pageContext.getOut().print("<head>");
      pageContext.getOut().print("<title>Hello World, Tag Style</title>");
      pageContext.getOut().print("</head>");
      pageContext.getOut().print("<body>");
      pageContext.getOut().print("<h1>Hello World!</h1>");
      pageContext.getOut().print("<hr/>");
      pageContext.getOut().print("</body>");
      pageContext.getOut().print("</html>");
    }catch(IOException iox){
      throw new JspException(iox.getMessage()) ;
    }
    return SKIP_BODY ;
  }

  public int doEndTag() throws JspException {
```

```
        return SKIP_PAGE ;
    }
}
```

Now that you have written the tag, you need to create the tld file. Right now, our library only has one tag, but we can always add more later. The tdl file can have any name you want, but the extension is .tld to indicate that it is a Tag Library descriptor. This file should be saved in the WEB-INF directory of the tags context.

This tld file has a few important items. First, the root attribute of this XML document is taglib, which has a fixed XML namespace. After the root element, you have several elements that describe the Tag Library. The rest of the XML document consists of the tag element that defines your new tag. The important item in the tag element is the name element, which is what you will use in your JSP page, and the tag-class element, which indicates the fully qualified class name of the implementation class. Listing 16.2 shows the complete tld file.

Listing 16.2   CIGTag.tld

```
<?xml version="1.0" encoding="UTF-8" ?>
<!DOCTYPE taglib
PUBLIC "-//Sun Microsystems, Inc.//DTD JSP Tag Library 1.2//EN"
"http://java.sun.com/dtd/web-jsptaglibrary_1_2.dtd">

<taglib xmlns="http://java.sun.com/JSP/TagLibraryDescriptor">
    <tlib-version>1.2</tlib-version>
    <jsp-version>1.2</jsp-version>
    <short-name>CIGTags</short-name>
    <uri>/tags</uri>
    <description>CIG JSP Book Tag Examples</description>

    <tag>
        <name>hi</name>
        <tag-class>com.persistentjava.tags.HelloWorldTag</tag-class>
        <body-content>empty</body-content>
        <description>HelloWorld, Tag Style</description>
    </tag>

</taglib>
```

The next step is to modify the deployment descriptor, web.xml, to map the Tag Library uri to the appropriate Tag Library file (see Listing 16.3). In this case, you map cig-tag to your new tld file, CIGTag.tld. The web.xml file resides, as always, in the WEB-INF subdirectory of our tags context. Listing 16.3 shows the deployment descriptor.

Listing 16.3 web.xml

```xml
<?xml version="1.0" encoding="ISO-8859-1"?>

<!DOCTYPE web-app
    PUBLIC "-//Sun Microsystems, Inc.//DTD Web Application 2.3//EN"
    "http://java.sun.com/dtd/web-app_2_3.dtd">

<web-app>

  <taglib>
    <taglib-uri>cig-tag</taglib-uri>
    <taglib-location>/WEB-INF/CIGTag.tld</taglib-location>
  </taglib>
</web-app>
```

After all of this, you can now write your JSP page that will use your new tag. Because the "hi" tag generates the complete HTML file, the JSP page is very simple. First you have the page directive to indicate the content type of the output. Next comes the taglib directive, which defines a prefix for the tags we will use in the CigTag Tag Library. After that, you just use your tag, and you are done, as shown in Listing 16.4.

Listing 16.4 hellotag.jsp

```jsp
<%@page contentType="text/html"%>

<%@ taglib uri="cig-tag" prefix="cig" %>
<cig:hi/>
```

The JSP page itself should be saved in the tags directory. But before you can test it out, you need to restart the web server. This is necessary, because the server needs to reload the deployment descriptor and load the new Java classes. After the server has been restarted, open a browser to localhost:8080/tags/hellotag.jsp. If you see the screen shown in Figure 16.1, you will have used your very first custom tag.

Figure 16.1

The result of viewing hellotag.jsp.

In case you are overwhelmed with all of the files and directories you've been using in building this example, Figure 16.2 shows the directory structure in the tags context. The

JSP page goes in the tags directory; the web.xml and the CIGTag.tld files go in the WEB-INF directory; and the HelloTag.class file goes in the WEB-INF\classes\com\ persistentjava\tags directory.

Figure 16.2

This figure shows the directory structure for the tags context, showing the full package hierarchy for the HelloWorldTag *class, and the WEB-INF directory that holds the deployment descriptor, web.xml, as well as the HelloTag.tld Tag Library descriptor.*

Building Full-Bodied Tags

The HelloTag example is useful, primarily because it demonstrates all of the steps and files that are required to make a custom tag work. But when it comes to functionality, it isn't exactly rocket science. In this section, you will build a custom tag that uses an attribute and is nonempty. To simplify deployment, you will place this new tag in your existing CIGTag Tag Library descriptor file. Listing 16.5 is the new code you'll be using.

Listing 16.5   TagTwo.java

```
package com.persistentjava.tags;

import java.io.* ;
import java.util.* ;

import javax.servlet.jsp.tagext.* ;
import javax.servlet.jsp.* ;
import javax.servlet.ServletRequest ;

public class TagTwo extends BodyTagSupport {

  private String listType ;

  private final static String cAttributeErrorMsg
  = "Invalid List Type Attribute, must be either ordered or unordered" ;

  private final static String cDelimiter = "," ;

  public void setListType(String type) {
    listType = type ;
  }
```

continues

Listing 16.5   TagTwo.java   (continued)

```java
   public int doStartTag() throws JspException {

     if((!listType.equals("ordered"))
     && (!listType.equals("unordered")))
       throw new JspException(cAttributeErrorMsg) ;

     return(EVAL_BODY_BUFFERED) ;
   }

   public int doAfterBody() throws JspException {
     try{
       String content = bodyContent.getString() ;
       bodyContent.clear() ;

       StringBuffer list = new StringBuffer() ;

       if(listType.equals("ordered")){
         list.append("<ol>\n") ;
       }else{
         list.append("<ul>\n") ;
       }

       StringTokenizer bodyToken = new StringTokenizer(content, cDelimiter,
false) ;

       while(bodyToken.hasMoreTokens())
         list.append("  <li>" + (String)bodyToken.nextToken() + "</li>\n") ;

       if(listType.equals("ordered")){
         list.append("</ol>\n") ;
       }else{
         list.append("</ul>\n") ;
       }

       bodyContent.print(list.toString());

       bodyContent.writeOut(getPreviousOut()) ;
     }catch(IOException iox){
       throw new JspException(iox.getMessage()) ;
     }
     return(SKIP_BODY) ;
   }

   public int doEndTag() throws JspException {
     return EVAL_PAGE ;
   }
}
```

Let's look at this listing a little at a time. First, because this custom tag uses its body content, you need to extend the `BodyTagSupport` class:

```
public class TagTwo extends BodyTagSupport {
```

To support an attribute, you need to have a JavaBean-type attribute and appropriate setter method:

```
public void setListType(String type) {
    listType = type ;
}
```

In this case, you have a `listType` attribute, which is used to specify if your tag should generate an ordered HTML list or an unordered HTML element.

You also have two constants for your class: an error message to report if the attribute has an illegal value and the character used to separate items in the body of your tag:

```
private final static String cAttributeErrorMsg
= "Invalid List Type Attribute, must be either ordered or unordered" ;

private final static String cDelimiter = "," ;
```

Your `doStartTag()` method just checks that the attribute has a legal value, and returns `EVAL_BODY_BUFFERED`, so that your tag class will have access to the body content:

```
public int doStartTag() throws JspException {

    if((!listType.equals("ordered"))
    && (!listType.equals("unordered")))
        throw new JspException(cAttributeErrorMsg) ;

    return(EVAL_BODY_BUFFERED) ;
}
```

You now use a new method, `doAfterBody()`, which allows processing to occur after the JSP container has processed the body of this tag. This method does most of the work, as it obtains a string value initialized to the body content of your tag:

```
String content = bodyContent.getString() ;
bodyContent.clear() ;
```

The appropriate start list tag is displayed, depending on whether the `listType` attribute indicates ordered or unordered HTML list:

```
StringBuffer list = new StringBuffer() ;

if(listType.equals("ordered")){
    list.append("<ol>\n") ;
```

```
}else{
  list.append("<ul>\n") ;
}
```

The method then tokenizes this string based on your constant delimiter character and steps through the generated tokens, creating a new HTML list item element for each token:

```
StringTokenizer bodyToken = new StringTokenizer(content, cDelimiter,
false) ;

while(bodyToken.hasMoreTokens())
  list.append("  <li>" + (String)bodyToken.nextToken() + "</li>\n") ;
```

After the body content has been completely tokenized, the method generates the end tag of your HTML list:

```
if(listType.equals("ordered")){
  list.append("</ol>\n") ;
}else{
  list.append("</ul>\n") ;
}
```

Then, the method writes out the generated HTML to the JSP page's `JspWriter` object:

```
bodyContent.print(list.toString());

bodyContent.writeOut(getPreviousOut()) ;
```

The method returns `SKIP_BODY`, because you only need to pass through the body content once:

```
return(SKIP_BODY) ;
```

The `doEndTag()` method doesn't need to do anything, but because the JSP page might have other useful content, it returns `EVAL_PAGE`:

```
public int doEndTag() throws JspException {
  return EVAL_PAGE ;
}
```

Besides `release()`, one additional method that you didn't implement is `doInitBody()`. This method enables you to perform processing after the start tag has been processed, but before the body content has been processed.

The next step is to modify your tld file to include the new tag. First name the new tag (for example, list), and associate the TagTwo implementation with the new name. Because the new tag takes an attribute, the tag element is slightly different, as it needs an attribute element. First, you name the attribute, and then you indicate that the attribute is required, and that a JSP expression cannot be used to initialize the attribute.

> **Hot Java**
>
> Be careful when deploying Tag Libraries, or writing them yourself. The Document Type Declaration (DTD) for the tld file changed between JSP version 1.1 and JSP version 1.2. If you aren't careful with your DTD declaration, the JSP container will report a parsing error when processing your tld file. This can be problematic if you are using an integrated development environment (IDE) to develop your own tags.

Listing 16.6   CIGTag.tld

```xml
<?xml version="1.0" encoding="UTF-8" ?>
<!DOCTYPE taglib
PUBLIC "-//Sun Microsystems, Inc.//DTD JSP Tag Library 1.2//EN"
"http://java.sun.com/dtd/web-jsptaglibrary_1_2.dtd">

<taglib xmlns="http://java.sun.com/JSP/TagLibraryDescriptor">
    <tlib-version>1.2</tlib-version>
    <jsp-version>1.2</jsp-version>
    <short-name>CIGTags</short-name>
    <uri>/tags</uri>
    <description>CIG JSP Book Tag Examples</description>

    <tag>
        <name>hi</name>
        <tag-class>com.persistentjava.tags.HelloWorldTag</tag-class>
        <body-content>empty</body-content>
        <description>HelloWorld, Tag Style</description>
    </tag>

    <tag>
        <name>list</name>
        <tag-class>com.persistentjava.tags.TagTwo</tag-class>
        <body-content>tagdependent</body-content>
        <description>Make A List</description>
        <attribute>
            <name>listType</name>
            <required>true</required>
            <rtexprvalue>false</rtexprvalue>
        </attribute>
    </tag>

</taglib>
```

Now you can write your JSP page, which is shown in Listing 16.7. First, you have your page and `taglib` directives, which are the same as before because you are loading the same Tag Library. You have the HTML elements that set up and finish your page wrapping your list custom tag. In this case, you specify an unordered list, and the body of your list tag has five different fruits, separated by commas, which was your item delimiter. If you restart the server, and browse to localhost:8080/tags/tagtwo.jsp, you should see Figure 16.3.

Listing 16.7 tagtwo.jsp

```
<%@ page contentType="text/html"%>
<%@ taglib uri="cig-tag" prefix="cig" %>

<html>
<head><title>Fruitstand JSP Page</title></head>
<body>

<h1> Robert's Fruit Stand</h1>
<hr/>

<cig:list listType="unordered">
Apples,Oranges,Bananas,
Pineapples,
Coconuts
</cig:list>

</body>
</html>
```

This concludes your tag tutorial. The next section introduces third-party Tag Libraries, which you can download and use directly.

Figure 16.3

This Fruit Stand website is generated by the tagtwo.jsp page. Notice how your tag evaluated the attribute and the body content of the custom action.

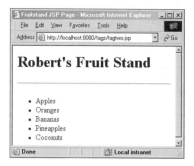

Utilizing Third-Party Tag Libraries

Since the tag extension has been part of the JSP specification for quite a while now, numerous developers and vendors have had sufficient time to build custom Tag Libraries that you can utilize to simplify your JSP development. A repository of open source Tag Libraries is maintained by the Apache Software Foundation's Jakarta project, under the name taglib.

CAUTION

Hot Java

Too much of anything, no matter how good, can become problematic—and Tag Libraries are no exception. In fact, some developers have become outspoken on what the potential for fragmentation within the JSP community as developers create new custom Tag Libraries. By using custom Tag Libraries, a developer is essentially using a new language, which may not be portable.

In order to minimize this effect, a standard Tag Library is being developed as part of the Java Community Process, as JSR 52. Eventually, this standard Tag Library will become part of the JSP specification. In any event, be cautious when adopting new Tag Libraries, you don't want to lose the portability of JSP web applications.

From the Jakarta taglib home page (jakarta.apache.org/taglibs/index.html) you can download a wide range of Tag Libraries that provide support for everything from database access to XML processing. In this section, you download the current version of the standard Tag Library, which eventually will become part of the JSP specification.

To get the standard Tag Library, you need to select "standard" from the left-hand taglib listing on the Jakarta taglib home page. This will take you to the home page for the Jakarta standard Tag Library (jakarta.apache.org/taglibs/doc/standard-doc/intro.html). You should download the latest binary release, and unzip it into a temporary directory.

To use the standard JSP Tag Library, you will want to place the standard-examples.war file in your Tomcat webapps directory. Restart your server, and browse to localhost:8080/standard-examples/—you should see the welcome screen, shown in Figure 16.4, for the Jakarta standard taglib. From here you can try out different tags that are included in the standard Tag Library.

Figure 16.4

The Welcome page for the Jakarta standard Tag Library. From here, you can test different tags that are part of the standard taglib, including XML, internationalization, and programming logic tags.

When you extract the standard-examples.war file from the archive into the webapps directory, be sure you do not use the folder hierarchy specified in the archive. Otherwise, the war file will not be in the webapps folder, but will instead be buried in the jakarta-taglib folder.

If you are worried that we are now done with custom tags, don't be. You will use custom actions later in the book for sending mail, processing XML, and accessing a database.

The Least You Need to Know

- Custom tags simplify JSP development by encapsulating Java code inside a valid XML element.
- Custom tags can be empty, they can have attributes, they can be nonempty, or they can have attributes and be nonempty.
- A Tag Library descriptor is an XML document that details the custom tags that are contained in the library. This file, among other things, maps a tag name to an implementing class.
- A wide range of Tag Libraries are available from the Apache Software Foundation's Jakarta project, including the standard JSP Tag Library.

Part 5

Entering the Real World

This part shows you how to make your JSP applications work in the real world. Learn how to make your application secure and how to talk to people around the globe in their own lingo. You also get a glimpse of how to work with XML.

Chapter 17

Locking It Down

In This Chapter

- ◆ Securing pages
- ◆ Implementing Servlet authentication mechanisms
- ◆ Introducing HTTP over SSL
- ◆ Auditing applications

Mention security to software developers, and most of the time they will throw up their hands, shake their heads, or respond with a blank stare. Let's face it: Security is a difficult concept to handle, and even harder to adequately implement. After all, the only secure computer is one that isn't running!

On the other hand, security is becoming increasingly important. With the pervasiveness of the Internet and the importance of online commerce, rare is the application that can safely ignore security. Fortunately, the Servlet specification defines basic security procedures, which when followed properly, can help increase your level of security. The specification is also flexible enough that you can add custom security procedures to complement or even replace the default mechanisms available to you from the Servlet container. In this chapter, you will see how to implement various types of security for your web applications.

Securing Pages

If you think about the complete process of interacting with a web application, security concerns can arise in several different areas, which are enumerated within the Servlet specification.

- ◆ **Authentication.** The communicating parties need to prove to each other that they are who they say they are. This is generally done using a username/password combination.

- ◆ **Access control.** A server must allow a developer to restrict access to specific resources, which can vary depending on the identity of the user.

- ◆ **Data integrity.** The Internet is a wild jungle, where data can be stolen or modified while in transit. An application can take steps to prevent this through encryption and the use of public/private key combinations.

- ◆ **Confidentiality.** A web application must guarantee that data is made available only to authorized users.

Two different security techniques have evolved to handle these requirements: declarative security and programmatic security. When using declarative security, the actual security structure exists separately from the web application. On the other hand, programmatic security is contained entirely within the application. Of these two, declarative security is the easiest to use, while programmatic security is generally the most secure. (Funny how the universe always forces us to make such choices, eh?) In this chapter, I will focus solely on declarative security, as provided by the Tomcat server.

Declaring Roles

The Servlet specification requires that a Servlet container support declarative security. In the specification, the mechanism to provide this support relies on the deployment descriptor for a web application to define what resources should be protected, and what type of authentication mechanism should be used to restrict access to those resources.

The first step in the process is to define roles for users of a web application. For example, if you are writing an e-commerce application, you might have a role for customers, a role for suppliers, and a role for administrators. When a user attempts to access a resource, the server will first require them to authenticate themselves. The server can use this information to assign them to a specific role.

The assignment process is handled by defining principals. This is just a fancy name for users—either individuals or groups of individuals—who belong to specific roles. For example, you might want to define that Jane is a principal who belongs to the administrator role, while Bill is a member of the supplier role. With Tomcat, you define principals in the tomcat_users.xml file, which is located in the conf subdirectory of your Tomcat installation. For the examples in this chapter, you need to add two principals to this file, as shown in Listing 17.1. To do this, load the existing tomcat_users.xml file into Notepad. Then, add the lines shown in bold in Listing 17.1. to the file and save the file.

Listing 17.1   tomcat_users.xml

```
<!--
   NOTE:  By default, no user is included in the "manager" role required
   to operate the "/manager" web application.  If you wish to use this app,
   you must define such a user - the username and password are arbitrary.
-->
<tomcat-users>
   <user name="tomcat" password="tomcat" roles="tomcat" />
   <user name="role1"  password="tomcat" roles="role1"  />
   <user name="both"   password="tomcat" roles="tomcat,role1" />
   <user name="rjbrunner" password="buyb00k" roles="cigjsp" />
   <user name="java" password="sun" roles="jdbc" />
</tomcat-users>
```

An application defines what roles it utilizes in its deployment descriptor. To define these roles, you add the name of the role to the deployment descriptor. Following the example, if you want the three roles—customers, suppliers, and administrators—you need to add the following to the relevant deployment descriptor, which, if you recall, is in your web.xml file for the current context. (Don't do this yet, though.)

```
<security-constraint>
  <web-resource-collection>
    <web-resource-name>CIGJSP Online Shopping</web-resource-name>
    <url-pattern>/store.jsp</url-pattern>
  </web-resource-collection>

  <auth-constraint>
    <role-name>customer</role-name>
    <role-name>supplier</role-name>
    <role-name>administrator</role-name>
  </auth-constraint>
</security-constraint>
```

This defines the three roles that are relevant to the collection of web resources that are listed in the same security constraint element. Obviously, for this to actually work, you will need to define the principals (and their passwords) who belong to these roles. The only other step is to define the type of authentication that the Servlet container should use. The Servlet specification defines four different authentication schemes, which are separately addressed in the following four sections:

- ◆ HTTP Basic authentication
- ◆ HTTP Digest authentication
- ◆ Form-based authentication
- ◆ HTTPS Client authentication

To keep the discussion straight, I created a new context for these four mechanisms, named basic, digest, form, and security, respectively. If you've forgotten how to create a context, I'll give you a quick refresher at the appropriate time.

The Basic Authentication Scheme

HTTP Basic authentication is defined in the HTTP version 1.0 specification, and is based on a username/password combination. When a client requests a resource that is protected using Basic authentication, the server passes a *realm*, which is a server-defined string that provides information to the user about the need for security back to the user. The web browser opens a new window that accepts a username and password from the user, and transmits this information back to the server. This information is transmitted in something called base64 encoding, which is not secure.

I promised you a refresher on creating a context. So here it is. Perform the following steps to create the "basic" context for the next example:

1. Open the Apache Tomcat configuration file, which is called server.xml and is located in the conf directory of your Tomcat installation directory.

2. Add the following entry to the server.xml file (add it right after the root context):

```
<Context
  path="/basic"
  docBase="basic"
  debug="0"
  reloadable="true"/>
```

3. Save the file.

4. Create the basic directory inside the webapps directory. For example, you might end up with this path: C:\jakarta-tomcat-4.0.1\webapps\basic.

5. Create a folder inside your basic folder and name this new folder WEB-INF.

That's it! Now, you're ready to move forward with the example. Listing 17.2 is the deployment descriptor for the basic-context example. This descriptor defines one role, jdbc, which is required for the secure-page.jsp resource. The final component indicates that this web application uses Basic authentication. Type web.xml, as shown in the listing, and then save it to the WEB-INF folder of the basic context.

Listing 17.2   web.xml

```xml
<?xml version="1.0" encoding="ISO-8859-1"?>
<!DOCTYPE web-app
  PUBLIC "-//Sun Microsystems, Inc.//DTD Web Application 2.2//EN"
  "http://java.sun.com/j2ee/dtds/web-app_2.2.dtd">
<web-app>
  <security-constraint>
    <web-resource-collection>
      <web-resource-name>Basic Security Page</web-resource-name>
      <url-pattern>/secure-page.jsp</url-pattern>
    </web-resource-collection>

    <auth-constraint>
      <role-name>jdbc</role-name>
    </auth-constraint>
  </security-constraint>

  <login-config>
    <auth-method>BASIC</auth-method>

    <realm-name>CIGJSP Basic authentication</realm-name>
  </login-config>
</web-app>
```

To demonstrate Basic authentication, you need two JSP pages. The first one is a welcome page, which is available to anyone. This would correspond to the home page for your bank, credit card, or online trading corporation. These pages always have a link, which allows you to "officially" log in to the site.

Listing 17.3 shows a simple demonstration of this concept. Type the listing, and then save it to the basic folder under the name Welcome.jsp. (For example, the complete path might end up being C:\jakarta-tomcat-4.0.1\webapps\basic\Welcome.jsp.) Before viewing this page, you will need to cycle Tomcat (that is, shut it down and restart it), so that it picks up the new deployment descriptor for the basic context. Once this is done, browse to localhost:8080/basic/Welcome.jsp, where you will see the welcome page in action, as shown in Figure 17.1.

Listing 17.3   Welcome.jsp

```jsp
<%@ page
  contentType="text/html"
%>

<html>
<head><title>Welcome to CIGJSP</title></head>
```

continues

Listing 17.3 Welcome.jsp (continued)

```
<body>
<h1>Greetings!</h1>
<hr/>
<h4> This page provides welcome information to the Site visitors. </h4>
<h4> Only unsecured data is provided here. </h4>
<p/>

<form method="post" action="secure-page.jsp"/>
  <h4>To access secure information, you must
  <input type="submit" value="Login" />
  first</h4>
</form>
<hr/>

</body>
</html>
```

Figure 17.1

The Welcome JSP page for the Basic authentication example.

The next step is to actually log in, which you can do by clicking the login button. This can also be implemented using a text hyperlink, or a clickable image, as shown in Chapter 12, "Controlling the Client." At this point, your browser will fire off a request for the secure-page.jsp resource, as shown in the following HTTP request:

```
POST /basic/secure-page.jsp HTTP/1.1
Referer: http://localhost:8080/basic/Welcome.jsp
Content-Type: application/x-www-form-urlencoded
```

The server receives the request, and in obeisance with the deployment descriptor, responds to the client that an unauthorized request was made. In addition to this, however, the server also indicates that the browser can allow the client to authenticate itself using Basic authentication, followed by the realm, as shown in the following HTTP response:

```
HTTP/1.1 401 Unauthorized
Content-Type: text/html
```

```
Date: Sat, 15 Dec 2001 17:08:19 GMT
WWW-Authenticate: Basic realm="CIGJSP Basic authentication"
Transfer-Encoding: chunked
Server: Apache Tomcat/4.0.1 (HTTP/1.1 Connector)
```

When the browser receives this response it should provide a login window that informs users that they are trying to access a secured resource named by the appropriate realm, and allow them to provide a username and password, as shown in Figure 17.2.

Figure 17.2

Here is the window displayed by Internet Explorer to authenticate the user. Notice the realm information that is displayed.

Before you try to log in, though, you need to add the page to display if you enter the correct username and password. Listing 17.4 shows this page. Type it and save it to your basic directory under the name secure-page.jsp.

If you use the right username and password, which are "java" and "sun" respectively, you will see the secure-page JSP page, as seen in Figure 17.3. This JSP page accesses the available security information, informing the client of the relevant values. You may notice a shorthand `<%= ((request.isSecure()) ? "YES" : "NO" ) %>`. What this does is the same as if we had coded an IF-THEN-ELSE statement. The ? is read as THEN and the : is the ELSE. So if the `request.isSecure() == true`, then the value is YES; otherwise, the value is NO.

Listing 17.4   secure-page.jsp

```
<%@ page
  contentType="text/html"
%>

<html>
<head><title>Security Check JSP Page</title></head>
<body>
<h2> Security Information: </h2>
<hr/>
<table border="2" width="100%">
  <tr>
    <th>Security Information</th>
    <th>Value</th>
  </tr>
```

continues

Listing 17.4 secure-page.jsp (continued)

```
    <tr>
      <td> Authentication Type </td>
      <td> <%= request.getAuthType() %> </td>
    </tr>
    <tr>
      <td> Secure Connection </td>
      <td> <b> <%= ((request.isSecure()) ? "YES" : "NO" ) %> </b> </td>
    </tr>
      <tr>
      <td> Principal  </td>
      <td> <%= request.getUserPrincipal().getName() %> </td>
    </tr>
    <tr>
      <td> In JDBC role </td>
      <td> <b> <%= ((request.isUserInRole("jdbc")) ? "YES" : "NO" ) %> </b>
</td>
    </tr>
    <tr>
      <td> Remote User </td>
      <td> <%= request.getRemoteUser() %> </td>
    </tr>
    <tr>
      <td> Remote Host </td>
      <td> <%= request.getServerName() %> </td>
    </tr>
    <tr>
      <td> Remote Address </td>
      <td> <%= request.getRemoteAddr() %> </td>
    </tr>
  </table>
  </body>
  </html>
```

Figure 17.3

The secure-page.jsp resource, after successfully logging in as the user "java" with password "sun", demonstrating the security information available to a resource form—the Servlet container.

If you remember, earlier I indicated that Basic authentication is insecure. To demonstrate this, the following snippet shows the actual HTTP request that was made when I used the proper username and password:

```
POST /basic/secure-page.jsp HTTP/1.1
Referer: http://localhost:8080/basic/Welcome.jsp
Content-Type: application/x-www-form-urlencoded
User-Agent: Mozilla/4.0 (compatible; MSIE 6.0; Windows NT 5.0; Q312461)
Connection: Keep-Alive
Cache-Control: no-cacheAuthorization: Basic amF2YTpzdW4=
Content-Length: 0
```

You may not notice it, but right there in the Authorization header is the username and password, albeit encoded in base64 format. Any base64 decoder can easily decode this encoding, and since these decoders are freely available on the Internet, this is not a good solution for securing sensitive resources.

The Digest Authentication Scheme

A better solution is to use Digest authentication, which encrypts the password before transmitting it across the Internet. First, you'll need to create your digest context. Follow the same procedure you used to create the basic context, except make the appropriate changes, which involves replacing all occurrences of "basic" in the steps with "digest." You can reuse most of the infrastructure from the basic context, so first you will want to copy those files over to the digest context. The only significant change comes in the deployment descriptor, which clearly demonstrates how declarative security sits outside the application.

The necessary changes are to replace Basic authentication with Digest authentication. There is no required second step! I did change the realm-name and the web-resource-name elements, however, to reflect that I am using Digest authentication and not Basic authentication in this example. With these changes, we have our new deployment descriptor, shown in Listing 17.5. Type this listing and save it to the WEB-INF folder of your digest context. Then, cycle the Tomcat server, browse to localhost:8080/digest/ Welcome.jsp, and you will see the welcome screen, as shown in Figure 17.4.

Listing 17.5　web.xml

```
<?xml version="1.0" encoding="ISO-8859-1"?>
<!DOCTYPE web-app
  PUBLIC "-//Sun Microsystems, Inc.//DTD Web Application 2.2//EN"
  "http://java.sun.com/j2ee/dtds/web-app_2.2.dtd"
>

<web-app>
```

continues

Listing 17.5 web.xml (continued)

```xml
<security-constraint>
  <web-resource-collection>
    <web-resource-name>DIGEST Security Page</web-resource-name>
    <url-pattern>/secure-page.jsp</url-pattern>
  </web-resource-collection>
  <auth-constraint>
    <role-name>jdbc</role-name>
  </auth-constraint>
</security-constraint>

<login-config>
  <auth-method>DIGEST</auth-method>
  <realm-name>CIGJSP Digest Authentication</realm-name>
</login-config>

</web-app>
```

Figure 17.4

This figure shows the Digest authentication Welcome page. The only difference is the URL in the browser window, demonstrating how declarative security doesn't impact the actual application.

When the client requests the secured resource, the server responds in a similar manner, but this time, the server indicates that Digest authentication is required, as shown in the following HTTP response:

```
HTTP/1.1 401 Unauthorized
Content-Type: text/html
Date: Sat, 15 Dec 2001 17:27:41 GMT
WWW-Authenticate: Digest realm="CIGJSP Digest Authentication", qop="auth",
nonce="c70fa24013e6d0d37aaf43a769d23647",
opaque="4ab054096cdbfa03f73fdd08d176b9d2"
Transfer-Encoding: chunked
Server: Apache Tomcat/4.0.1 (HTTP/1.1 Connector)
```

The browser receives this response and displays a login window, shown in Figure 17.5, that is nearly identical to the Basic authentication example. The only clear difference is that the new realm is shown.

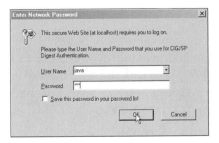

Figure 17.5

This figure shows the window displayed by Internet Explorer to authenticate the user.

If you enter the correct username and password, which are the same as the previous example, the server will accept the request and respond with the secured resource, as shown in Figure 17.6. With Digest authentication, however, the password is not visible, as you can see in the following HTTP request.

```
POST /digest/secure-page.jsp HTTP/1.1
Referer: http://localhost:8080/digest/Welcome.jsp
Content-Type: application/x-www-form-urlencoded
User-Agent: Mozilla/4.0 (compatible; MSIE 6.0; Windows NT 5.0; Q312461)
Connection: Keep-Alive
Cache-Control: no-cache
Authorization: Digest username="java", realm="CIGJSP Digest Authentication",
qop="auth", algorithm="MD5", uri="/digest/secure-page.jsp",
nonce="c70fa24013e6d0d37aaf43a769d23647", nc=00000001,
cnonce="7b57682e7b0a447b6177ab80a2051b0a",
opaque="4ab054096cdbfa03f73fdd08d176b9d2",
response="2680d43195fd9f431a314d53d0d2924e"
Content-Length: 0
```

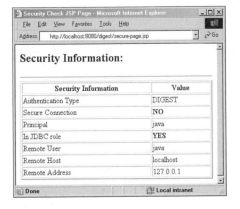

Figure 17.6

The server responds with a secured resource to the user's authentication response.

As you can clearly see, the Authorization HTTP Header is considerably more complex than the Basic authorization example. While a packet-sniffing hacker could steal this header, he would be hard-pressed to crack the encryption and will likely not try, opting for easier targets. If so, why doesn't everyone just use Digest instead of Basic authentication? Because Digest authentication is not as widely supported among the available browsers, it isn't always an option.

What about handling incorrect or invalid information? If you enter an incorrect username/password combination, the server responds with the same original request. The only way to get out of the loop is to click Cancel, at which point, you are presented with an error page, which can easily be customized for your web application, as shown in Chapter 9, "Wrapping It Up!"

Figure 17.7

Here is the web page that is returned by the server when the user clicks Cancel on the login dialog. This page and the information contained on this page can be customized by the web application.

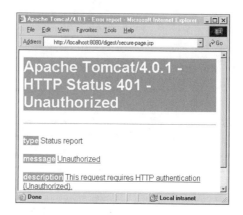

The Form-Based Authentication Scheme

The previous two authentication mechanisms were very simple to use, requiring no change to your application. As a developer, however, you have no control over how the user is prompted for the authenticating information; that is entirely the purvey of the web browser. If you want to control how the application looks, you need to use Form-based authentication.

To use Form-based authentication, however, you have to do a little more work. I suggest that you follow along with this example by creating a special context named form. First, you will want to copy the files from either the basic or digest context to this new one, as you will reuse them.

In order to control the look and feel, you need to write the login form yourself. You also need to write an error-handling page, which is only used to handle incorrect logins, not application errors. In order for the Servlet container to know about these two JSP pages, you need to explicitly name them in the deployment descriptor, as shown in Listing 17.6.

If you take a look at this web.xml file, you'll notice that it is very similar to the previous two examples. The only required modifications are the FORM authentication method and the inclusion of the login and error pages. I also changed the name of the web resource to indicate that this is a Form authentication. Type this listing and save it to the WEB-INF folder of your form context. Then, if you restart the Tomcat server and browse to local-host:8080/form/Welcome.jsp, as shown in Figure 17.8, you are ready to start.

Listing 17.6   web.xml

```xml
<?xml version="1.0" encoding="ISO-8859-1"?>
<!DOCTYPE web-app
PUBLIC "-//Sun Microsystems, Inc.//DTD Web Application 2.2//EN"
"http://java.sun.com/j2ee/dtds/web-app_2.2.dtd">
<web-app>
    <security-constraint>
        <web-resource-collection>
            <web-resource-name>FORM Security Page</web-resource-name>

            <url-pattern>/secure-page.jsp</url-pattern>
        </web-resource-collection>

        <auth-constraint>
            <role-name>cigjsp</role-name>
        </auth-constraint>
    </security-constraint>

    <login-config>
        <auth-method>FORM</auth-method>

        <form-login-config>
            <form-login-page>/login.jsp</form-login-page>

            <form-error-page>/error.jsp</form-error-page>
        </form-login-config>
    </login-config>

</web-app>
```

Figure 17.8

This figure shows the Welcome web page for the Form-based authentication demonstration. Notice the form context in the browser's location window.

Next step is to type Listing 17.7 and save it in your form directory under the name login.jsp. This will be your custom login page.

Listing 17.7 login.jsp

```
<%@ page
   contentType="text/html"
%>

<html>
<head><title>FORM Login JSP Page</title></head>
<body>
<h1>Please Login</h1>
<hr/>
<h2>Before proceeding, you need to be verified</h2>

<form method="post" action="j_security_check">
   <input type="text" name="j_username"/> Username <p/>
   <input type="password" name="j_password"/> Password <p/>
   <p/>
   <input type="submit" value="Login"/>
</form>
</body>
</html>
```

Finally, you need to type Listing 17.8 and save it to your form folder under the name error.jsp. This is the error page that the user will see if he types in an incorrect username or password.

Listing 17.8 error.jsp

```
<%@ page
   contentType="text/html"
%>

<html>
<head><title>FORM Login Error JSP Page</title></head>
<body>

<h1>Error: Invalid Login</h1>
<hr/>

The authorites have been notified, big brother is on his way.
<p/>
```

```
If you feel you just mistyped your password, feel free to
<a href='<%= response.encodeURL("login.jsp") %>'> login </a> again.

</body>
</html>
```

Now, if you click the Login button, you will be shown the login web page, not a separate login window. As Figure 17.9 demonstrates, this is a regular web page, and can be customized to suit the needs or desires of the application developer. This shows how the developer can customize the appearance of the login page. While I am not especially graphically oriented, you might be. Because this is a JSP-generated web page, you can do just about anything you might want to from here.

Figure 17.9

This figure shows the web page that is returned by the server when the user clicks Login on the Welcome JSP page.

When the server processes the client's request for the secured resource, it responds with a redirection to the login page. The login page is very simple, as shown in Listing 17.7. You might notice the funny names for the form action, and the username and password input controls. These are standard names that you have to use for Form-based authentication. These names enable the server to uniformly process the Form-based authentication.

The correct username and password are different for this example, because I changed the role-name that is used in the form context deployment descriptor. To successfully log in, you need to use "rjbrunner" for the username and "buyb00k" for the password. If you do this, you will be directed to the secure-page.jsp resource, shown in Figure 17.10, which shows you the security information related to your request.

Form-based authentication has the same security problem as Basic authentication, in that the password is transmitted in unencrypted form across the Internet. To make it more secure, you must use a more secure transport, like Secure Sockets Layer (SSL), which is discussed in the next section.

Figure 17.10

The web page that is returned by the server when the user successfully logs in using Form-based authentication.

On the other hand, if the data is invalid, you will be sent to the error.jsp page, which you created from Listing 17.8. As you can see in Figure 17.11, this page should inform the user of what went wrong and provide a means to go to the login page, without having to use the browser's Back button.

Notice how you don't directly place the link to the login JSP page in the HTML element, but instead encode it first. This ensures that all of the proper HTTP headers are sent along with the new request for the login page.

Figure 17.11

The web page that is returned by the server when the user does not enter the correct information into the login form.

Hot Java _____

All three of these authentication methods utilize HTTP sessions for maintaining the security clearances of clients. Generally, this also requires that the clients accept cookies, which are used to maintain the session. If you do not use SSL, these cookies are visible over the Internet, allowing someone to spoof someone else's security clearance. This is a strong argument for not only using SSL, but also for requiring all sessions to have a small timeout period, generally on the order of 10 minutes. This further complicates the task of spoofing someone else.

Securing Your Sockets

All of the previous methods provide the basic framework, but they rely on standard HTTP to communicate, which can be easily intercepted and processed. A more secure communication mechanism would be to first encrypt the important communiqués, like login information, before sending them out across the Internet.

Engineers at Netscape, early on in the development of web browsers, conceived this same idea. In order to implement it, they developed the Secure Socket Layer (SSL). This enabled HTTP communication over an encrypted channel, commonly known as HTTPS. Tomcat version 4.0 supports SSL, and setting it up is very simple.

The first step in the process is to generate a certificate that your server will send to the web browser, indicating who you are and that you want to utilize SSL for communication. Normally, you would purchase a certificate from a recognized certificate agency (CA). Two companies that provide this sort of service are Verisign and Thawte. Typically, these certificates cost several hundred dollars or more for an individual, and significantly more for a corporation. These companies are supposed to do a thorough background check to verify the requestor's identity, allowing the ordinary public to be confident when accepting "official" certificates.

However, I don't have an official certificate, and I doubt you do either, so you need to make your own. This task is extremely simple, because Java provides the tools you need, as part of the standard Java 2 version 1.4 development kit. The main tool is called keytool, and is installed in the bin directory of your JDK installation directory. In order to simplify things, you will create a keystore in the security context. Of course, first you have to create your security context. You should be an expert at this by now, so get to it, and then meet me at the next paragraph.

> **Fresh Brew**
>
> If you don't have JDK version 1.4 or higher, you can always download the necessary tools separately. You will need to get the Java Secure Sockets Extension (JSSE). It is available from Sun at java.sun.com/products/jsse/.

To do this, change directories to the security context, and issue the following command. (You may first have to set the PATH system variable to your Java installation's bin directory.)

```
>keytool -genkey -alias cigjsp -keyalg RSA -keystore WEB-INF/.keystore
Enter keystore password:  buyb00k
What is your first and last name?
  [Unknown]:  Robert Brunner
What is the name of your organizational unit?
  [Unknown]:  Alpha Books
```

```
What is the name of your organization?
  [Unknown]:  Pearson Publishing
What is the name of your City or Locality?
  [Unknown]:  Indianapolis
What is the name of your State or Province?
  [Unknown]:  IN
What is the two-letter country code for this unit?
  [Unknown]:  US
Is <CN=Robert Brunner, OU=Alpha Books, O=Pearson Publishing, L=Indianapolis,
ST=
IN, C=US> correct?
  [no]:  yes


Enter key password for <cigjsp>
        (RETURN if same as keystore password):
```

As you can see, you will be prompted for various items, including your name, corporation, and location. You can put whatever you want here; I merely show an example of what I entered. At the very end, you are prompted for a second password. In order for SSL to work with Tomcat, you should just hit enter, so both passwords are the same. Notice how I used the -keystore flag to the keytool command. This specified that the keystore should be stored in the WEB-INF directory with the filename .keystore.

The second step is to modify the Tomcat configuration to indicate that you want Tomcat to support SSL connections. The relevant file is the familiar server.xml and is located in the conf subdirectory of the Tomcat installation directory. As you've learned, this file controls the behavior of the Tomcat server, including the port number the server listens to, as well as whether SSL is supported or not.

By default, the relevant XML elements are commented out. All you need to do is find the relevant section, remove the comments, and add two attributes that indicate the password you used and the location of the keystore file. In Listing 17.9, I show the relevant elements from my server.xml file. To make the changes, perform these steps:

1. Load the server.xml file into Notepad.
2. Find the comment <!-- Define an SSL HTTP/1.1 Connector on port 8443 --> in the file.
3. Remove the <!-- from the line following the comment you located in step 2.
4. Replace the entire connector statement with the one shown in Listing 17.8.
5. Remove the --> from the line following the </Connector> end tag.
6. Save the file changes.

Listing 17.8   server.xml

```
<Connector className="org.apache.catalina.connector.http.HttpConnector"
           port="8443" minProcessors="5" maxProcessors="75"
           enableLookups="true"
           acceptCount="10" debug="0" scheme="https" secure="true">
    <Factory className="org.apache.catalina.net.SSLServerSocketFactory"
           clientAuth="false"
           keystoreFile="webapps/security/WEB-INF/.keystore"
           keystorePass="buyb00k"
           protocol="TLS"/>
</Connector>
```

Once you make the changes to the server.xml file, you need to restart your Tomcat server. Then, you can start using HTTP over SSL (HTTPS). To demonstrate this, you should first browse to the Tomcat home page, localhost:8443/. From this URL, you will first notice that you are now using the HTTPS protocol, and second, you are now connecting to port 8443. If you see the Tomcat home page, everything is working fine.

If you see a Security Alert appear when trying to access Welcome.jsp, make sure you have correctly installed the JSSE version 1.0.2 or a later version. Once you have the JAR file downloaded, just put it in your $JAVA_HOME/jre/lib/ext directory.

The next step is to try out any of the three previous authentication mechanisms. For example, in Figure 17.12, I show the result of Form-based authentication using SSL. If you want to try this, browse to localhost:8443/basic/Welcome.jsp. When you click the Login button, you will be presented with a certificate notice, as shown in Figure 17.12.

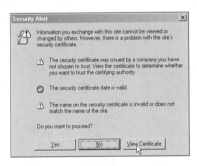

Figure 17.12

Here is the certificate notice that displays the certificate I just created using keytool. The Tomcat server is presenting it to the client for authorization.

If you click on View Certificate, you can see the details of the certificate holder, as shown in Figure 17.13. This information is, of course, what I just entered when creating the certificate using keytool. This demonstrates the difference between signed certificates and simple certificates like what you just created.

Hot Java

Now that you know how easy it is to create certificates, you will hopefully be more careful when you are asked to accept one from a website.

If you enter a URL like https://localhost:8443/basic/show-message.jsp instead of just plain http, you notice that the secure resource now indicates that you are using a secure connection. This is shown in the browser as a little locked icon to signal HTTPS is being used.

Figure 17.13

The information that Tomcat provided to the web browser regarding the particular certificate that was presented.

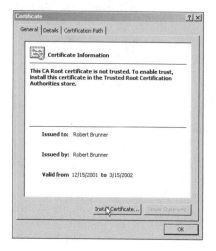

If you accept the certificate and successfully log in, you will see the new security information regarding your connection. You will now notice that you are using a secure connection, as shown in Figure 17.14.

Figure 17.14

The security information when connecting to the secure-page resource using Basic authentication over HTTPS.

Auditing Your Application

When trying to make your site secure, the obvious solution is to build big walls and reinforce the front door. Of course, no matter how careful you are, you are only as strong as your weakest link. As a result, many sites also employ auditing techniques, which keep track of who is trying to do what. As you saw in Chapter 6, "Getting a Free Lunch," a web browser sends a lot of information along with the client's request. You can record this information, along with other details, in order to improve your site, including not only security, but also performance as you can optimally cache heavily used information or resources.

Tomcat, as do most servers, automatically records basic information, like the time of every request and what was requested. You can supplement this data by adding your own information to the log files. The server.xml file that you modified in the previous section also defines the names and locations of log files used by Tomcat. The default location for the log files is the log subdirectory of your Tomcat installation. The log files also record information for a single day, and a new one is created for each day.

There are two log files that you may find useful. The first is the log file that records the standard information and has a base name of localhost_access_log, with a file extension that is the date the log was recorded. The second log file is called localhost_log, with a file extension of the date the log was recorded. This second log file contains any output that you write using the log() method of the application object. For example, you can dump any information you want regarding any client request into this log file, as shown in Listing 17.9.

Coffee Break

While auditing is very useful and can be a sound business practice, there are potential legal implications. Be sure to consult a proper legal authority if you start collecting data. Generally, you have nothing to worry about, but if you want to sell or trade this type of data, you can quickly run into trouble.

Listing 17.9   audit.jsp

```
<%@ page
   contentType="text/html"
%>


<%
   application.log("*********************") ;
   application.log("Locale:" + request.getLocale()) ;
   application.log("Remote Server:" + request.getRemoteHost()) ;
   application.log("Remote User:" + request.getRemoteUser()) ;
   application.log("Query String:" + request.getQueryString()) ;
   application.log("User Agent:" + request.getHeader("User-Agent")) ;
   application.log("Referer:" + request.getHeader("Referer")) ;
   application.log("*********************") ;
%>


<html>
<head><title>Audit JSP Page</title></head>
<body>
```

continues

Listing 17.9 audit.jsp (continued)

```
<h1>Your presence has been noted</h1>
</body>
</html>
```

When this page is requested, it records various audit information, and generates a simple message back to the client, as shown in Figure 17.15. More importantly, for this exercise, is the data that is logged. First, the following entry is logged into localhost_access_ log.2001-12-15:

```
127.0.0.1 - - [15/Dec/2001:10:31:57 -0800] "GET /security/audit.jsp HTTP/1.1"
200 129
```

In addition, the information you wrote is in the file "localhost_log.2001-12-15".

```
2001-12-15 10:31:57 ***********************
2001-12-15 10:31:57 Locale:en_US
2001-12-15 10:31:57 Remote Server:127.0.0.1
2001-12-15 10:31:57 Remote User:null
2001-12-15 10:31:57 Query String:null
2001-12-15 10:31:57 User Agent:Mozilla/4.0 (compatible; MSIE 6.0; Windows NT
5.0; Q312461)
2001-12-15 10:31:57 Referer:null
2001-12-15 10:31:57 ***********************
```

When using this technique, you can quickly eat up disk space, so you might look into other options, like rotating log files, or using a database for storing the information.

Figure 17.15

The auditing web page showing the client that you are watching them.

The Least You Need to Know

◆ Security is very important, especially on systems that are open to the Internet.

◆ Servlet containers support three different authentication mechanisms: Basic, Digest, and Form-based authentication.

◆ Servlet containers also support HTTP over SSL, also known as HTTPS. This communication protocol encrypts information before it is transmitted.

◆ Auditing can provide important information, especially if you are trying to improve performance or track down crackers who are trying to break into your system.

Chapter **18**

Go Global, Stay Local

In This Chapter

◆ Localizing resources

◆ Setting and detecting locales

◆ Bundling resources

When the web first started to grow and evolve, the majority of websites were all in English. As the number of Internet users has grown, however, websites have developed that speak to the new clients in their own language. This process is even more important for e-commerce sites, which often live or die based on any potential marketing edge—obviously, speaking a native tongue correctly is a huge potential benefit.

The process of making software applications available to people that speak different languages and have different customs is known as internationalization, or i18n. The first step in this process is identifying the components of a software application that are unique to a specific region, either because of language or cultural issues. This is known as localization, or l10n. (In case you're wondering why the shorthand is i18n and l10n, the answer is simple: There are 18 characters between the "i" and the "n" in internationalization. Likewise, there are 10 characters between the "l" and the "n" in localization.)

In this chapter, I will show you how to use Java's built-in localization and internationalization capabilities to make a JSP application "globally aware." First, I will describe locale-specific functionality, some of which may surprise you. After that, I will show you how to let your JSP application dynamically configure itself for users around the world.

What's Your Locale?

All of the information that is specific to a location is encapsulated in the `java.util.Locale` class. You specify a particular locale by using a language code together with a country code. These codes are an international standard, governed by the International Organization for Standardization (ISO). The ISO standard enables developers worldwide to write software that will work where and how it is intended. (For more information on the ISO go to www.iso.org.)

For example, to specify the United States locale, you would use en_US, where the en stands for English, and the US for the United States. Likewise, for the United Kingdom, you use en_UK. Some countries, however, have more than one language, and thus more than one locale. For example, Canada has both English- and French-speaking locations, thus they each have their own locale specifications, which are en_CA and fr_CA, respectively.

Coffee Break ————————————————————————————————

While some of the language and country codes seem easy to understand, some of them might seem strange, especially if you are not familiar with a particular language or country. If so, this is demonstrating why internationalization is important, and also difficult. Remember, people in the locales that seem odd to you probably feel the same way about your locale.

To simplify life, these standards are available online. The country code, which is handled in ISO standard 3166-1, is available at www.din.de/gremien/nas/nabd/iso3166ma/. Likewise, the language code, which is handled in ISO standard 639-1, is available at www.oasis-open.org/cover/iso639a.html.

The Locale class contains special constants that simplify the creation or indication of specific locales. For example, you can indicate the U.S. locale by using Locale.US. Likewise, you can use Locale.FRANCE instead of fr_FR, Locale.GERMANY instead of de_DE, and Locale.CHINA instead of zh_CN.

Finding Locales

Of course, none of this matters if your current platform doesn't support your desired locale. The JSP page in Listing 18.1 demonstrates how to check what locales are supported on the server that executes the JSP page. In order to keep the examples in this section organized, I suggest you create a special context called i18n in your Tomcat webapps directory.

Listing 18.1   locales.jsp

```
<%@ page
  contentType="text/html"
  import="java.util.*"
%>

<html>
<head><title>Server Locale JSP Page</title></head>
<body>

<h1> Available Server  Locales </h1>
<hr/>

<%
  Locale[] lc = Locale.getAvailableLocales() ;
%>

<ul>

<%
  for(int i = 0 ; i < lc.length ; i++) {
%>

  <li> <%= lc[i] %> </li>

<% } %>

</ul>

</body>
</html>
```

As you can see, this JSP page is very simple. All you need to do is call the getAvailable
Locales() method, and iterate through the resulting array of Locale objects. On my PC
running Windows 2000, with Java version 1.4beta3 installed, the list of available locales
is rather long, as shown in Figure 18.1. This list was generated by browsing to
localhost:8080/i18n/locales.jsp.

Numerical Formatting

When you first think about locales, you probably think primarily of handling language
issues, such as translation, and perhaps even topics like which direction the text flows, and
character encodings. While these are very important, they are not the only part of a locale.
Different countries have different formats for representing dates, currency, and even per-
centages.

Figure 18.1

This figure shows the list of available locales from the Tomcat server.

To simplify the handling of these issues, Java provides the DateFormat and the NumberFormat classes, in the java.util package. The NumberFormat class provides specific formatting capabilities for formatting numbers, currencies, and percents in different locales. The JSP page shown in Listing 18.2 demonstrates the differences in how three different locales—France, Germany, and the United States—differ when it comes to displaying dates, numbers, currency, and percents.

Listing 18.2   test-locales.jsp

```
<%@ page
  contentType="text/html"
  import="java.util.*"
%>

<%@ page import="java.text.DateFormat" %>
<%@ page import="java.text.NumberFormat"%>

<html>
<head><title>Test Locale JSP Page</title></head>
<body>

<h1> Locale Number Formatting </h1>
<hr/>

<%
  int cNumber = 1234567890 ;
  double cCurrency = 1234567.89 ;
  double cPercent = 0.1234 ;

  Locale[] lc = {Locale.FRANCE, Locale.GERMANY, Locale.US} ;
```

```
DateFormat[] df = new DateFormat[lc.length] ;

for(int i = 0 ; i < lc.length ; i++) {
    df[i] = DateFormat.getDateTimeInstance(DateFormat.FULL, DateFormat.FULL,
lc[i]) ;
%>


<%= lc[i].getDisplayName() %>

<ul>
  <li> <%= df[i].format(new Date()) %> </li>
  <li> <%= NumberFormat.getNumberInstance(lc[i]).format(cNumber) %> </li>
  <li> <%= NumberFormat.getCurrencyInstance(lc[i]).format(cCurrency) %> </li>
  <li> <%= NumberFormat.getPercentInstance(lc[i]).format(cPercent) %> </li>
</ul>

<% } %>

</body>
</html>
```

Again, the code itself is rather straightforward. First, you create the appropriate `Locale` objects. You can easily change this to different locales; just change the initialization of the `Locale` array. Next, define three constants that will be used to compare the different number-formatting techniques. Then create a `DateFormat` array and initialize it to the current date in all three locales. Finally, for each locale, the current date, the constant number, the constant currency, and the constant percentage are all formatted according to the rules of the particular locale and displayed appropriately, as shown in Figure 18.2.

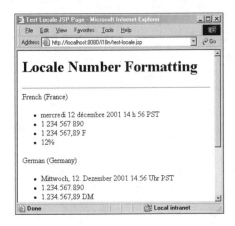

Figure 18.2

A demonstration of the number-formatting capabilities provided by Java.

Specifying Locales

So far, all I have showed you is how to find what locales a server can handle and how different locales format dates and numbers. Conceptually, however, you will have users, or customers, from different locales requesting the same resource. You might wonder how you can simulate this in order to test out your application, without the obvious choice of hiring testers from around the world.

Fortunately, this problem has already been solved, as the popular web browsers provide significant support for users in different locales. When the browser connects to a website, or in this example, a JSP page, as part of the request, it can specify a list of acceptable languages, in a preferred order. This list can be retrieved from the request object using the getLocales() method, as shown in Listing 18.3.

Listing 18.3 client-locales.jsp

```
<%@ page
  contentType="text/html"
  import="java.util.*"
%>

<html>
<head><title>Client Locale JSP Page</title></head>
<body>

<h1> Available Client Locales </h1>
<hr/>

<%
  Enumeration en = request.getLocales() ;
%>

<ul>

<%
  while(en.hasMoreElements()) {
%>

  <li> <%= ((Locale)en.nextElement()).getDisplayName() %> </li>

<% } %>

</ul>

</body>
</html>
```

Unless you have already played with your language settings in your browser, you probably only have one language listed, as I did (see Figure 18.3). Before you proceed, check your current locale settings by calling this JSP page, localhost:8080/i18n/client-locales.jsp.

Figure 18.3

The original (default) locale for Internet Explorer on my computer.

You can add, delete, and reorder the preferred languages for your browser, however, which allows you to test your website. Of course, making sure that the translation of your website is correct is an entirely different matter.

Hot Java

Translation is a tricky business, and if you're not careful, you can actually make matters worse. For the examples in this chapter, I used an online translation service at babelfish.altavista.com. This approach is generally sufficient for simple examples; if you want a correct translation for a complex website, you need to hire a good translator who is also familiar with the culture of the intended audience.

The rest of this section demonstrates how to customize the locale settings for the Internet Explorer web browser. First, you need to open the Internet Options window, which is accomplished by selecting the Tools menu, followed by Internet Options. The Internet Options window is shown in Figure 18.4.

This window provides you with the ability to customize the appearance and behavior of your web browser, so be careful what you do. For this example, all you need to do is modify the language settings, which can be done by clicking on the Languages button, which is one of four buttons at the bottom of the Internet Options window. This brings up the Language Preference window, shown in Figure 18.5.

Figure 18.4

This figure shows the Internet Options dialog, which enables you to change the languages or locales that IE will accept.

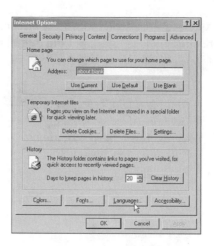

Figure 18.5

This figure shows the original list of selected languages for my Internet Explorer. Notice how this matches the list shown in Figure 18.3.

As you can clearly see, when I started, all I had was the U.S. locale. In order to add more locales, you need to click the Add button. This will bring up the Add Language window, as shown in Figure 18.6. From here, you can select as many new locales as you want, and more important, control their order.

Figure 18.6

Here is the list of available languages that Internet Explorer recognizes.

After you have selected several locales, click the OK button, which will take you back to the Select Languages window. Before you close the Language Preference window, be sure to move one of your new locales to the top of the list, using the Move Up or Move Down buttons. My list is shown in Figure 18.7, but yours is probably different. Feel free to experiment—this is the fun part.

Figure 18.7

This figure shows the new list of accepted languages that my Internet Explorer will recognize.

You should now click OK to close the Language Preference window, and also click OK to close the Internet Options window. If you reload the client-locales.jsp page, you should see all your new locales listed. For example, Figure 18.8 shows my new list of locales, which, if you compare it to Figure 18.7, is identical to the list I set in my web browser.

For testing purposes, this is a powerful trick. Be sure to change your settings back to their original order, however, as you may have unintended consequences when you are surfing the web later.

Figure 18.8

The updated list of available locales as presented by my Internet Explorer. Notice how it matches the list in Figure 18.7.

Bundling Resources

So far all you have seen is how to detect and change locales, as well as how to format items differently, depending on the selected locale. The next step is to bundle any locale-specific resources, so that you can more easily add support for new locales into your application. In Java, the ResourceBundle class, which is located in the `java.util` package, handles this for you.

To demonstrate how you can use `ResourceBundle` objects, the following simple web application uses two JSP pages—select-locale.jsp shown in Listing 18.4, and show-locale.jsp shown in Listing 18.5—to first select a locale, and then display a JSP page, whose contents change according to the selected locale.

First, the select locale JSP page is rather straightforward, and consists entirely of a FORM element that allows the user to select a locale from a list, as shown in Figure 18.9. When the user clicks the Show Locale button, the browser is sent to the show locale JSP page.

Listing 18.4   select-locale.jsp

```
<%@ page
   contentType="text/html"
   import="java.util.Locale"
%>

<html>
  <head>
    <title>Select Locale JSP Page</title>
  </head>
<body>

<h1> Select a Locale </h1>
<hr/>
<p/>

<form method="get" action="show-locale.jsp">
  <select name="locale">
    <option value="fr">France
    <option value="de">Germany
    <option value="uk">United Kingdon
    <option value="us">United States
  </select>
  <p/>
  <input type="submit" value="Show Locale"/>
  <p/>
</form>

</body>
</html>
```

The heart of the action is located in the show-locale.jsp page, shown in Listing 18.5.

Listing 18.5   show-locale.jsp

```
<%@ page
  contentType="text/html"
  import="java.util.*"
%>

<html>
  <head>
    <title> Show Locale JSP Page</title>
  </head>
<body>

<%
  String locale = request.getParameter("locale") ;
  Locale userLocale = new Locale(locale, "") ;

  ResourceBundle helloBundle
    = ResourceBundle.getBundle("hello", userLocale) ;
%>

  <h1> <%= helloBundle.getString("hello.greeting") %> </h1>
  <hr/>
  <p/>
  <img src="<%= helloBundle.getString("hello.flag") %>" />

</body>
</html>
```

In this page, you need to find the selected locale. Notice how you grab the locale using the getParameter() method, and not the getLocale() method, like this:

```
String locale = request.getParameter("locale") ;
```

This allows your JSP page to use the locale selected in the select-locale.jsp page, and not whatever is indicated by the web browser as part of its HTTP request.

Using the locale name, you can create a new `Locale` object:

```
Locale userLocale = new Locale(locale, "") ;
```

The next step is to create the `ResourceBundle` object:

```
ResourceBundle helloBundle
    = ResourceBundle.getBundle("hello", userLocale) ;
```

The appropriate `factory()` method for creating this object takes two parameters. The first one is the base name of the file that contains the actual resource bundle. The second one is the newly created `Locale` object. What actually happens in this method is that the JVM goes out and finds the resource bundle by appending the locale name to the base name together with a file extension of "properties." For example, if the United States locale is selected, the resource bundle is found in the hello_en_US.properties file, while for the France locale, it would be hello_fr_FR.properties.

Once you've created the `ResourceBundle` object, you can use it to obtain locale specific resources, such as messages or image names. You indicate a specific resource by providing the resource name used in the properties file. In this JSP page, I use hello.greeting to find the appropriate greeting, and hello.flag to indicate the name of the appropriate flag:

```
<h1> <%= helloBundle.getString("hello.greeting") %> </h1>
<hr/>
<p/>
<img src="<%= helloBundle.getString("hello.flag") %>" />
```

In order to use these two JSP pages, you need to create the necessary property files. Because there are only two required properties, they are rather short. The U.S. locale property file was the first one I created, and it only consists of two lines ...

```
hello.greeting=Hello World!
hello.flag=images/flag_us.jpg
```

The other property files have the same property names, but different property values. For example, the France locale property file has the following two lines ...

```
hello.greeting=Bonjour Monde!
hello.flag=images/flag_fr.jpg
```

... while the Germany locale property file has these two lines:

```
hello.greeting=Hallo Welt!
hello.flag=images/flag_de.jpg
```

In this simple example, I placed the locale-specific information in a property file. Another option is to place the locale-specific data in a list resource bundle, which is handled by the

ListResourceBundle class, located in the java.util package. You use ListResourceBundle objects the same way that I used the ResourceBundle property files; the only difference is that you place the localized information in a list array, instead of a file. Personally, I find the property files to be easier to work with, thus I only demonstrated how to use them in this chapter.

Coffee Break

Some locales use characters that are not representable in the standard character encodings that are used by default in many applications. For example, the default character encoding used in JSP, as specified by either the contentType or the pageEncoding attribute of the page directive, is ISO-8859-1.

This character encoding is useful for Latin-based character encodings, like English, French, and Spanish, but can't handle other character sets, like Korean, Chinese, or Hebrew. In order to handle these other languages, ISO created a Universal Character Set (UCS) that can handle all characters and symbols of all written languages. Most applications can't handle UCS, which requires 4 bytes, or 32 bits, to represent characters (and thus can represent over 2 billion characters).

Fortunately, many applications, including both Java and XML, can handle the Unicode character coding system. In order to handle UCS, several Unicode transformations have been developed, the most popular of which is probably UTF-8, or UCS Transformation Format 8. To represent a character in Unicode, you use the Unicode escape sequence, which is of the form \uXXXX, where the X symbols are replaced by the appropriate numerical sequence for the desired character.

For more information on Unicode go to www.unicode.org. Unicode has lists of Unicode escape sequences for a wide range of different characters.

In order for the Tomcat server to find these property files, they need to be individually stored in the WEB-INF\classes directory. If you use the book's sample code, you can select the different locales and see the resulting JSP pages. Figures 18.10 and 18.11 show the French and German locales, respectively.

Figure 18.10

The message shown in the French locale.

Figure 18.11

The message shown in the German locale.

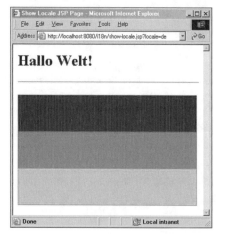

The Rest of the Story

You can probably guess that I have only highlighted the basics required to properly internationalize an application. While true, the basics are rather simple, and once you understand them, the bulk of the work is in identifying locale-specific data, and creating the appropriate resource bundles. To simplify the development of Internationalized Java applications, Sun has created a Java Internationalization and Localization toolkit, which is available at java.sun.com/products/jilkit/.

Of course, another option is to utilize custom Tag Libraries, which can handle some of the burden of making your application i18n compliant. An example of this type of Tag Library is the i18n custom Tag Library available from the Jakarta-taglibs project. Now that you have a better understanding of what is necessary to localize your JSP application, you can probably make better use of these tags.

The Least You Need to Know

- ◆ The process of making your application available to people across languages and cultures is known as internationalization, or i18n.

- ◆ The first step in this process is to localize any resources, such as messages, numbers, currency, dates, or images. This process is known as localization, or l10n.

- ◆ To use localized information, you place it in resource bundles.

Chapter 19

You've Got Mail

In This Chapter

- ◆ An e-mail primer
- ◆ Sending e-mails
- ◆ Receiving e-mail

Have you ever been surfing the Internet, maybe shopping for a new book, or searching for a great deal at an auction site, when suddenly something goes wrong? The first thing you probably want to do is to contact someone to find out what happened, or maybe just to vent. Rarely are you able to contact a live human being anymore; everything is automated, including customer service, it seems.

In fact, you often don't even get the actual e-mail address, just an HTML form that you can use to send a message to someone. While this may irritate you, you probably also think it is pretty cool and wish you knew how to do it. In this chapter, you will learn how to do that, as well as how to view messages, all from a JSP application.

An E-Mail Primer

Before jumping in with both feet, however, you need to review what actually goes on when you send and receive e-mail. First, unlike web communication that rides on HTTP, e-mail communication rides on Simple Mail Transport Protocol (SMTP). SMTP is one of the most, if not *the* most, used Internet protocols.

Fresh Brew

Formally, SMTP, POP, and IMAP are all defined in different Request for Comments (RFC), which are available at www.rfc-editor.org. If you want to learn the nitty-gritty details, you should check them out. SMTP is defined in RFC 821, POP is defined in RFC 1939, and IMAP is defined in RFC 2060.

Basically, SMTP is all about sending messages between servers. E-mail is initially sent from the originating client to an SMTP server. The message travels from SMTP server to SMTP server, until finally it reaches the destination server, where it is stored in a mailbox, called the inbox, until the client can retrieve it.

To retrieve a message, a client connects to the SMTP server and grabs the message. This process is more complicated than the initial sending, and it turns out that there are two competing protocols for handling the receiving of new messages. The first one is Post Office Protocol (POP). Currently, POP is in version 3, so it is sometimes referred to as POP3. POP is the dominant method used for retrieving messages, due primarily to its simplicity.

The POP protocol supports a single mailbox for every user, which is the inbox. When a server receives an e-mail, it places it in the user's inbox. A POP e-mail client connects to the server and grabs the messages in the inbox. Fundamentally, POP requires users to store their e-mails on their own computer.

The alternative protocol is the Internet Message Access Protocol (IMAP). Currently, IMAP is in version 4, so it is sometimes referred to as IMAP4. IMAP operates in a similar manner to POP, in that a user can connect to a mail server and retrieve any message in the inbox. IMAP, however, also allows users to store their e-mail on the server, resulting in a centralized mail repository, which can easily be archived. This places a larger burden on the mail server; hence, it is not always available.

Coffee Break

When SMTP was originally designed, all messages were composed entirely of US-ASCII characters, or equivalently, plain old English text. Only 7 bits were available to represent characters, which limits you to 128 characters. In order to represent binary data, the data had to be encoded, which was handled by uuencode, short for UNIX to UNIX encode. To pull the binary data out of the message, you had to run uudecode.

As long as everyone used the same versions of the encoder/decoder, the users were computer literate, no problems occurred when the message was transmitted, the planets were all aligned, your rabbit's foot was properly shined, and so on, you could send binary messages.

Fortunately, this problem was recognized and a solution was developed, called Multipurpose Internet Mail Extensions (MIME). With MIME, you could send data in a variety of formats and have it reliably received at the other end. MIME is defined in a variety of RFCs, including 822, 2045, 2046, and 2047.

To send and receive e-mails using Java, you need the JavaMail API, which does two things. First, it defines how to send and receive messages from Java. The second part of the API defines how to create a provider for a particular protocol, such as POP or IMAP. As part of the JavaMail download, Sun includes good implementations for the providers, thus you don't need to worry about them.

If you are using the Enterprise Edition of the Java 2 platform (J2EE), you already have JavaMail. If not, you can download the JavaMail API from java.sun.com/products/javamail, which is currently version 1.2. While you don't need it for the examples in this chapter, if you plan on working more with JavaMail, including sending or receiving attachments, you will also need the JavaBeans Activation Framework, which you can find atjava.sun.com/products/javabeans/glasgow/jaf.html.

If you download the JavaMail zip file, inside you will find several jar files. To use JavaMail from a JSP page, you will need to place these jar files into the WEB-INF\lib subdirectory of whatever context you plan on using for your JSP mail pages.

Coffee Break

The JavaMail API enables you to build what is called a Mail User Agent (MUA) that can send and receive messages. More familiar examples of MUAs are Microsoft Outlook, Eudora, Pine, and Elm. JavaMail is not about transporting, delivering, or forwarding messages, which is accomplished by Mail Transport Agents (MTAs). MTAs, like Sendmail or Microsoft Exchange, are used by your Internet Service Provider to enable you to send and receive e-mails.

Making Messages

Now that the preliminaries are out of the way, you can jump right into an example. While you could place all of the code inside a JSP, I have taken a Model 2 approach in this chapter and use JSP pages to interact with the user, while a Servlet provides the functionality. An alternative approach would be to develop custom tags to provide e-mail capabilities. In fact, you can download a custom Tag Library from the Jakarta-taglib project, which does just that. Of course, the problem with using a custom Tag Library is that you don't understand what is actually going on, you just learn how to use the tags.

To send e-mail, you first need to create the message. The JSP shown in Listing 19.1 creates an HTML form that enables the user to specify the necessary information to send an e-mail. This includes the to field, an optional cc field, the subject line, and the actual message body. A hidden input field specifies the from line—you should change this to whatever is appropriate.

The first step toward getting this example running is to type Listing 19.1 and save it to your cigjsp folder. Then you can see the mail form by browsing to localhost:8080/cigjsp/send-mail.jsp. Don't try to do anything with the form yet, though. All the parts of this example are not in place yet.

Listing 19.1   send-mail.jsp

```
<%@ page contentType="text/html" %>

<%!
  String cFrom = "rjbrunner@pacbell.net" ;
%>

<html>
<head><title>JSP Page</title></head>
<body>

<h1> Send Mail </h1>
<hr/>

<form method="post" action="SendMailServlet">

<table>
  <tr>
    <td align="left">To:</td>
    <td><input type="text" name="to" size="40" maxlength="80"/></td>
  </tr>
  <input type="hidden" name="from" value="<%= cFrom %>"/>
  <tr>
    <td align="left">CC:</td>
    <td><input type="text" name="cc" size="40" maxlength="80"/></td>
  </tr>
  <tr>
    <td align="left">Subject:</td>
    <td><input type="text" name="subject" size="40" maxlength="80"/></td>
  </tr>
</table>
<hr/>
<textarea rows="5" cols="40" name="body">
</textarea>
<p/>
<input type="submit" value="Send Mail"/>
</form>

</body>
</html>
```

This JSP page does not do any error checking. In production sites, you should add some JavaScript function to perform some client-side validation, such as making sure the to field isn't blank. You also should verify the data on the server, because the client may not have JavaScript support enabled, and to perform stricter field checking.

When the user clicks Submit, the form data is sent to SendMailServlet. I didn't use a JavaBean to encapsulate the data in order to keep things simple. One thing you might notice, however, is the use of the size and maxlength attributes for the input controls. This is a good idea as it both enables you to control the appearance of your form and restricts the amount and type of information that can be uploaded in the POST request to your server.

Fresh Brew

In order for this example to work on your site, you need to change the mail.isp.net in the SendMailServlet code (see Listing 19.2) to the DNS name of your actual ISP mail host. A simple way to do this is to open your mail tool and find out what values it is using. For Microsoft Outlook, you can do this by going to the Tools menu and selecting Accounts. From here, select the actual mail account you want to use and click Properties. The Servers tab contains the relevant information.

Listing 19.2 shows the SendMailServlet Java source code. Type the listing, and then save it to your cigjsp\WEB-INF\classes folder under the name SendMailServlet.java. You then must compile the listing. In case you've forgotten how to do all this stuff, here's Ye Olde Step By Step:

1. Start a DOS command-prompt window and enter **set PATH=X:*Java*\bin**, where *X* is the drive on which you installed the Java SDK, and *Java* is the folder into which you installed the SDK. For example, you might type **set PATH=C:\j2sdk1.4.0-beta3\ bin**. This tells your system where to find the Java compiler.

2. Now, type **set CLASSPATH=X:*Jakarta*\common\lib\servlet.jar; X:*Jakarta*\common\lib\mail.jar**, where *X* is the drive on which you installed Tomcat, and *Jakarta* is the folder into which you installed Tomcat. For example, you might type **set CLASSPATH=C:\jakarta-tomcat-4.0.1\common\lib\servlet.jar; C:\jakarta-tomcat-4.0.1\common\lib\mail.jar;%CLASSPATH%**. This tells Java where to find the packages that the Servlet imports and preserves your current CLASSPATH environment variable.

3. Move to the directory in which you stored the SendMailServlet.java file. To do this, you might type **cd C:\jakarta-tomcat-4.0.1\webapps\cigjsp\WEB-INF\classes**.

4. Type **javac SendMailServlet.java** to compile the Servlet. You'll then end up with a file named SendMailServlet.class, which is the compiled form of SendMailServlet. java.

Listing 19.2   SendMailServlet.java

```java
import java.util.* ;
import javax.servlet.*;
import javax.servlet.http.*;

import javax.mail.* ;
import javax.mail.internet.* ;

public class SendMailServlet extends HttpServlet {

  private final static String mailServer = "mail.ISP.net" ;
  private Session mailSession = null ;

  public void init(ServletConfig config) throws ServletException {
    super.init(config);
    try{

      Properties props = System.getProperties() ;
      props.put("mail.smtp.host", mailServer) ;
      mailSession = Session.getDefaultInstance(props, null) ;

    }catch(Exception ex) {
      throw new ServletException("Mail Error: Unable to initialize Session.")
;
    }
  }

  protected void processRequest(HttpServletRequest request, HttpServletResponse
response)
  throws ServletException, java.io.IOException {
    try{

      String to = (String)request.getParameter("to") ;
      String from = (String)request.getParameter("from") ;
      String cc = (String)request.getParameter("cc") ;
      String subject = (String)request.getParameter("subject") ;
      String body = (String)request.getParameter("body") ;

      Message msg = new MimeMessage(mailSession) ;
      msg.setFrom(new InternetAddress(from)) ;
      msg.addRecipient(Message.RecipientType.TO, new InternetAddress(to)) ;

      msg.setSubject(subject) ;
      msg.setText(body) ;
      msg.setHeader("X-Header", "SendMailServlet") ;
```

```
        msg.setSentDate(new Date()) ;

        Transport.send(msg) ;

        response.setContentType("text/html");
        java.io.PrintWriter out = response.getWriter();

        out.println("<html>");
        out.println("<head>");
        out.println("<title>Send Mail Servlet</title>");
        out.println("</head>");
        out.println("<body>");

        out.println("<h2> To: " + to + "</h2>") ;
        out.println("<h2> From:" + from + "</h2>") ;
        out.println("<h2> CC: " + cc + "</h2>") ;
        out.println("<h2> Subject: " + subject + "</h2>") ;
        out.println("<h2> Body: " + body + "</h2>") ;

        out.println("</body>");
        out.println("</html>");

        out.close();

      }catch(Exception ex) {
        System.err.println(ex.getMessage()) ;
        throw new ServletException("Mail Error: Unable to send message.") ;
      }
    }

  protected void doGet(HttpServletRequest request, HttpServletResponse response)
  throws ServletException, java.io.IOException {
    processRequest(request, response);
  }

  protected void doPost(HttpServletRequest request, HttpServletResponse
response)
  throws ServletException, java.io.IOException {
    processRequest(request, response);
  }

  public String getServletInfo() {
    return "Send Mail Servlet";
  }
}
```

The basic steps in sending an e-mail using the JavaMail API are rather simple. First, you need to obtain a Session object that encapsulates a basic mail session:

```
Properties props = System.getProperties() ;
props.put("mail.smtp.host", mailServer) ;
mailSession = Session.getDefaultInstance(props, null) ;
```

Generally, you will just use the default session instance, although you can create a special session instance that can be useful for a high-traffic server. The factory method for obtaining the session instance takes a Java Property object, which includes basic information like the name of the mail server. In this example, I specify the key name of mail.smtp.host, which indicates that you want to use the SMTP protocol to send messages. You need to change the value of this property to match your mail server.

The next step is to create a message. The Message class in the javax.mail API is an abstract class; therefore, in order to actually create a message, you need to create a subclass of the Message class, which generally will be the MimeMessage class. Once you have a Message object, you can set the relevant fields, which you grab from the request parameters:

```
String to = (String)request.getParameter("to") ;
String from = (String)request.getParameter("from") ;
String cc = (String)request.getParameter("cc") ;
String subject = (String)request.getParameter("subject") ;
String body = (String)request.getParameter("body") ;

Message msg = new MimeMessage(mailSession) ;
msg.setFrom(new InternetAddress(from)) ;
msg.addRecipient(Message.RecipientType.TO, new InternetAddress(to)) ;

msg.setSubject(subject) ;
msg.setText(body) ;
msg.setHeader("X-Header", "SendMailServlet") ;
msg.setSentDate(new Date()) ;
```

You might notice that the addressing is handled by the InternetAddress class. While you are using the constructor that only takes one argument, an alternative constructor takes a second argument that is a name you want to appear along with the e-mail address. For example, to specify that John A. Doe should prefix the john.doe@nowhere.com e-mail address, you use the following constructor:

```
Address to = new InternetAddress("john.doe@nowhere.com", "John A. Doe") ;
```

Once the message is composed, you can send the message, which is handled by the transport class:

```
Transport.send(msg) ;
```

The simplest technique is to use the static `send()` method, which just takes the message as its parameter. Alternatively, you open a full connection to the mail server, by obtaining a new `Transport` instance from your `Session` object. This approach is useful if you need to send a large number of e-mails all at once. The Servlet finishes by printing out an HTML page that contains the data entered by the user, sort of a poor man's receipt.

Because you are using a Servlet, you need to have a deployment descriptor to tell our server to map a URL request to the appropriate Servlet. In Listing 19.3, I show the descriptor I used to deploy this mail demonstration. Type this listing, and save it to the WEB-INF folder of the cigjsp context. Once that is done, restart your Tomcat server and browse to localhost:8080/cigjsp/send-mail.jsp. An example of a message that I composed is shown in Figure 19.1. When you click Send Mail, you will have sent your first mail message from Java.

Listing 19.3   web.xml

```
<?xml version="1.0" encoding="ISO-8859-1"?>
<!DOCTYPE web-app
PUBLIC "-//Sun Microsystems, Inc.//DTD Web Application 2.3//EN"
"http://java.sun.com/dtd/web-app_2_3.dtd">

<web-app>
  <servlet>
    <servlet-name>SendMailServlet</servlet-name>
    <servlet-class> SendMailServlet</servlet-class>
  </servlet>
  <servlet-mapping>
    <servlet-name>SendMailServlet</servlet-name>
    <url-pattern>/SendMailServlet</url-pattern>
  </servlet-mapping>
</web-app>
```

Figure 19.1

This figure shows the Send Mail screen where you can enter a mail message, including header information, before sending it off.

Checking Your List

Once you can send e-mail, the next step is to receive it. In reality, I doubt you will want to do this very often using Java, especially from a JSP page. This is not because it is inherently complicated, but because you probably already have a perfectly good mail reader, which you may have been using for some time now. Just for fun, however, Listing 19.4 demonstrates how to connect to a mail server and download a list of mail messages that are in your inbox.

Listing 19.4   check-mail.jsp

```
<%@ page
   contentType="text/html"
%>

<html>
<head><title>Check Mail JSP Page</title></head>
<body>

<h1> Check Mail </h1>
<hr/>

<form method="post" action="ReceiveMailServlet">
<input type="text" name="user" size="20" maxlength="20"/> Username <p/>
<input type="password" name="passwd" size="20" maxlength="20"/> Password <p/>
<input type="submit" value="Check Mail"/>
</form>

</body>
</html>
```

CAUTION

Hot Java _____

In reality, you would want to be more careful about security than I have been in this simple example. You should only send passwords over an encrypted channel, which can be done using Secure Sockets Layer (SSL).

First, since you generally need to log in to your mail server in order to access your inbox, you need a login JSP page, as shown in Listing 19.4. Again, you would generally want some client-side validation JavaScript, but this is merely a simple demonstration. A sample view of the check mail JSP page is shown in Figure 19.2.

Once the user has entered a username and password, the check-mail JSP page contacts the ReceiveMailServlet, shown in Listing 19.5.

Figure 19.2

*The Check Mail login
screen, where users can enter
the username and password
for their mail server.*

Listing 19.5   ReceiveMailServlet.java

```java
import java.util.* ;

import javax.servlet.*;
import javax.servlet.http.*;

import javax.mail.* ;
import javax.mail.internet.* ;

public class ReceiveMailServlet extends HttpServlet {

  private final static String mailServer = "mail.isp.net" ;

  private Session mailSession = null ;
  private Folder folder = null ;
  private Store store = null ;

  public void init(ServletConfig config) throws ServletException {
    super.init(config);
    try{

      Properties props = new Properties() ;
      mailSession = Session.getDefaultInstance(props, null) ;

    }catch(Exception ex) {
      throw new ServletException("Mail Error: Unable to initialize Session.")
;
    }
  }

  protected void processRequest(HttpServletRequest request, HttpServletResponse
response)
    throws ServletException, java.io.IOException {
    try {
```

continues

Listing 19.5 ReceiveMailServlet.java (continued)

```java
      String user = request.getParameter("user") ;
      String passwd = request.getParameter("passwd") ;

      store = mailSession.getStore("pop3") ;
      store.connect(mailServer, user, passwd) ;

      folder = store.getFolder("INBOX") ;
      if(folder == null) {
        throw new ServletException("Unable to retreive inbox.") ;
      }

      folder.open(Folder.READ_ONLY) ;

      Message[] msgs = folder.getMessages() ;

      MailBean mb = null ;
      Vector mbv = new Vector() ;

      for(int i = 0 ; i < msgs.length ; i++){
        mb = new MailBean() ;
        mb.setFrom((msgs[i].getFrom()[0]).toString()) ;
        mb.setSubject(msgs[i].getSubject()) ;

        mbv.addElement(mb) ;
      }

      HttpSession session = request.getSession() ;
      session.setAttribute("mbv", mbv) ;

      RequestDispatcher dispatcher = request.getRequestDispatcher("list-
mail.jsp") ;
      dispatcher.forward(request, response) ;

    }catch(Exception ex) {
      throw new ServletException(ex) ;
    }finally {
      try {
        if(folder != null)
          folder.close(false) ;
        if(store != null)
          store.close() ;
      }catch(Exception ex) {
        throw new ServletException(ex) ;
      }
    }
  }
```

```
  protected void doGet(HttpServletRequest request, HttpServletResponse
response)
    throws ServletException, java.io.IOException {
      processRequest(request, response);
  }

  protected void doPost(HttpServletRequest request, HttpServletResponse
response)
    throws ServletException, java.io.IOException {
      processRequest(request, response);
  }

  public String getServletInfo() {
    return "Receive Mail Servlet";
  }
}
```

As before, the first thing you must do is create a mail session:

```
      Properties props = new Properties() ;
      mailSession = Session.getDefaultInstance(props, null) ;
```

To connect to your mail server, you obtain a `Store` object, which you can obtain from your mail session using the DNS name of your mail server, your username, and password as parameters. Once you have the `Store` object, you use its `connect()` method to actually connect to the mail server:

```
      String user = request.getParameter("user") ;
      String passwd = request.getParameter("passwd") ;

      store = mailSession.getStore("pop3") ;
      store.connect(mailServer, user, passwd) ;
```

The next step is to create a `Folder` object that represents your inbox. In this Servlet, you open the inbox folder in `READ_ONLY` mode:

```
      folder = store.getFolder("INBOX") ;
      if(folder == null) {
        throw new ServletException("Unable to retreive inbox.") ;
      }

      folder.open(Folder.READ_ONLY) ;
```

If you want to remove a message from the server, you need to open the folder in READ_WRITE mode. If you are using POP as your provider, you only have access to the inbox folder. IMAP, on the other hand, would provide access to more folders.

Once you have the inbox folder, grab all messages that are in the folder using the getMessages() method:

```
Message[] msgs = folder.getMessages() ;
```

You can then grab the relevant fields from each message. In Listing 19.5, I only grab the from and subject lines, store them in a JavaBean called MailBean, and store all MailBean objects in a Vector object:

```
MailBean mb = null ;
Vector mbv = new Vector() ;

for(int i = 0 ; i < msgs.length ; i++){
  mb = new MailBean() ;
  mb.setFrom((msgs[i].getFrom()[0]).toString()) ;
  mb.setSubject(msgs[i].getSubject()) ;

  mbv.addElement(mb) ;
}
```

This Vector object is added as an attribute to the current HTTP Session, and the request is redirected to the list-mail JSP page:

```
HttpSession session = request.getSession() ;
session.setAttribute("mbv", mbv) ;

RequestDispatcher dispatcher = request.getRequestDispatcher("list-
mail.jsp") ;
dispatcher.forward(request, response) ;
```

One last point about this Servlet is that you might have noticed the getFrom() method is appended with an array operator that retrieves element zero. In this example, you are only dealing with one Internet address. In reality, you can have multiple e-mail recipients in a given recipient field, hence the need for the array. In order to make this Servlet operational, you need to add the following lines to your deployment descriptor.

```
<servlet>
  <servlet-name>ReceiveMailServlet</servlet-name>
  <servlet-class>ReceiveMailServlet</servlet-class>
</servlet>
<servlet-mapping>
  <servlet-name>ReceiveMailServlet</servlet-name>
  <url-pattern>/ReceiveMailServlet</url-pattern>
</servlet-mapping>
```

The MailBean is rather simple, as shown in Listing 19.6. All it does is wrap the message subject and the person who sent the mail into a Java component.

Listing 19.6   MailBean.java

```java
package com.persistentjava ;

import java.beans.* ;
import java.io.Serializable ;

public class MailBean implements Serializable {

  private String _from ;
  private String _subject ;
  private String _body ;

  public MailBean() {
  }

  public String getFrom() {
    return(_from) ;
  }

  public void setFrom(String from) {
    _from = from ;
  }

  public String getSubject() {
    return(_subject) ;
  }

  public void setSubject(String subject) {
    _subject = subject ;
  }
}
```

The last step in the chain is the list mail JSP page. All it does is iterate through all of the
MailBean objects that are stored in the Vector that was attached to the HTTP Session. To
make things look nicer, I wrap everything in a nice HTML table. After using the send-
mail.jsp page several times, I call the check-mail.jsp page, which produces Figure 19.3.

Listing 19.7   list-mail.jsp

```jsp
<%@ page
  contentType="text/html"
  import="com.persistentjava.MailBean"
%>

<html>
```

continues

Listing 19.7   list-mail.jsp   (continued)

```
<head><title> Mail Digest JSP Page</title></head>
<body>
<h1> Mail Digest </h1>
<hr/>

<jsp:useBean id="mbv" scope="session" class="java.util.Vector" />

<table border="4">
  <tr>
     <th align="center">ID</th>
     <th align="center">From</th>
     <th align="center">Subject</th>
  </tr>

<%
  MailBean mb = null ;

  for(int i = 0 ; i < mbv.size() ; i++) {
    mb = (MailBean)mbv.elementAt(i) ;
%>
    <tr>
      <td> <%= i %> </td>
      <td> <%= mb.getFrom() %> </td>
      <td> <%= mb.getSubject() %> </td>
    </tr>
<% } %>

</table>
<hr/>
</form>
</body>
</html>
```

Figure 19.3

This figure shows the list of available mail as displayed by list-mail.jsp after being called by ReceiveMailServlet.

While these examples are rather simple, they actually demonstrate how to send and receive e-mail using Java, and JSP technology in particular. In the list-mail.jsp page, you didn't actually view the mail messages, which is a simple task once you have the messages. All you need to do is call the writeTo() method for any message you want to see. Other features that we didn't address, but that are possible with the JavaMail API, include replying to messages, forwarding messages, and handling multipart messages, which can have different MIME types. If you want to do it, the JavaMail API probably will let you do it.

The Least You Need to Know

- ◆ JavaMail provides you with the tools you need to send and receive e-mail.
- ◆ You send e-mail by obtaining a mail Session object, creating messages, and using a Transport object to actually send the message to your mail server.
- ◆ You receive e-mail by obtaining a mail Session object, creating a Store object, obtaining a Folder object for your inbox, and grabbing an array of your messages.

Don't Forget to XML

In This Chapter

◆ Introducing XML and XSL

◆ Making XML using JSP pages

◆ Processing XML using JSP technology

Since its creation, Java has generated a great deal of hype, followed by predictions on how the world will forever be changed. Just when you thought you would never find another technology that could possibly be more hyped than Java, along came XML, and suddenly an even bigger buzz was generated—after all, even Microsoft was behind XML.

In both cases, some of the hype was just hot air, but as they say, "Where there's a spark there's a fire," and both Java and XML do have enormous potential to change how we do things. After all, you are reading this book! Together, Java and XML are a powerful combination. By using both of these technologies together, applications can be built that put the golden ring of object-oriented development within reach. That golden ring is the reuse of components in multiple applications. In this chapter, I will show you how you can use JSP pages to generate XML and also to process it. But first, how about a short discussion on XML?

Extensible What?

XML stands for Extensible Markup Language. Without telling you, I have been working with not one, but two XML applications throughout this book. The first is XHTML, which was discussed in Chapter 10, "Extending HTML." This is what you have been generating with your JSP pages. The second are the JSP pages themselves.

It's important to note that XML represents data; it does not represent how that data appears. In other words, the power of XML is that you can pass data between applications, and the XML tags define what the data actually represents. How the data appears is left to the view. Remember my earlier discussion on the MVC model? Well, now you can see how it's all coming into place.

While I have generally used the JSP notation, you can also write JSP pages in a valid, well-formed XML notation. Well-formed notation just means that for every opening tag, there is a closing tag. For example …

```
<sampleTag></sampleTag>
```

… is well-formed XML, while …

```
<sampleTag><SomeOtherTag>
```

… is not well-formed because there is no closing tag for `<sampleTag>`. A closing tag consists of the same element name preceded by a forware slash (/), as you can see in the well-formed sampleTag example. If you have an XML notation that is not well formed, you will get some nasty errors from the XML parser. The XML parser (or processor, as it's sometimes called) is what reads and interprets the XML language.

Fresh Brew

XML is developed by the W3C. You can find more information, including links to online XML tutorials and articles at www.w3c.org/XML/.

You might wonder what the big deal is about having JSP pages in XML notation. Simple: If you want a JSP page to be processed by an XML processor, it must be well formed, and preferentially valid, XML. This capability enables you to dynamically generate JSP pages and pass them around, possibly to new servers, where they can be translated and processed. It also simplifies development—JSP tools can more easily parse and process XML documents, because they must follow a well-defined set of rules.

XML is a language used to create other languages. Hence, it is sometimes referred to as a meta-language. As such, XML has strict rules about what you can and can't do. For example, XML is case-sensitive. In XML, all attributes must be quoted. In XML, a start tag must be followed by an end tag; and if an element does not have body content, it can use the empty element shorthand. Finally, in XML, you must properly nest elements.

Examples speak louder than words, so take a look at the XML document shown in Listing 20.1. This XML document encapsulates a weather report and has a base element of current-weather. This element has two child elements, data and condition. Each of these two elements has its own children elements. Some of the elements have attributes, like the time element, which has a zone element.

Listing 20.1   current-weather.xml

```
<?xml version="1.0" encoding="UTF-8"?>

<!DOCTYPE current-weather SYSTEM "weather.dtd">

<current-weather>
    <date>
        <month>December</month>
        <day>14</day>
        <year>2001</year>
        <time zone="PST">10:09</time>
    </date>
    <condition>
        <observation>Light Rain</observation>
        <temperature unit="F">54</temperature>
        <windspeed unit="mph" direction="variable">5</windspeed>
        <humidity>72</humidity>
        <visibility unit="miles">5.00</visibility>
        <dewpoint unit="F">45</dewpoint>
        <barometer unit="inches" direction="falling">29.92</barometer>
    </condition>
</current-weather>
```

As you can see, the tags used to indicate specific elements do not tell you how to display the data, as is the case with HTML. Instead, the tags describe the data. For example, you know that the data element contains a date, and not a stock price. Internet Explorer can render XML documents using this treelike representation, as shown in Figure 20.1.

If IE can't display a document properly, it complains, showing you the line that violates a particular rule of XML. If a document obeys the rules of XML, it is called well formed. But for a document to be really useful, it must also be valid. A valid document has the additional qualification that it follows a predefined grammar.

The first format for describing a grammar for an XML language was the Document Type Declaration (DTD). A DTD is used to describe the rules that a certain XML document will follow. You frequently see DTDs defined by Standard-based groups. This is so that anyone who attempts to follow a well-known Standard follows the same rules. Usually it's not necessary to create your own DTD. However, if you have an application that others will be creating—new XML documents, for example—it is always a good idea to provide the rules for your XML.

Figure 20.1

This figure shows how Internet Explorer displays an XML document, providing a treelike view of all the elements.

DTDs have their own syntax that is used to describe these rules. I'm not going to go into the syntax on how to write your own DTDs. However, Listing 20.2 provides an example so you can see what it looks like. In this listing, I show part of the DTD that is used in the weather XML documents to give you a sense of what the DTD actually contains. This DTD defines what elements can appear in a weather XML document, their order, their cardinality, and the allowed attributes.

Listing 20.2   weather.dtd

```
<?xml version='1.0' encoding='UTF-8'?>

  <!ELEMENT windspeed (#PCDATA)>
  <!ATTLIST windspeed
    direction CDATA #IMPLIED
    unit CDATA #IMPLIED
  >


  <!ELEMENT temperature (#PCDATA)>
  <!ATTLIST temperature
    unit CDATA #IMPLIED
  >
```

An XML parser can check an XML document, like current-weather.xml, against this DTD to verify that it is valid. You can share a valid XML document, allowing others to use this information however they see fit. This means that if you have two different applications, they can each access the data contained in the XML document and present it in whatever ways is fit for that application. A second, and more powerful, technique for describing the contents of an XML document is called XML Schema. XML Schema closely mirrors Java in allowing inheritance and the definition of complex data types. By inheritance I mean that the attributes and methods present in one object are included and available in another. As an analogy to the weather example, if you had a Java object called WeatherCondition, and a Storm is a type of `WeatherCondition`, then you would say that Storm inherits from `WeatherCondition` and Storm has access to any attributes and methods that a `WeatherCondition` might have. By using XML Schema, it becomes possible to turn Java classes into XML documents and vice-versa. This all comes into play when using JSP pages, because it allows for input from a user to be saved or retrieved as XML documents and at the same time to use Java classes within the application on the Server to perform some operation with that data. Go back to thinking about the MVC strategy I mentioned earlier. The Java classes are the part that fit into the Model portion.

While XML is a great format for describing data, if you want to display or render it, you need another tool. In Chapter 11, "Using Cascading Style Sheets," you learned about cascading style sheets, which are one possibility. The designers of XML, however, also created the Extensible Stylesheet Language (XSL) to provide presentation capabilities to XML documents. XSL style sheets are themselves valid XML documents but have some added features that tell a processor how to display the information. Let's look further into this powerful feature.

XSL is actually composed of two different parts: XSL Transformations (XSLT) and XSL Formatting Objects (XSL-FO). XSLT can be used to transform an XML document into another document. The output of an XSL transformation can be another XML document or any type of mark-up language that is needed by the application. This includes XHTML for browsers, or WML (Wireless Markup Language) for cell phones. This is an incredibly powerful feature because you can have all sorts of ways to view the data, and it is all defined separate from the way the data is actually represented. If you refer back to the weather example, you can take the same XML document and have XSL transform the output so that it can be viewed through a web browser one way and on a cell phone another without ever changing the way the application sends the data. Pretty cool!

Fresh Brew

XSL is also developed by the W3C. You can find more information, including links to online tutorials and articles, at www.w3c.org/Style/XSL/.

XSL-FO, on the other hand, is more like CSS, albeit considerably more powerful, in that it can be used to control the presentation of an XML document. Usually, XSL-FO is used for producing actual documents, like Microsoft Word documents or Adobe PDF files. XSL-FO is more complex to use, but if you have to support multiple types of documents in your application, it makes sense to use it.

XSLT has a whole syntax associated with it, and is an entire book unto itself! I'm not going to go into all the details to learn and write XSLT. Instead, let's briefly walk through a simple example to give you a flavor for what is possible.

To demonstrate XSLT, Listing 20.3 contains an XSL style sheet that transforms an XML weather document into an XHTML document. While it may seem rather daunting at first glance, it is actually rather simple. Looking over weather.xsl, you notice first that the output() method is set to HTML:

```
<xsl:output method="html"/>
```

Following that are a bunch of xsl:template elements, which contain HTML elements and xsl:apply-template elements. Any element that is part of the XSL DTD, has the prefix of xsl. Here's one example:

```
<xsl:template match="/">
  <html>
    <xsl:apply-templates/>
  </html>
</xsl:template>
```

XSL is also known as a template, or pattern, language. When a transformation happens on an XSL file, think of it as comparing the current element to a set of patterns. Each pattern is then looked at to see if there are other patterns contained within it. The process continues down in a treelike structure until all the elements in the XML document have been looked at. The template elements define a pattern and a corresponding action that should be performed when that pattern is found. The first template element (the one I just pointed out to you in the previous code snippet) shows what to do when the root element is found in a document. When the root element is found, the transformation goes ahead, looks at all the templates that are defined, and applies the appropriate one. The second one shows what happens when the current-weather element is found:

```
<xsl:template match="current-weather">
  <head>
    <title> Weather Report </title>
  </head>
  <body>
    <xsl:apply-templates select="date"/>
    <xsl:apply-templates select="condition"/>
  </body>
</xsl:template>
```

This continues down the XML tree until leaf elements are reached, at which point xsl:value-of elements are encountered. These elements grab a value out of the XML document and put it into the output document. This allows the element and attribute values in the current-weather.xml document to be pulled out and placed into the

XHTML table. There would be XSL templates for each and every element that could be present in the XML document. However, to keep the example simple, I'll just present the date and condition template so you can get a feel for what's involved and how the patterns and templates are applied.

Listing 20.3   weather.xsl

```
<?xml version="1.0" encoding="UTF-8" ?>

<xsl:stylesheet version="1.0"
  xmlns:xsl="http://www.w3.org/1999/XSL/Transform"
  >

  <xsl:output method="html"/>

  <xsl:template match="/">
    <html>
      <xsl:apply-templates/>
    </html>
  </xsl:template>

  <xsl:template match="current-weather">
    <head>
      <title> Weather Report </title>
    </head>
    <body>
      <xsl:apply-templates select="date"/>
      <xsl:apply-templates select="condition"/>
    </body>
  </xsl:template>

  <xsl:template match="date">
    <h2> Weather Report for
    <xsl:value-of select="concat(month, ' ', day, ', ', year)"/>
    </h2>
    <hr/>
    <h4><xsl:apply-templates select="time"/></h4>
    <p/>
  </xsl:template>

  <xsl:template match="time">
    Data accurate as of
    <xsl:value-of select="."/> (<xsl:value-of select="@zone"/>)
  </xsl:template>

  <xsl:template match="condition">
```

continues

Listing 20.3 weather.xsl (continued)

```
    <table border="2" width="100%">
      <xsl:apply-templates/>
    </table>
  </xsl:template>

  </xsl:template>

</xsl:stylesheet>
```

One more thing to note: If you want to add special characters into XML documents, you need to specify them with their Unicode value. Unicode is a defined set of values for all symbols and characters for any language that exists on the planet. Quite a task. For example, if you want to display the degree symbol, the string value will be &#x0B00. This is how to encode non-ASCII characters into an XML document.

If this is all gibberish, perhaps a demonstration will help. You can download any number of free XSL processors, including one from the Apache Software foundation called Xalan. But Internet Explorer also includes one, and by modifying current-weather.xml, it will automatically render the XML document using the indicated XSL style sheet. Essentially, all you need to do is add the following line right after the XML declaration in current-weather.xml:

```
<?xml-stylesheet type="text/xsl" href="weather.xsl"?>
```

If you now display current-weather.xml in your browser, it will render its XHTML per the XSLT style sheet, as shown in Figure 20.2. I placed all these files in the XML context of my Tomcat installation. If you do the same, you can either use Tomcat to serve the documents to you—localhost:8080/xml/current-weather.xml—or you can open the file from the file system. Either way, it should be properly rendered as XHTML. Take a look at the XHTML source for this web page, and you will see how the XSL transformed the XML.

Figure 20.2

This figure shows how Internet Explorer will dynamically transform an XML document when the XML document specifies an appropriate XSL style sheet.

Making XML

Okay, the XML discussion was interesting, but who wants to sit around writing XML documents all day by hand? The real action is in making and processing XML documents dynamically. Well, once again, I have to tell you that you have already been making XML documents throughout this book. For example, take a look at Listing 20.4, which generates current-weather.xml. The only difference between this JSP page and the XML document shown in Listing 20.1 is the page directive, which sets the content type to be text/xml, instead of text/html. If you start up Tomcat and browse to localhost:8080/xml/get-weather. jsp, you will see the XHTML table automatically generated by the browser, which read the XML file, requested the XSL file, and then transformed the XML into the XHTML that is displayed.

Listing 20.4   get-weather.jsp

```
<%@page contentType="text/xml"%>

<?xml version="1.0" encoding="UTF-8"?>

<?xml-stylesheet type="text/xsl" href="weather.xsl"?>

<!DOCTYPE current-weather SYSTEM "weather.dtd">

<current-weather>
    <date>
        <month>December</month>
        <day>14</day>
        <year>2001</year>
        <time zone="PST">10:09</time>
    </date>
    <condition>
        <observation>Light Rain</observation>
        <temperature unit="F">54</temperature>
        <windspeed unit="mph" direction="variable">5</windspeed>
        <humidity>72</humidity>
        <visibility unit="miles">5.00</visibility>
        <dewpoint unit="F">45</dewpoint>
        <barometer unit="inches" direction="falling">29.92</barometer>
    </condition>
</current-weather>
```

The next example demonstrates how to generate the XML dynamically, in case you feel cheated by the previous example—after all, there wasn't any Java code in the JSP page. First, take a look at Listing 20.5, which is a JavaBean that encapsulates a weather report. Notice how the data and time are dynamically generated, while the conditions can only be set using the Bean's properties.

Figure 20.3

This figure shows the result of generating an XML document from a JSP page.

While it's possible to include all the information in the JavaBean that appears on the weather web page, to keep things simple, I will just look at a few of the properties.

Listing 20.5   WeatherBean.java

```java
package com.persistentjava;

import java.lang.String ;
import java.lang.Integer ;
import java.util.Calendar ;

import java.beans.* ;
import java.io.Serializable ;

public class WeatherBean implements Serializable {

  private final static String[] months =
  {"January", "February", "March", "April", "May", "June",
   "July", "August", "September", "October", "November", "December"} ;

  private String month ;
  private int day ;
  private int year ;
  private String time ;

  private String observation ;

  public WeatherBean() {
    Calendar today = Calendar.getInstance() ;

    month = months[today.get(Calendar.MONTH)] ;
    day = today.get(Calendar.DAY_OF_MONTH) ;
```

```java
      year = today.get(Calendar.YEAR) ;
      time = new Integer(today.get(Calendar.HOUR_OF_DAY)).toString() + ":" +
        new Integer(today.get(Calendar.MINUTE)).toString() ;

    observation = "Heavy Rain" ;
  }

  public String getMonth() {
    return(month) ;
  }

  public void setMonth(String m) {
    month = m ;
  }

  public int getDay() {
    return(day) ;
  }

  public void setDay(int d) {
    day = d ;
  }

  public int getYear() {
    return(year) ;
  }

  public void setYear(int y) {
    year = y ;
  }

  public String getTime() {
    return(time) ;
  }

  public void setTime(String t) {
    time = t ;
  }

  public String getObservation() {
    return(observation) ;
  }

  public void setObservation(String obs) {
    observation = obs ;
  }

}
```

Much of this Bean should look familiar to you from the chapter where we walked through a sample Bean. You should recognize the constructor and setter and getter methods. One thing to note in case you aren't a Java expert is that this Bean allows for the current date to be retrieved, which is what all the Calendar business is about in the constructor.

With this JavaBean, you can now write a JSP page that dynamically creates the XML weather document. You should notice in Listing 20.6 how I mix XML declarations with JSP JavaBean actions. You could do the same thing with JSP custom actions, or you could generate the whole XML document from a Bean or Tag. When this JSP page is requested, the current-weather document is generated, and displayed as shown in Figure 20.4.

Listing 20.6   current-weather.jsp

```
<%@ page
  contentType="text/xml"
%>

<?xml version="1.0" encoding="UTF-8"?>

<?xml-stylesheet type="text/xsl" href="weather.xsl"?>

<!DOCTYPE current-weather SYSTEM "weather.dtd">

<jsp:useBean id="weather" scope="session"
class="com.persistentjava.WeatherBean" />

<current-weather>
    <date>
        <month><jsp:getProperty name="weather" property="month" /></month>
        <day><jsp:getProperty name="weather" property="day" /></day>
        <year><jsp:getProperty name="weather" property="year" /></year>
        <time zone="PST">
          <jsp:getProperty name="weather" property="time" />
        </time>
    </date>
    <condition>
        <observation>
          <jsp:getProperty name="weather" property="observation" />
        </observation>
    </condition>
</current-weather>
```

You may wonder what the big deal is. After all, you still end up with the same weather report looking like an XHTML table. Well, I can give you two important reasons why this is a very important step. First, as the viewer of the weather web page, you have no idea how the data was obtained. It could be a canned XML document, it could be a canned JSP page, or it could be dynamically obtained, with the current data and time, and perhaps the conditions being read from a database or a news wire.

Figure 20.4

This figure shows the result of dynamically generating XML, in this case by creating a JavaBean and extracting the relevant properties.

Second, using JSP pages, you can custom-tailor the appearance of your document, only needing to change one line. As I discussed in Chapter 6, "Getting a Free Lunch," part of an HTTP request is the "User-Agent" Header. You can have different style sheets for different user agents, customizing the appearance of the weather report for recent web browsers, old web browsers, and even mobile phones. Furthermore, it is a small step to move from a JSP weather service to a weather web service, allowing even more clients to connect and utilize your service.

Processing XML

There are a number of ways to handle dynamic data in XML while using JSP pages. It does require a more detailed understanding and comfort level with Java. The parsers that are used are provided as part of a Java XML pack, also called JAX. It takes a fair amount of study to understand the workings of the parsers and how to use them to meet your needs. More detailed information on this is provided in the Appendix C, "Processing XML," but if you want a 30,000-foot overview, here you go.

There are three types of models that are used to parse XML. They are called Simple API for XML (SAX), the Document Object Model (DOM), and XSL Transformations (XSLT). We've already looked at XSLT. SAX is used to parse each line of XML as it is encountered. It requires more programming on the developer's part, but is faster and uses less memory. DOM reads an entire XML document all at once so that the programmer can access any part of it that is needed. This is easier to program, but it's a bit slower and uses lots of memory. There are pros and cons to each model, and it's usually a matter of what best suits your needs. Again, for all the gory details, refer to the Appendix C on this topic.

So there you go. This concludes your introduction to XML. More important, this chapter concludes your introduction to JSP and the related technologies. You've covered a lot of material in a short time, and while you should now have a good understanding of how all these web technologies work together, I suggest that you continue your studies by picking up a few more advanced books that cover not only JSP but also related technologies like Java, JavaBeans, and XML. The better you understand these technologies, the better you can use them to create your own web masterpieces.

The Least You Need to Know

- XML is a meta-language that is used to define new vocabularies. Together Java and XML form a powerful combination.

- JavaServer Pages can easily generate XML, and can themselves be valid, well-formed XML documents.

- The JAXP interface simplifies the task of parsing and transforming XML documents from Java applications.

Help, It Doesn't Work

Sometimes, no matter how good your intentions are, the computer just doesn't want to cooperate. When this happens and you are just one step short of pulling your hair out, maybe some of these suggestions will help. Or better yet, take a look over these common problems first and prevent yourself from even wanting to pull your hair out. While these aren't hard and fast fixes, they will probably help in resolving some common problems that you might run into.

These are in no particular order, since I have no way of knowing which problem you might run into first. But give them all a look. Sooner or later, you'll probably hit one or more of these issues, and maybe something you read here will ring a bell.

Changes Not Showing Up on a JSP

Problem: You made a change to a JSP page, like maybe you added a new link or reformatted a layout, but nothing new is appearing when you view the page in your web browser.

Solution: This can happen when the JSP page is not being re-compiled into a Servlet that includes the new changes. Try deleting the Servlets on the web server.

The location of these files depends on the server you are using. For example, with Tomcat they are located in the tomcat\work directory. Within the work directory, there will be a subdirectory for your web application. That subdirectory will contain a number of files, all with long, generated filenames.

These are the Servlets that are compiled from the JSP pages. Delete all the Servlets in that subdirectory. The next time you access the JSP, a new Servlet will be created and will include your new changes.

The Dreaded HTTP 500 Error

Problem: You access a JSP and get a very informative error message: HTTP 500 error, Internal Servlet Error. Helpful, huh? This error is like looking for a needle in a haystack. A 505 error represents an "internal server error" encountered while processing your request. To find out more about the error, study the trace at the server window. These errors can occur when translating JSP source to a Servlet. Translation-time errors typically occur because of a syntax error in the JSP file or in the generated Java file. Use the error message at the server window for debugging. Errors can also occur at request time. Refer to the server-side trace for information about the specific problem or exception.

Solution: Try some of these resolutions and see if they help fix the problem:

- There will usually be an ugly-looking stack trace in the browser window or in the server log file to help you find out more about the error. See if you can glean any information from that, like the method name or a line number that might be causing the problem. These errors can occur when translating JSP source to a Servlet.

- If you see an error in the Translation-time of the JSP and you also notice some offending Java code that prevents the Servlet from being compiled, check for missing ";" and other syntax errors.

- The filename of the JSP page was entered in the wrong case. If you try to access a JSP as Weather.jsp instead of weather.jsp, the file won't be found.

- Check the CLASSPATH of the web server. You might be trying to access a Java class that can't be found by the web server.

The No-Less-Dreaded 404 Error

Problem: I'm sure you have seen this error on one web page or another. HTTP 404 means that the server was not able to locate the resource requested in the URL. Usually this is a web page, or in this case, a JSP page.

Solution: To resolve this annoyance, check to ensure that you entered the URL correctly and didn't make a typo. If that doesn't fix it, check the document root of the web server you are using. Make sure that your application is configured under the correct document root. If you need help with this, there is usually good documentation provided with the web server on setting up the document root.

Servlets Gone Haywire

Problem: There's a problem running a Servlet and you see a FileNotFoundException error.

Solution: Run! Well, maybe there are a couple of things you can try. First, check the application server console or log file. There will usually be a Java stack trace. This error occurs when a Servlet is trying to access a resource or file that it can't find. There are places that files typically go, so check to see if the offending file is in the wrong location. Try the local directory; if a path was hard-coded (which is really poor programming practice, so don't do that!) try that, or the web server document root, or the classes directory of your application. Also, check to make sure that your CLASSPATH of the web server is set up to find the files that you need.

JSP Syntax Errors

Problem: It's really easy to make syntax errors when coding JSP pages. Typically, in the case of syntax errors, your browser simply goes on strike and refuses to display your page.

Resolution: If your browser refuses to display your page, check for the following:

- The value of an attribute is not enclosed within quotes (" "). The error message should tell you the name of the attribute.
- The JSP file refers to a Bean that does not exist or is not accessible. The error message indicates the values of the name and type attributes for the <BEAN> tag.
- You're using a Bean and forgot some of the required attributes.
- The <BEAN> tag specifies attributes that are not valid for a given Bean. Usually, this is a spelling mistake. The message indicates the unknown attributes.
- The JSP file refers to a variable that is not declared in the correct scope or in the <SCRIPT> tag.
- The JSP file contains Java code that is not valid. The message indicates the line number of the compilation error.

Compiling JSP Files

Problem: I've written a JSP that gets a compile error. What's wrong?

Resolution: The JSP compilation step may produce compiler errors. The JSP engine should provide the error messages from the compiler so that you can debug the problem. Most compiler errors are caused by mistakes in scriptlet (Java) code. One common error is naming your JSP page using a Java-reserved word. Such a name causes an error that looks something like "Identifier expected instead of this token." An example would be naming your JSP page default.jsp—default is a Java-reserved word and cannot be used.

Throw Me a Life-Preserver

The resolutions provided should get you through a fair amount of the problems that you might encounter. However, there are some errors that take hours of staring at a screen before you figure out what the problem is. If you really get stuck, go to the Sun Java site (java.sun.com) and look at the JSP user mailing list or JSP sections. More than likely, there's someone who ran into the same problem before and might have posted a solution.

The Jakarta Project Taglib: An Overview

Throughout this book, you've read about the Taglib Tag Library. This appendix provides a brief overview of the functionality provided by this library.

Jakarta Application Taglib

jakarta.apache.org/taglibs/doc/application-doc/intro.html
The Application custom Tag Library contains tags that can be used to access information contained in the ServletContext for a web application.

Jakarta BSF Taglib

jakarta.apache.org/taglibs/doc/bsf-doc/intro.html
The Bean Scripting Framework (BSF) integrates scripting languages such as JavaScript, VB Script, Perl, Tcl, Python, NetRexx, and Rexx.

Jakarta DateTime Taglib

jakarta.apache.org/taglibs/doc/datetime-doc/intro.html
Contains tags for date- and time-related functions such as formatting, parsing from form input, using time zones and localization.

Jakarta I18N Taglib

jakarta.apache.org/taglibs/doc/i18n-doc/intro.html
Contains tags that help manage the complexity of creating internationalized web applications.

Jakarta Input Taglib

jakarta.apache.org/taglibs/doc/input-doc/intro.html
Generates HTML form elements that preset their values from the ServletRequest.

Jakarta JDBC Taglib

jakarta.apache.org/taglibs/doc/jdbc-doc/intro.html
The JDBC custom Tag Library contains tags that can be used to read from and write to
an SQL database.

Jakarta JNDI Taglib

jakarta.apache.org/taglibs/doc/jndi-doc/intro.html
The JNDI Tag Library creates an instance of a javax.naming.Context based on the values
of the attributes providing some of the standard values. In addition to the System properties and the jndi.properties, some standard properties are scanned in the pageContext
attributes.

Jakarta JSP Spec Taglib

jakarta.apache.org/taglibs/doc/jspspec-doc/intro.html
Includes working examples of the tags described in the JavaServerPages specification,
Version 1.1.

Jakarta Mailer Taglib

jakarta.apache.org/taglibs/doc/mailer-doc/intro.html
Used to send e-mail.

Jakarta Page Taglib

jakarta.apache.org/taglibs/doc/page-doc/intro.html
Contains tags that can be used to access all the information about the PageContext for a
JSP page.

Jakarta Request Taglib

jakarta.apache.org/taglibs/doc/response-doc/intro.html
Contains tags that can be used to access all the information about the HTTP request for
a JSP page.

Jakarta Response Taglib

Has tags that can be used to set all the information for an HTTP response for a JSP page.

Jakarta Rexexp Taglib

jakarta.apache.org/taglibs/doc/regexp-doc/intro.html
Includes tags that can be used to perform Perl syntax regular expressions.

Jakarta SQL Taglib

jakarta.apache.org/taglibs/doc/sql-doc/intro.html
Provides an implementation of the SQL tags discussed in Sections A.2.1 and A.2.2 of the
JavaServer Pages 1.1 Specification.

Jakarta Scrape Taglib

jakarta.apache.org/taglibs/doc/scrape-doc/intro.html
Can scrape or extract content from web documents and display the content in your JSP. For example, you could scrape stock quotes from other websites and display them in your pages.

Jakarta Session Taglib

jakarta.apache.org/taglibs/doc/session-doc/intro.html
Contains tags for reading or modifying client HttpSession information.

Jakarta Utility Taglib

jakarta.apache.org/taglibs/doc/utility-doc/intro.html
Provides examples of some basic tags. It illustrates several custom Tag Library code techniques.

Jakarta XSL Taglib

jakarta.apache.org/taglibs/doc/xsl-doc/intro.html
Contains tags to process XML documents with an XSL style sheet and insert it in place.

Jakarta/Struts Bean Tags

jakarta.apache.org/struts/struts-bean.html
Includes tags useful in accessing Beans and their properties, as well as defining new Beans (based on these accesses) that are accessible to the remainder of the page via scripting variables and page scope attributes. Convenient mechanisms to create new Beans based on the value of request cookies, headers, and parameters are also provided.

Jakarta/Struts Logic Tags

jakarta.apache.org/struts/struts-logic.html
Provides tags that are useful in managing conditional generation of output text, looping over object collections for repetitive generation of output text, and application flow management.

Jakarta/Struts Template Tags

jakarta.apache.org/struts/struts-template.html
Contains three tags: put, get, and insert. Put tags put content into request scope, which is retrieved by a get tag in a different JSP page (the template). That template is included with the insert tag.

Appendix C

Processing XML

Realizing how important XML is, Sun Microsystems along with other members of the Java Community Process, is developing a set of Java APIs, called the Java XML (JAX) Pack. These APIs simplify the development of XML applications using Java. In this appendix, I will show you how to use one of those APIs, called JAXP, for the Java API for XML processing, to process XML documents. First, you need to download the JAXP API and a parser that implements this API. The easiest solution is to go to the JAX Pack home page at java.sun.com/xml/ and download the latest release, which is currently called the winter pack. This package contains all the JAX Pack APIs, of which the JAXP API is the most stable, because it's at version 1.1.

Although this download contains a lot of information and resources, all you really need is to place the jaxp.jar and crimson.jar files into the lib subdirectory of your Tomcat installation directory. The jaxp.jar file provides the JAXP API, while the crimson jar file contains an implementation of the JAXP API. After placing these jar files in the lib directory, you need to restart Tomcat for it to be able to use them.

The JAXP API provides three different mechanisms for processing an XML document: Simple API for XML (SAX), the Document Object Model (DOM), and XSL Transformations (XSLT). In this appendix, I will use each of these to generate the weather report. The JAXP API hides the actual details of any individual parser, like crimson, behind a standard interface. In this approach, to obtain a reference to an actual parser implementation, you first create a factory object and have it create a parser for you. A factory object is a standard way in Java to have an object created for you. The factory simply stamps out an object just like in an assembly line, hence the word *factory*. To specify an actual implementation, you use a special property that the JVM uses to determine which parser to instantiate.

When you reach the point of doing XML parsing, there's a good reason why there are two different technologies that do basically the same thing. SAX is faster (performance-wise), but more cumbersome for the programmer. DOM is slower, takes up more memory, but allows the programmer to have all the needed information available. When deciding which parser to use, it really comes down to what you are trying to accomplish, or for that matter, which technology you know better. For more information on SAX go to www.saxproject.org/.

The first example uses SAX to parse the current-weather.xml document, informing the user of the result. You can change the URL to any XML page to check if it is well formed and valid. SAX processes XML documents serially and generates events indicating the start of an element, the end of an element, the start of character data, and so on. As a developer using SAX, you can provide event handlers that will be called when these events are generated. In this example, I just use the default event handler, because I am only interested in parsing the XML document, not actually reading the data out of it. If you browse to localhost:8080/xml/sax-weather.jsp, you will see the resulting web page, shown in Figure C.1.

Listing C.1   sax-weather.jsp

```
<%@ page
   contentType="text/html"
   errorPage="error.jsp"
%>

<%@ page import="org.xml.sax.*" %>
<%@ page import="org.xml.sax.helpers.*" %>
<%@ page import="javax.xml.parsers.*" %>

<html>
<head><title>SAX Parse JSP Page</title></head>
<body>

<%
   String weather = "http://localhost:8080/xml/current-weather.xml" ;

   SAXParserFactory spf = SAXParserFactory.newInstance() ;
   spf.setValidating(true);
```

```
    SAXParser sp = spf.newSAXParser() ;
    sp.parse(weather, new DefaultHandler()) ;
%>


<h1> Congratulations! </h1>
<hr/>
<h2> SAX Validation Successful </h2>
<hr/>
<h4> Date: <%= new java.util.Date() %> </h4>
<h4> <%= weather %> </h4>
</body>
</html>
```

Figure C.1

This figure shows the result of parsing and validating the current-weather.xml using the JAXP API with the SAX parser.

The other parsing model is the Document Object Model, where the entire XML document is read, and a parse tree is constructed that contains the entire XML document. That's why I mentioned earlier that DOM takes up a lot more memory because the entire XML document is read at once. Usually this isn't a problem, but you can see how it can become a problem with really large XML files. This approach has the advantage of allowing random access, unlike the serial approach provided by SAX, but the disadvantage is that it requires significant memory resources for very large XML documents. As a result, SAX is the preferred approach when you only need to process an XML document serially, but DOM is the preferred approach when you need to have random access to the XML document. For more information on DOM go to www.w3c.org/DOM/.

Using a DOM parser is simplified by using the JAXP interfaces. First, you create a DOMBuilderFactroy object and use it to obtain the actual DOM parser, known as a DOMBuilder by JAXP. Unlike SAX, when you parse an XML document using DOM, you obtain the DOM tree, allowing you to randomly traverse through the elements and attributes of the XML document. In both this example and the previous SAX example, I tell the factory to obtain a validating parser. Because we have specified a DTD, we can do this. If, on the other hand, you do not have a DTD or an XML Schema, you should set this to false. Browsing to localhost:8080/xml/dom-weather.jsp generates a web page, as seen in Figure C.2.

Listing C.2   dom-weather.jsp

```
<%@ page
   contentType="text/html"
   errorPage="error.jsp"
%>

<%@ page import="org.w3c.dom.*" %>
<%@ page import="javax.xml.parsers.*" %>

<html>
<head><title>DOM Parse JSP Page</title></head>
<body>

<%
   String weather = "http://localhost:8080/xml/current-weather.xml" ;

   DocumentBuilderFactory dbf = DocumentBuilderFactory.newInstance() ;
   dbf.setValidating(true);

   DocumentBuilder db = dbf.newDocumentBuilder() ;
   Document doc = db.parse(weather) ;
%>

<h1> Congratulations! </h1>
<hr/>
<h2> DOM Validation Successful </h2>
<hr/>
<h4> Date: <%= new java.util.Date() %> </h4>
<h4> <%= weather %> </h4>
</body>
</html>
```

Figure C.2

This figure shows the result of parsing and validating the current-weather.xml using the JAXP API with the DOM parser.

The last example uses an XSL transformer to convert the XML document into a different XML document, in this case, an XHTML document. Because XSL does not specify how to parse an XML document, you first use DOM, as in the previous example, to obtain a DOM tree. This allows XSLT to randomly grab elements and attributes as needed. We saw how this is possible in the earlier examples using value-of in the XSL file. Following the factory model, JAXP defines the TransformFactory, which I use to obtain an XSL transformer, which requires both an XML document and an XSL document.

When creating an actual XSL transformer object, you can specify the XSL document. To make a more general model, the JAXP API dictates that these methods take StreamSource objects instead of a String or a URL object. Thus, we create a StreamSource to represent our XSL document and create our XSL transformer. The transform() method takes two parameters, one of which is a StreamSource that represents the XML document, and the second is a StreamResult object, which I set to the implicit JSP out object. This makes the transform() method transform the XML document directly into the response output stream. If you browse to localhost:8080/xml/xslt-weather.jsp, you will see Figure C.3.

Listing C.3   xslt-weather.jsp

```
<%@ page
  contentType="text/html"
  errorPage="error.jsp"
%>


<%@ page import="org.w3c.dom.*" %>
<%@ page import="javax.xml.transform.*" %>
<%@ page import="javax.xml.transform.stream.*" %>
<%@ page import="javax.xml.parsers.*" %>


<%
  String weather = "http://localhost:8080/xml/current-weather.xml" ;
  String weatherstyle = "http://localhost:8080/xml/weather.xsl" ;

  DocumentBuilderFactory dbf = DocumentBuilderFactory.newInstance() ;
  dbf.setValidating(true);

  DocumentBuilder db = dbf.newDocumentBuilder() ;

  Document doc = db.parse(weather) ;

  TransformerFactory tf = TransformerFactory.newInstance() ;

  StreamSource wdoc = new StreamSource(weather);
  StreamSource wstyle = new StreamSource(weatherstyle);
```

continues

Listing C.3   xslt-weather.jsp   (continued)

```
Transformer transformer = tf.newTransformer(wstyle);

StreamResult result = new StreamResult(out);
transformer.transform(wdoc, result);
%>
```

Figure C.3

This figure shows the result of using the xslt-weather.jsp page, which dynamically transforms the current-weather.xml using the weather.xsl XSL style sheet.

The real power of JSPs is now apparent. When we are dealing with dynamic data and real-world applications, the combination of XML and Java can provide a great deal of flexibility when building an application.

Speak Like a Geek:
The Complete Archive

Apache   The name of the most popular web server, currently exceeding the market share of all other web servers in use. The name is actually derived from a euphemism—"A Patchy Server"—used to describe the NCSA HTTP web server by developers who took over the software development.

Applets   A Java application that is executed inside a web browser.

ASF   The acronym of the Apache Software Foundation, which was created to promote the development of open-source software. ASF currently supports the development of the Apache web server and PHP, as well as some of the most popular Java and XML open-source projects.

auditing   The process of methodically reviewing the records of a web application. Often used to improve performance, provide better client service, or track down attempts to infiltrate an application.

Beans   A shorthand description for JavaBeans. Also used to make an addictive elixir that helps authors and developers stay awake.

body content   The data that is between an element's start tag and end tag.

buffering   The process of holding data in a temporary storage and writing it into a stream all at once, rather than writing every character individually.

character encoding A numerical scheme for representing a set of characters.

class file The compiled version of a Java source file. The class file is compiled to run in a Java Virtual Machine (JVM), and is inherently portable.

comment A programming element that is used to communicate information about the program to the reader of the source code.

container An application that manages the life cycle of a JSP or Servlet and supports their runtime execution.

content type The Multipurpose Internet Mail Extensions (MIME) type that describes the data being returned by a JSP or Servlet.

context The view of a web application provided to a JSP page or a Servlet by a container.

cookie A small piece of data that is exchanged between a web server and a browser, enabling the server to recognize the client during later client requests.

CSS (cascading style sheets) Encapsulate how data should be presented and include descriptions for the colors, fonts, borders, and sizes of rendered elements.

custom action A user-defined action that is implemented with a custom tag.

declaration A scripting element that can introduce methods and variables into a JSP page.

deployment descriptor An XML document that dictates to a web server the contents of a web application, allowing the web server to provide access to the web application without any administrative intervention.

directive A communication from a JSP page to the JSP container.

DNS (Domain Name Service) Provides a mechanism for mapping human-readable names to IP addresses. DNS allows you to enter www.persistentjava.com into your web browser and see the appropriate web page.

DOM (Document Object Model) Provides a treelike representation for a document. For example, an HTML file has a root HTML element, which has branches for the HEAD and BODY elements, which themselves have branches, etc.

DTD (Document Type Description) Provides a mechanism for constraining the content of an XML document. An XML document that adheres to a DTD is described as being valid.

EAR (Enterprise Archive) file A Java Archive file that is used to deploy Java Enterprise Applications. Basically, this requires that the jar file include special directories and files.

ECMAScript   The standardized name for JavaScript. ECMA stands for European Computer Manufacturers' Association.

element   A set of characters that are collectively recognized as forming a distinct entity.

empty element   An element that does not have any data in its body. An empty element can have both a start tag and an end tag, or it can be written using the empty element shorthand.

error page   A JSP page that is registered with a different JSP page to handle any exceptions that might be thrown during the evaluation of the primary JSP page.

event handler   A method that is registered to be called when a particular event or condition is generated.

exception   A Java object that encapsulates an error condition.

expression   A Java scripting element that is evaluated, the result converted to a string, and placed in the JSP page's output.

filters   Servlets that can preprocess client requests or post-process server responses.

focus   The process by which a control becomes active. For example, before you can enter data into a text field control, that control must have focus, which is generally done by clicking in the text field with the mouse.

font   A design for displaying a set of characters, including the typeface, size, pitch, and spacing.

form   A mechanism for a web application to dynamically obtain input from a user.

forward   An action taken by a server, without notifying the client, where a request is passed on to a new server.

hexadecimal   A syntax for writing numbers that has 16 digits, as opposed to decimal that only has 10. The 16 digits are encoded using 0 through 9 and A through F. Hexadecimal is popular since it results in a smaller mapping to the natural architecture of a computer, which is built in binary.

HTML (HyperText Markup Language)   Currently the *lingua franca* of the web. HTML describes how data should be presented in a web browser.

HTTP (HyperText Transmission Protocol)   The dominant protocol used on the Internet to enable web communication. It is a stateless protocol and follows the client-server model, with client requests being answered with server responses.

i18n   The shorthand for internationalization, it is used since there are 18 characters between the i and the n, thus i18n.

IANA   Internet Assigned Numbers Authority manages the assignment of IP addresses.

ICANN   The Internet Corporation for Assigned Names and Numbers oversees the process of assigning names and IP addresses.

IDE   Integrated Development Editor simplifies the task of developing applications by hiding the complexities of compiling, deploying, and testing applications from the user. Most Java IDEs support JSP development, allowing you to write and test your JSP, JavaBeans, Servlets, and custom tags.

IMAP   Internet Message Access Protocol can be used to access a mailbox remotely. IMAP allows the user to store e-mail messages on the e-mail server.

implicit objects   Objects that encapsulate specific functionality, such as the client's request and the server's response, that are made available to the JSP page automatically by the JSP container.

include   A JSP standard action that allows a JSP page to dynamically include content.

include directive   A communication between a JSP page and the JSP container that allows a JSP page to include content at page-translation time.

internationalization   The process of making an application accessible to people of various cultures or locales.

IP (Internet Protocol)   Provides the backbone of Internet communication, identifying target machines the same way your phone number targets your phone.

IPv6 (Internet Protocol version 6)   Increases the number of available IP addresses, enabling IP connections to be expanded worldwide into a wider range of devices.

Jakarta   A project of the Apache Software Foundation that develops open-source Java tools.

jar file   Java Archive file is used to collect and compress multiple Java class files and associated manifest information to simplify application deployment.

Java plugin   A web browser component that provides a Java Runtime Environment (JRE) inside a web browser. This allows Applets to be run in any browser that supports the plugin architecture.

JavaBean   A discrete Java object that can easily be reused.

JavaScript   A scripting language invented by Netscape that utilizes a Javalike syntax.

JCP (Java Community Process)   Is used to make changes to the Java language.

JDBC (Java Database Connectivity)   Allows Java programs to interact with data-storage programs, such as relational databases, using SQL.

JDK (Java Development Kit)   Provides all the tools you need to build and execute Java applications.

JDO (Java Data Objects)   Is a new Java API that allows developers to utilize persistent Java objects without directly using JDBC.

JDOM (Java Document Object Model)   A relatively new XML processing API that provides a natural Java implementation to utilizing the DOM API.

JMS (Java Messaging Service)   A Java interface for building message-based applications.

JNDI (Java Naming and Directory Interface)   An API that allows Java programs to associate and use a name with a Java object.

JRE (Java Runtime Environment)   Provides the implementation for a JVM, allowing you to run Java applications on a specific type of hardware. A JRE does not provide the tools necessary to build Java applications; for that you need a JDK.

JSP (JavaServer Pages)   Are what this book is all about!

JSR (Java Specification Request)   The method for proposing and defining additions and modifications to the Java programming language.

JVM (Java Virtual Machine)   Provides a portable execution environment for Java applications. Unlike traditional programming languages, Java programs are not compiled into a machine-specific language.

l11n   The shorthand for localization; there are 11 characters between the l and the n, thus l11n.

life cycle   The complete process that a Java object, such as a Servlet, JSP page, JavaBean, or even a custom JSP tag, follows as it is created, utilized, and then destroyed.

localization   The process of modifying an application so that any content or data that is particular to a specific location is encapsulated, allowing an application to be easily modified to support other locales.

MIME (Multipurpose Internet Mail Extensions)   Defined by RFC 1341; allow divergent file types to be packaged and communicated across the Internet.

Model 1   A design approach to building JSP web applications that utilizes JSP pages and JavaBeans.

Model 2   A design approach to building JSP web applications that utilizes the MVC design pattern. The view is generated using JSP pages, the model is implemented using JavaBeans, and the controller is implemented using Servlets.

MVC (Model-View-Controller) An architecture for building user-interfaced applications, in which the data is encapsulated in the model, the presentation of the data is encapsulated in the view, and the data processing is encapsulated in the controller.

nonempty element An element that has data inside the body of the element.

page directive A mechanism for communicating specific instructions between a JSP page and a JSP container that controls the appearance and functionality of the JSP-generated output.

param A JSP standard action that associates a parameter value with a name, allowing a JSP developer to pass data between JSP pages and Servlets.

parser An application that reads a document, optionally verifies the legality of the document, and breaks the document up into tokens for further processing.

POP (Post Office Protocol) Currently in version 3, thus it is often written as POP3. POP is a remote e-mail accessing protocol that enables the user to store e-mails locally.

port number A number that, along with the host IP address, uniquely associates a service on the Internet.

property An attribute that defines the behavior of a Java application, such as a JSP page.

quoting rules A mapping between a specific set of characters and the corresponding escape characters that allows the desired characters to be used in places they would otherwise be misinterpreted.

redirect A communication from a server to a client that indicates the client should request the resource from a different server.

request A communication between a client and the server where the client asks for a particular resource.

response A communication between a server and a client where the server either provides a requested resource or indicates the appropriate response code.

response code A numerical value that is returned to a client to indicate the status of the server after processing the client's request. The value must be from the standard mapping of numerical value and server conditions.

RFC (Request For Comment) A document that defines an Internet standard.

role A functional grouping of the users of an application.

SAX The Simple API for XML is an event-handling alternative to DOM for processing documents. Using SAX, you define events that should happen when specific elements are encountered in a document.

scope   The region within an application in which an object is visible to other objects.

scriptlet   A small snippet of Java code that is executed inside a JSP page.

selector   The part of a stylesheet rule that selects elements to which the appropriate style rule must be applied.

servlet   A Java web component that provides dynamic responses to client requests.

session   A series of client-server interactions that are tracked by the server to maintain client identity and persist the state of an interaction.

SMTP   Simple Mail Transport Protocol is the dominant protocol used on the Internet for exchanging messages (such as e-mail) between servers.

SOAP   Simple Object Access Protocol enables disparate remote objects to communicate with each other. SOAP is one of the fundamental technologies that enable web services.

standard action   JSP tags that are defined as part of the JSP specification. Includes actions for forwarding requests, including content, and using JavaBeans and Applets.

struts   An open-source JSP Tag Library that is designed to simplify the development of MVC applications using JavaServer Pages.

tag   A set of characters that occurs between a less-than sign, <, and a greater-than sign, >, that has a name, optional attributes, and forms the basis for an element.

Tag Library   A collection of related custom tags collected together to simplify their deployment and use.

Tag Library descriptor   An XML document that describes a Tag Library and its constituent tags.

taglib   Shorthand for Tag Library.

TCP   Transmission Control Protocol is a layer over IP that simplifies the development of Internet communications.

TLD   Tag Library Descriptor is an XML document that defines a group of custom JSP tags.

Tomcat   The official reference implementation for the Servlet and JavaServer Pages specifications. Available form the Apache Software Foundation's Jakarta project.

UDDI   Universal Description, Discovery, and Integration provides a phone book–like service that allows users to locate and connect to web services.

Unicode   A standard method for representing every character in any language with a number. Developed and supported by the Unicode Consortium.

URI   Uniform Resource Identifier, as defined in RFC2396, is a compact string of characters used to identify a resource.

URL   Uniform Resource Locator, as defined in RFC1738, specifies the syntax and semantics of formalized information, as well as the location and access of resources via the Internet.

UTF-8   Unicode Transformation Format, 8-bit encoding form.

UTF-16   Unicode Transformation Format, 16-bit encoding form.

valid   A term used to indicate that an XML document adheres to its DTD, or Schema.

validation   The process of checking that data entered by the user conforms to the proper datatype. For example, you can check that an e-mail address has the @ character or that a phone number only contains numerical characters.

verification   The process of checking that data entered by the user is correct. For example, you might e-mail the password to the user, verifying that the e-mail is correct.

W3C   World Wide Web Consortium was created in 1994 to develop and promote common protocols that enable the web to grow and evolve.

war file   Web application archive is a jar file that contains additional files, such as a deployment descriptor, that are necessary to deploy the web application in a J2EE compliant server.

Web Service   An application that is accessible via the web and conforms to standards for receiving client requests and generating responses.

well-formed   A term used to describe an XML document that obeys the syntactical rules of XML.

WSDL   Web Service Description Language; used to programmatically describe a Web Service.

XHTML   Extensible HyperText Markup Language, a reformulation of HTML as an XML application.

XML   Extensible Markup Language, the universal format for storing and using data and documents on the web.

XSL   Extensible Stylesheet Language is an XML application that allows a developer to express stylesheets.

XSL-FO   Extensible Stylesheet Language Formatting Objects; used to convert XML documents into other document formats.

XSLT   Extensible Stylesheet Language Transformations; used to transform an XML document into another XML document, including an HTML document.

Index

B

Q-R

S

T

X–Y–Z

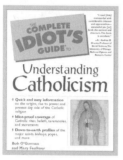

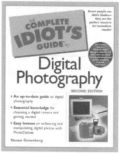
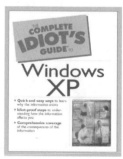